PENGUIN BOOKS
TELL ME I'M HERE

Anne Deveson is an Australian writer, broadcaster and documentary
film-maker. Her films have won awards in the United States, Australia,
Italy, England and Ireland. She is a three-time winner of the United Na-
tions Media Peace Prize. *Tell Me I'm Here* was the recipient of the 1991
non-fiction Australian Human Rights Award.

Deveson has also been a member of many major inquiries concerning
social justice issues. When her elder son developed schizophrenia, she
helped establish the NSW Schizophrenia Fellowship and the national organization Schizophrenia Australia, of which she is deputy chairperson.
In 1991 she chaired a special ministerial committee on the NSW Mental
Health Act and produced and directed a one-hour documentary on
schizophrenia, *Spinning Out*.

# *Tell Me I'm Here*

Anne Deveson

Penguin Books

To Georgia and Joshua
and to the memory of Jonathan

PENGUIN BOOKS
Published by the Penguin Group
Viking Penguin, a division of Penguin Books USA Inc.,
375 Hudson Street, New York, New York 10014, U.S.A.
Penguin Books Ltd, 27 Wrights Lane,
London W8 5TZ, England
Penguin Books Australia Ltd, Ringwood,
Victoria, Australia
Penguin Books Canada Ltd, 10 Alcorn Avenue, Suite 300,
Toronto, Ontario, Canada M4V 3B2
Penguin Books (N.Z.) Ltd, 182–190 Wairau Road,
Auckland 10, New Zealand

Penguin Books Ltd, Registered Offices:
Harmondsworth, Middlesex, England

First published in Australia by Penguin Books Australia Ltd 1991
This edition with an introduction by
E. Fuller Torrey published in Penguin Books (U.S.A.) 1992

10  9  8  7  6  5  4  3  2  1

LIBRARY OF CONGRESS CATALOGING IN PUBLICATION DATA
Deveson, Anne.
Tell me I'm here / Anne Deveson: introduction by E. Fuller Torrey.
p.  cm.
Originally published: Australia: Penguin Books, 1991.
Includes bibliographical references.
ISBN 0 14 01.7339 0
1. Deveson, Jonathan—Mental health.   2. Schizophrenics—
    Australia—Biography.   I. Title.
RC514.D43   1992
616.89'82'0092—dc20     92–9587

Printed in the United States of America

# Foreword

Schizophrenia is surely the cruelest disease. Imagine having a condition in which you are a normal person for the first fifteen to twenty years of your life. Then, slowly and insidiously, your brain begins playing tricks on you. Your thoughts become intermittently confused. Things you hear on the radio or passing comments of strangers on the street seem to refer to you. Voices from inside your head assail and berate you—voices as real as those you heard around you, but voices apparently not audible to others. Your emotions acquire a life of their own so that sometimes you laugh and sometimes you cry for no reason at all. It is as if your brain has been invaded by a foreign being, perhaps one from another planet. It is, in the words of Anne Deveson's son Jonathan, like "rats, they're eating my brain."

Anne Deveson has given us a poignant and powerful account of what schizophrenia was like for her son, her family and herself. She is an astute observer and meticulous recorder of the nuances of tragedy; the product is the best account of schizophrenia which I have seen. One can share her son's confusion, his delusions that he was being watched, the voices that followed him day and night, and his graveside giggling at his father's funeral. The narrative is much more terrifying than the worst horror movie or book available because it is real. You cannot walk out, switch to another channel, or close the book, as much as you might wish to do so.

In addition to the disease itself, Ms. Deveson has captured the scandal of psychiatry's failings. Like many individuals who have schizophrenia, her son had little insight into his condition or his need for treatment. That is not surprising since schizophrenia is a disease of the brain, the same organ we use to think about ourselves. To say that someone with schizophrenia can only be treated if they request it voluntarily is as silly as saying that a man with a failing heart cannot be treated until his heart again becomes normal. In misguided efforts to protect an individual's right to be sick, the ignorance of lawyers, judges and "patient advocates" is astounding.

Current medical research has clearly established that schizophrenia is a brain disease in exactly the same way that Alzheimer's disease, Parkinson's disease, and multiple sclerosis are brain diseases. Do we allow people with Alzheimer's disease to wander the streets and be randomly victimized just because they do not have insight into their condition and do not realize that they need care? We do this to people with schizophrenia every day, by the thousands, in Seattle and Akron just as Ms. Deveson describes it in Sydney and Adelaide.

There is almost certainly going to be a special place in Hell reserved for the lawyers, psychiatrists, and public officials who, by failing to insure treatment, have consigned individuals with schizophrenia to a Hell on earth. Some sufferers, like Jonathan, eventually give up and commit suicide. Nobody can blame them. It is a response that is far more rational than the non-treatment system usually offered to them.

We should be grateful to Anne Deveson for sharing her tears and her trials with us. It should motivate us to do what is necessary to improve the treatment system. Merely watching the ongoing tragedy of schizophrenia is voyeurism; salvation can only come by action.

*E. Fuller Torrey, M.D.*

# Acknowledgements

I thank Georgia and Joshua for their love and courage through-out such a difficult period in their lives, and for their under-standing of my need to write this book. I am grateful to Georgia for allowing me to use some of her poetry.

Many of those who helped us during the years with Jonathan are named in this book; countless others also assisted. I look back with wonder at the extent of love and support we so often received, and at the ongoing help I have had since. I am par-ticularly grateful to those people with schizophrenia and their families whose encouragement has so often sustained me, and whose friendship I enjoy.

# Contents

# Prologue

*A thing is not impossible merely because it is inconceivable.*
LEWIS CARROLL

This is a story about a journey into madness. It was a journey where my son became a will-o'-the wisp, leading us all into brambles and boglands. Now you see him, now you don't.

'Tell me, tell me, Anne, tell me I'm here. Open your right eye only when you're telling the truth.'

Jonathan had schizophrenia. He was seventeen when he first became ill. His journey took him to lands of mythical happenings. The demons that plagued him were capricious, and he could not order their behaviour. Sometimes they brought him delight; more often they plunged him into horror.

My journey after him took me down a labyrinth of passageways, each labelled 'cure'. I never found one. Jonathan died of a drug overdose when he was twenty-four.

In the beginning I had intended writing a book about schizophrenia. After Jonathan's death I wanted to write a more personal book, a book about what happens when someone you love goes mad. The journey led me to question love's power, and out of the questioning to discover love's essence. It led me to seek other alchemies, and to journey but never arrive. And it led me to realise that there is never one reality, but many.

I remember listening to a conversation between three young people who had schizophrenia, and marvelling at their sense of irony.

'When I was in hospital, three women thought I was Jesus Christ and one of them kept kissing my feet. They put her in isolation for behaviour modification.'

'What'll I call my poem?'

'Call it "The Bird of Paradise – Plucked".'

'Call it "Schizophrenia".'

'Call it "Nothing".'

'I can't go into a shop and ask for "Nothing".'

'Why not?'

'They'll think I'm mad.'

We do not use the word 'mad' any more. We have banished it, together with words like 'lunatic' and 'asylum'; even the word 'insane' is rarely heard. These words evoke oppressions of the past; today the terminology has changed, become more technical and distancing, yet our oppressions remain. They are the oppressions of neglect.

For too long, mental illness has been a shadow that we like to pretend is not there. Perhaps many of us recognise that our own grasp on sanity is at times precarious. Perhaps we are fearful that madness will catapult us into melodrama, and we are frightened of losing control. Perhaps it is simply because we do not understand madness, just as we understand very little of our universe within.

The ordeal of insanity, and the struggle of the human spirit to rise out of it, has a universal core, one that has been written about since earliest times, as the Book of Job shows:

> *For the thing which*
> *I greatly feared is come upon me,*
> *and that which I was afraid of*
> *is come into me.*
> *I was not in safety, neither*
> *had I rest, neither was I quiet:*
> *yet trouble came.*

We would like to believe that insanity happens only in other people's families, and never to us. But any one of us can brush wings with madness. We can choose to hide it, and in the hiding give it shame. Or we can recognise it as part of the human condition and learn from it. So this book about schizophrenia became a story, with all the elements of story: birth and death, love and hate, passion and denial.

The story could begin at a time when Jonathan is seventeen years old. It is 1978. Jonathan paints; he likes music from Pink Floyd to Mozart; he enjoys cooking; he reads Tolkien and *Playboy*; he is uncompetitive and argues about social justice. He sometimes behaves erratically: he may think people are against him and, if challenged, can change from being quiet and gentle to shouting aggressively. This has only been happening in the last two years.

A major character in this story is the mother. I am the mother. I am journalist, broadcaster, writer, film-maker. I am also to become Demeter trying to save her child from the underworld.

The father is called Ellis. He has been a broadcaster of some distinction, a pioneer of jazz radio, who loved all kinds of music, a volatile man. He was married once before our marriage, and once after, and was to die less than a year after this story begins.

There are two other children, Georgia and Joshua. They are not 'other' in the sense that they are less, but for a time Jonathan's madness pushes them into the shadows which, in turn, becomes part of their story. They will have to grow up too fast, and, in that growing, lose much of their childhood.

And there is the architect, with whom I lived in the earlier part of the story. I call him 'the architect', not because I wish to distance myself from him, but because he is a private person and found himself an unwitting player in a drama that had its roots in other people's lives. The architect was dark, reticent and intense.

Writing this book has meant re-living periods I would rather forget. We all remember them differently: we each experienced only our part. The part I tell is recounted as openly as I can. Sometimes I have altered names, sometimes I have captured the essence of what happened rather than the specific detail. I have worked from diaries, records and notes of the time and from scraps of paper I kept as I tried to make sense of the chaos around us.

Jonathan is dead. But our stories need to be told. How else

can we know that others tread the same pathways? How else can we find our healing?

So I write this book for Jonathan, who was graceful and funny and lovely, but who for his last seven years lived a life of torment.

I write it for those millions of others with schizophrenia, who daily walk a tightrope, courageously trying to balance between their world and ours.

I write it for their families who struggle to hold on to hope when often they are scourged by despair, and who suffer from our ignorance and neglect.

And I write it for Georgia and Joshua, who are loving, brave and honest. Out of the sadness, they grew wise.

# One
# *A Beginning*

*There ariseth a little cloud out of the sea, like a man's hand.*
                                                    1 KINGS 18.44

*7 September 1961*   I have this newborn baby in my arms. First-born. Born of astounding energy, like something I could never have imagined, and over which I had no control. As if an earthquake were heaving inside me, as if I were exploding into infinity. Anyway, it was quick, perhaps too quick. The baby seemed to bump his head on the way out.

But, as I hold him in my arms, I decide I like him. I like the soft smell of his skin. I like his downy hair. I like the feel of him nestling against me. I am worried by only one thing. He keeps crying: a small, high-pitched cry. I ask the nurse and the doctor if there is anything wrong, but they both say, 'Of course not.' His father is also worried about the crying, and wonders if he should not, after all, go to see his son in Tasmania, as arranged weeks ago. I encourage Ellis to go, and then wish that I hadn't.

The following morning, three doctors stand at the foot of my bed, like the three Magi. But there is no star and no baby.

'Your baby has cerebral irritability.'

'We are taking him to the Children's Hospital for a check-up.'

'Nothing to worry about.'

Later, one of the pink ladies runs in, beaming joyously. She is a voluntary aide and full of good intent. Her white tennis shoes squeak on the lino floor. She is pushing a trolley before her and the cups are rattling. 'Your baby's arrived. He's alive.'

I have been rigidly balanced on a high-wire of anxiety which stretches from 'cerebral irritability' at one end to a question-mark

5

at the other. Now I plummet. The general practitioner, ambles in. He is a cheerful, matter-of-fact man who subsequently gives up doctoring to drive a tourist bus. He asks if I want my baby christened.

'Just in case', he says, trying not to sound worried.

I refuse and plummet further. After he has left the room, I cry.

The following day the obstetrician enters and says solemnly that the cerebral irritability has been caused by a cerebral haemorrhage. A cerebral haemorrhage means bleeding inside the brain. Why would a newborn baby have bleeding inside the brain? I am too scared to say anything more than 'Oh' and 'Thank you', but, after he has gone, I reflect that people rarely ask the questions they most need answering when they are in shock. Both the nurse on duty and the matron offer me sedatives, and I say 'No'. I am suspicious of their proposal. I want to stay alert.

Ellis gets back the following day, and I am relieved to see him. We drive to the Children's Hospital where they have taken the baby. It is early spring, and thin rain stings our faces as we leave our parked car and run across the road. I feel hollow inside, and as if I am in some curious state of suspension outside.

The Children's Hospital is an ugly, brick building. We find our way up lifts and down corridors into a ward full of incubators, like sterilised wombs of glass. Each incubator contains a baby, each baby is pierced by needles which are attached to tubes which are attached to bottles. The babies have small white patches of sticking-plaster under their noses and on their bodies, in order to secure the needles and the tubes. I am shocked by their shrivelled vulnerability.

Immediately, the baby is no longer 'the baby'; he becomes 'our baby'. I long to put my hands inside the humidicrib, and to stroke him, to reassure him that everything will be all right. But I am not allowed. The longing is so intense that I pace round and round the incubator.

The student nurse hovers with a pen, asking for the baby's name. We have not yet settled on one, but I do not like admitting this; it seems unwelcoming. So when Ellis vaguely mentions

'Jonathan', she writes it down, and I am relieved and pleased.

The following day we return to the hospital to talk with the paediatrician, who arrives with a procession of student doctors and nurses. He tells us it is impossible to say what caused the cerebral haemorrhage, and it is also impossible to say whether there has been any damage. He looks at me for a short while, then pronounces, 'You may feed your baby.'

Everyone stands around, gravely observing me as I nervously hold the baby. He is so bundled up in the checked hospital blanket that I am not even sure I've got hold of the right end. *Oh God, he'll reject me. He'll die and it will all be my fault.* But the baby gets the idea and feeds quite calmly.

The paediatrician says, 'Good girl, you may now come and feed your baby every day. Nurse, give her a breast pump to take home.'

We are broke at the time that Jonathan is born, and we live over an hour's drive out of town. Our small car needs new tyres but we cannot afford them, so we drive to the hospital very slowly each day, clutching a milk bottle of best human milk, wrapped around with newspaper and nestled in a waste-paper basket. A cane basket. New.

A few weeks later, we are allowed to bring Jonathan home. I feel a fierce protectiveness towards him. I will save him from ghoulies and ghosties and long-leggedy beasties, and things that go bump in the night. I will nurture him and feed him till he is the finest baby in the world.

But when we get home, Jonathan cries. He cries during the day, he cries during the night. The only time he isn't crying is when he is feeding. When I get up in the middle of the night, I am all alone with him and with the tall trees that push their shadowy fingers against the glass. I gaze down at his eyes. They look back, dark and unblinking. I want to shake him.

When he is six months old, give or take, Jonathan smiles. The event seems so miraculous, so bathed in light, that I rush out to call the neighbours. Better still, the more he smiles, the less he cries, as if he has decided it is safe now to unpack his life. At about the same time, the paediatrician detects that Jonathan has some physical disability. The paediatrician still does not know whether there is any intellectual damage. The muscles on one side of Jonathan's body are weak. He has a weak left leg, a weak left arm, and weak muscles in the left side of his neck, so his head flops to one side. I give him daily exercises; after several months, his muscles have grown strong and he has put on weight. He feeds properly. He walks at the time when most babies start walking. He talks at the time most babies start talking.

When he is two, the paediatrician gives him the all-clear. But I notice that Jonathan's head still leans to one side, just a little. By day, he has become a remarkably placid child. At night, he is tormented with night terrors, which become articulated nightmares as he gets older, and these haunt him for the rest of his life. He begins walking in his sleep. For a while he insists on wearing several jumpers even in mid-summer. He is five years old.

I see him on the beach one day with a group of friends. He is on the outside, hovering around them, separated in some way. I feel a quiver of anxiety. He is seven years old.

Sometimes he walks to school and doesn't get there. Sometimes he walks back from school and doesn't get home either. He is talking to the birds, or listening to the trees. He is here but not here.

Once he sits on my lap after school and says, 'When I look at you, your face keeps turning into a witch.' He whispers this and hangs on to me tightly. He says, 'Do people's faces often do that, turn into nasty faces?'

Sometimes he is timid; other times he seems robust and reassuringly normal, a loving, thoughtful child, and, when he is older, a delightful companion.

Yet, years later, when I am looking at early family photographs, I see Jonathan standing behind everyone else, his head pitched awkwardly to one side. He seems anxious.

# Two
## *I Think He's Sick*

*and everything under the sun is in tune*
*but the sun is eclipsed by the moon*
PINK FLOYD

**April 1979**  We had just moved to South Australia, and I was in the kitchen one Sunday night in early autumn. The church bells had just rung, and I was making soup.

Adelaide is an ordered, gracious city, with roads in straight lines and houses with walled gardens. Every now and then I longed to drop my knickers in the main street and say something rude.

The architect was due for dinner and my two younger children, Georgia and Joshua, were in the garden.

The front door opened, banged shut, and Jonathan appeared with a friend called Paul, who led the way. They had been camping for the weekend. At this stage of the story, Jonathan was seventeen, Georgia fourteen and Joshua ten.

Paul jerked his head toward Jonathan and said, 'I think he's sick.'

Jonathan wore a beige beanie on his long fair hair and had pulled it down so it almost covered his eyes and nose. His nose was long and straight but the bridge was a bit crooked from where a gang had jumped him at a swimming pool two years earlier. He had sensitive features, fair skin and brown eyes. He was very tall and getting taller.

Sometimes he looked truly beautiful, like one of those angels in Italian Renaissance paintings. I nearly do not write this, because I think it might sound mawkish. But at this time in his life, Jonathan was beautiful. He still held his head on one side, and had a dimple when he smiled. Tonight, he ignored everyone and wandered up and down the room talking to himself, and giggling. When I went

9

up and hugged him, he looked over my head and his arms hung stiffly by his side.

We sat at the table. It was one of those evenings that was going to be lumpy. The architect, who liked his meals to be candle-lit with Mozart, instead of with rowdy teenagers and wheezy dogs, tried valiantly to sustain an intelligent conversation. He asked us what we thought of Norman Mailer.

Georgia said Mailer was passé.

Jonathan turned his soup bowl upside-down on the table and made patterns on the polished wood. 'Yair, yair,' he said conspiratorially. He kept nodding his head. His eyes darted round the room. He looked frightened. I felt alarm, a lurch in my stomach.

Jonathan stood up suddenly, and the table shook. He strode purposefully into the garden like someone embarking on a marathon race. His head was thrust forward, his elbows were flapping, and his lips were moving as if he were having this intense conversation with himself. There was immense energy about this sudden action of his. It stopped just as suddenly. He came to rest beneath a plum tree. Under a darkening sky, he stood there for a moment like a stork, one leg tucked under the other. The plum tree was brazenly beautiful, its fruit dark red and ripe. Lots of plums had fallen on the ground, and he began systematically squashing them.

The architect echoed Paul's earlier remark. He said in a concerned voice (because he was, and is, a kindly man), 'I think he *is* sick.'

Jonathan wandered back in. He had been eating one of the plums and its red juice stained his mouth. The architect took his leave as soon as he could gracefully manage.

We all went to bed. I lay and worried. I don't usually worry, but tonight was different. My bed didn't help. It was pear-shaped and the sheets were black satin. This was an improbable feature of an improbable house which was built by a Russian in the 1950s and which the architect had rented for us so that we could have one year of settling in before we all lived together.

This house had a glass-brick facade and part of it was painted lime green. It was bow-fronted like a ship and belonged to a man who had spent his life in the South Seas and a mild-looking woman who was said to have been waiting for him. While she waited she had filled her cupboards full of hair rollers, and bird-seed for the pigeons.

Lying in my pear-shaped splendour, I dozed off, still uneasy. I was wakened to a sound that thrummed through my ears, my eyes, my head, my whole body. The house was shaking. At first I wasn't sure what was happening, then I realised it was music, loud music.

I fumbled my way downstairs and opened the door of the living-room. It was a big L-shaped room with a parquet floor, plastic armchairs and several hideous metal sculptures on the wall which moved when you wound them up. The music was Pink Floyd, 'Dark Side of the Moon', and it was thundering into such distortion that I had to put my hands over my ears. Although it was a warm night, Jonathan sat hunched up over the electric fire. All bars were blazing and his sneakers smelt of burning rubber. He was rocking back and forth, his arms tightly wrapped around himself as if he were holding himself together. His lips were moving. I turned off the music. He jumped up, turned it on again, and grabbed me by the wrists. Then he spat in my face.

'Fucking bitch,' he hissed. There was a ferocity about his anger that alarmed me.

I wiped my face. I was angry. 'Don't!' I shouted.

'Fucking bitch!' he shouted again. He began banging his head with his hands, and then banging his head against the wall. He was screaming something about rats, only I couldn't hear him properly above the din. 'Rats, they're eating my brain,' I thought he said. I rushed to put my arms around him. 'There aren't any rats. No rats. No rats,' I crooned.

He pushed me away, so hard that I fell backwards on the floor. I looked up and saw the other two children standing in the doorway. Georgia had her hand to her mouth. I think she was screaming 'Don't Jonathan, don't Jonathan.' But then he was screaming too. And all the while the music was pounding through the room, through our heads, through the screaming. Joshua turned it off, and Jonathan went to grab him but changed his mind. He stood with his hands tucked in the top of his jeans, his feet apart.

'The PLO will get you,' he said, and spat on the floor. 'Now piss off,' he roared. 'Piss off!'

We retreated. Georgia and Joshua went back to bed and I returned to the living-room. Jonathan was back at the radiator, rocking to and fro. There was no music, only his keening, a strange high lament. When he saw me he became agitated, and I withdrew. I thought about calling a doctor, but the whole incident had been so bizarre, so unexpected that I felt shocked and bemused. My head ached, but I guess I must have dropped off to sleep because I woke, startled. It was the silence that disturbed me, made me stumble down the stairs, to find Jonathan sprawled out in an armchair. His face was flushed, but otherwise he looked like a boy who had fallen asleep on an ordinary night in an ordinary house in an ordinary town. I turned off the fire and closed the door.

Next day, we were exhausted. Jonathan was no longer in the living-room. He had gone up to his bedroom and crashed, fully clothed, on his bed. He came downstairs at about two in the afternoon, and went straight to the bread crock. He made himself large hunks of bread and jam and sat cross-legged on the floor, shoving the bread into his mouth as if he hadn't eaten in days.

'What happened last night?' I asked him.

He giggled.

'You said rats were eating your brain.'

He giggled again, and walked out of the house.

I followed him, but he was too fast for me and I had to let him go. I watched him as he padded barefoot down the road, hands in his pockets. He was wearing an old, grey, Tibetan wool jacket I had bought him, striped with many different coloured braids.

I had tried to ring the architect earlier in the day, but he was out on a job. Georgia and Joshua were at school. I barely knew anyone else in Adelaide. I comforted myself by eating almost as many hunks of bread and jam as Jonathan had.

Then I remembered I had seen a Youth Refuge at the end of our street. I went straight there.

The staff were young and confident. They said that I did not have to put up with such aggressive behaviour and I agreed. They also said that it could be a drug reaction, and they gave me the name of a general practitioner and a drug-and-alcohol counselling service. The general practitioner said to bring the boy in. The counselling service said the boy had to want to come in. But Jonathan had disappeared.

The architect arrived for dinner, and I told him what had happened. He said, not unreasonably, 'Oh Lord, I hope it doesn't happen tonight.' That night would be one of the nights the architect stayed. He was a man given to regularity in his life.

During dinner in the garden, Jonathan joined us and sat with his eyes downcast. His lips were tightly held together and he spoke in monosyllables. The other two children were also quiet. We all felt tense. I went to bed in apprehension but all was well. The house was quiet. Everyone slept or appeared to sleep. A pale moon hovered low in the sky.

For the next week or so, Jonathan flitted through the house like a grey moth. He was supposed to be looking for a job, but he rarely appeared before early afternoon, when he would dart into the kitchen, make himself some food and return to his room. At night, he paced up and down, talking and laughing, or he went downstairs and played Pink Floyd, over and over again. I bought him headphones which he sometimes remembered to use. Often, as he listened to the music, he rocked and repeated his lament. Several times, he went out in the early hours of the morning, leaving the front door swinging wide open. His hair was matted and he refused to change his clothes. Most worrying of all was his withdrawal from everyone around him. If we tried to break through to him, he would either walk right past us, or erupt in a rage. I sensed a build-up of energy inside him, as if there were an engine racing inside his head that was about to explode.

When I suggested that he visit a doctor because I was worried about him, he looked at me as if I had offered him a visit to a torture chamber. Then he became obsequious, ringing his hands like Uriah Heap. 'No thank you,' he said. 'No thank you, I do not think that would be a good idea. But thank you.'

I tackled him about drugs. When Jonathan first went to high school we were at the end of the flower-power era, and drugs – mainly marijuana – were readily available. He hung his head, mumbling 'No, nothing like that.' Then he scuttled off giggling.

This endless giggling was driving us all up the wall. We did not know whether to join in or to tell him to shut up. And what would we have said: 'Laughing is forbidden around here'?

I contacted his friend Paul, who was defensive. He said they had smoked some dope while they were camping, but not much, and after all he, Paul, was okay. No, he didn't know what had happened except that when they woke up on Sunday morning Jonathan had begun trembling and behaving strangely.

When I rang Jonathan's father in Sydney, Ellis said he was sorry, and that it must be very worrying for me. Ellis and Jenny (his new wife) had spent Easter with us, just a few days earlier. 'Get him to a doctor,' Ellis advised. I said that I was trying to get Jonathan to a doctor but he kept refusing. 'My heart bleeds for you,' said Ellis, who was given to hyperbole, but had also just learned he had cancer. In the same circumstances, I doubt if I would have done any better. I put the telephone down and felt very alone. This was a time I needed family, but both my parents had died when the children were very young, and my brothers lived overseas.

I climbed the stairs to Jonathan's room which looked out at tree tops and sky. Since he was a child, Jonathan had drawn and painted. His images were usually bold. But today, he had a piece of charcoal clenched in his hand and was making small cramped marks on the paper. His face was bent so low over his desk that I wondered how he could see. He was drawing snakes and spiders and strange tormented faces, swastikas and machine guns, mushroom clouds and knives. When the charcoal disintegrated because he was pressing so hard, he picked up another piece as if he hadn't noticed what had occurred. He was giggling.

I said, 'Tell me . . .' My voice sounded desperate.

'Yes?'

'Tell me what's happening for you.'

'Nothing.'

'But I feel . . .' Oh God, what did I feel? Frightened, confused, needing to convince him that he was behaving strangely, when either he did not want to know about it, or did not comprehend it.

He thrust his face and body so close to mine that I could feel his breath on my forehead. Then he spun me round several times and peered at me. 'Mars Bar,' he said. 'You're a fucking Mars Bar.'

He rocked me backwards and forwards. I began crying. He stopped, and put his arms around me. 'I'm sorry.'

'Jonathan, are you all right?'

'I'm all right. And now get out before I kill you.' He said it casually, and then continued his drawing.

He looked up when I didn't leave. '*Get out!*' he yelled.

A friend gave me the name of two psychiatrists but they were booked up for many weeks. One of them said Jonathan should be making his own appointments. The other, a psychiatrist at a public hospital, said he would see Jonathan but that I would have to bring him in. He said it was probably youthful rebellion. Later that day, Jonathan threw two plates across the kitchen, emptied a cordial bottle over the floor, said that Jane Fonda was his mother, and pushed past me into the street. That night we heard him running up and down the living-room, howling. These were not howls of rebellion; these were howls of pain.

I made an appointment for Jonathan to see one of the psychiatrists but Jonathan was nowhere to be found when I went to take him. So I went myself. The psychiatrist was young and earnest. He made copious notes as I proffered up every detail of my life. Afterwards, I felt disembowelled. The psychiatrists and the general practitioner all declined to make home visits.

I found a social worker and then wished I hadn't. She wore sandals and a denim skirt, touched my arm several times, and spoke with a rising inflection at the end of every sentence. I decided she had taken a counselling course by correspondence.

'Try not to be down-hearted.'

'What am I going to do?'

'Show him you love him.'

'But what-am-I-going-to-do?'

I know its a cliché to write about people talking through gritted teeth but my teeth were so gritted that my jaws felt like a clam shell.

The social worker had a fixed, indefatigable smile. 'It is true that he does appear to have some inappropriate social responses. And some discomfort in his thought processes.' She was beginning to sound nervous. 'But he's probably merely acting out.'

'Why?'

'To pay you back.'

'Why?'

'For coming to Adelaide.'

'But he wanted to come.'

'My dear,' she said with a hint of a sigh, 'teenagers don't always give meaningful responses.'

I stared at her. I could feel tears of frustration pricking behind my eyes.

'It's not like that,' I shouted.

The social worker hopped in quickly. 'Why don't you draw up a contract together and stick it up somewhere handy? Like the door of your fridge.' She smiled graciously.

I am wary of such contracts. They sounded a good idea in the parenting manuals, but whenever I tried them on my children, they said, 'You're weird.'

Jonathan was more pungent. 'You're brain-damaged,' he snarled.

The following day I found a note left by the telephone. It read:
*To Queen Anne from Kinky Joe*

*Nobody wants to play with me any more, all Joe wants is to have some friends and dance round the tree and sing Noel.*

I wept. Because we had only just moved to Adelaide, the children had made few friends. Paul had been keeping away. No one else had called for Jonathan. His isolation was growing.

I am reminded now of a Hockney drawing of a boy crouched inside an egg-shell, walled off from the rest of the world. Some years later, I bought a print of the drawing but I had to stack it away; it made me feel too sad.

Sometimes I felt enraged by Jonathan's behaviour, other times distressed. Mostly I was confused and worried. Adolescence can be a time of extremes, from rebellious independence to agonising vulnerability; a time to burst through into the adult world and find your own identity. Jonathan wasn't finding his identity. He was losing it. In front of our eyes, his personality was slowly changing. I felt as if he were caught in a maze of terror, and I was on the outside struggling to free him but I could not find the way.

Georgia and Joshua were also having a rough time. There they were, in a new city, at a new school, and suddenly their elder brother was turning into some monster who terrorised them at unpredictable times and in unpredictable ways. One of them said, 'I hate him,' and burst into tears. They began to scuttle around the house trying to avoid him. They looked white-faced and strained. I knew that

I was short-changing them but I did not know what else to do. It was like coming across an accident where one person has been blown up, and the other two appear merely stunned. So you put all your energies into the one who is in pieces, and tell the others you'll turn to them in a minute. The trouble was that the minute never came. It was to be a long time before Georgia and Joshua got the attention they needed and deserved.

One morning, Georgia came down to breakfast in the pink kitchen, and banged plates and cups down on the table with a sharpness that made me look up. There was this blonde blue-eyed daughter of mine, paragon of good behaviour, looking cold and angry.

'I had a bad dream,' she said tartly. 'I dreamed Jonathan had a gun and was going to shoot me. I yelled for you, and you came running. You ignored me. You didn't even take the gun. You said, "Jonathan, but how are you *feeling?*" '

I was becoming obsessed by Jonathan and consumed by guilt. Maybe it was all my fault that Jonathan was turning into some rogue delinquent. Maybe I had demanded too much of him. Maybe I had demanded too little. Maybe it was because I worked. Maybe it was because of the divorce. Maybe I should never have uprooted everyone and come to Adelaide. Maybe. The days and nights became prey to 'maybes' that floated around like comic-strip bubbles, each one becoming increasingly judgemental. Maybe it was even punishment for thinking I could be happy again. Maybe I didn't deserve happiness.

One of the fantasies I carried into adult life was that the house I had grown up in, in England, had a mother, a father, and a large kitchen with homemade bread on a scrubbed table and a large pot of soup on the stove. The soul searches for myths to nourish it. By either side of the fireplace there were shelves of bottled fruit. Plump golden peaches, ruby coloured plums, apricots and quinces. They were never sour.

Then one day I was crossing a main highway in the middle of Sydney when, right in the middle of the road, for no apparent reason, I suddenly realised that my own childhood was about as far from the norm as the norm is from Mills and Boon.

The reality was that I had had a father who was a rubber planter in Malaya, who could recite prodigious amounts of poetry and sing Victorian music-hall songs. But I rarely saw him. And a mother who was a fashion designer and wore French silk lingerie and took us for walks in the rain eating buttered brazil nuts. But I didn't see much more of her. My brother, who was three years older, was sent to boarding school at the age of seven, which was the quaint middle-class English custom of the time, and I was looked after by an old-fashioned nanny who taught me to read the *Times* newspaper when I was four, and who told me 'A stitch in time saves nine', and 'Satan finds mischief for idle hands to do'. Good girls didn't get cake until they had eaten all their bread and butter, and good girls always finished their dinner otherwise it wasn't fair on all those starving Indians.

When I was nine, my mother, my brother and I sailed from England to Malaya to join my father. He felt we should be saved from the war with Germany. We arrived in time for war with Japan. We became refugees in Western Australia, where my father joined the Army to teach Malay, in preparation for the great counter-invasion that never came. I spent the rest of my childhood in a household with three refugee families – six children, three mothers, no fathers (except for mine who only came home on leave very occasionally), and no money.

The cosy image of my early family life stayed with me until that day in Sydney when I suddenly realised it was all a fantasy. Maybe this was one of the reasons I had stayed around too long in a marriage that had begun well but ended badly. Even though I had known it was time to move on, I clung to the picture frame around my childhood dream, long after the canvas had been ripped to shreds.

I had come to Adelaide two years after my marriage ended to be with the architect. I was going to paint another canvas to put inside the family frame. The problem was that the architect and I had different pictures in mind. We thought they were the same, but his prussian blue turned out to be my burnt sienna. The moral of the story is: lay your paints out on the table before you begin.

But all this was unknown to me when, on Boxing Day, I had bundled the three children, two dogs and a cat into the car, loaded the roof-rack with luggage, pots and pans, and set out to drive the several thousand kilometres from Sydney to Adelaide.

When we arrived in Adelaide, I had prowled around in concern at the alien environment of the strange green house. The architect kept telling us it had design integrity, but he did not have to live in it. And then I had spotted the plum tree. The plums were not yet ripe, but I watched them in anticipation and, sometime in February, I cajoled all three children into helping me pick them. I washed the fruit, rubbed up the bottling jars, and then realised I had neither rubber bands nor clips to make the lids stay shut. It was Saturday afternoon. We had to wait till Monday till the shops were opened before I could continue with my sugar-plum dream.

By Monday the purple mounds of fruit had begun to ooze and some of the plums were mouldy. I had to throw most of them away. I picked the next lot on my own. The fruit was smaller and not as good. But what the hell, once it was bottled, no one would ever know.

The plums were gently poaching, and I was bored. I went upstairs to write. When I came downstairs, the kitchen was full of steam and a pungent smell. The plums had overcooked. Some had disintegrated into yellow streamers. Damn, damn, damn! But I bottled them, every one of them, and came down next morning to find all the fruit had floated to the top. They looked like small embryos in a sea of pale blood.

I had bottled the plums without sugar. This was in deference to the architect who didn't like sweet food. I now decided that this meant they might be unsafe – and would probably taste revolting.

'Aren't we going to eat them?' said Joshua, who was always hungry.

'No.'

'S'pose we're just going to look at them, are we? S'pose they're going to sit there for ever, are they?'

'Why can't we eat them?' said Georgia.

'Botulism,' I said, with a sudden rush of memory. Botulism, that's why we couldn't eat them. I had remembered being in a boarding house in Western Australia when I was nine years old, and listening in fascination to the fat landlady telling us about the death of her niece. 'Ate some of her own bottled peaches, and dropped down dead,' said the landlady. 'In front of my eyes.'

So we never ate the plums. We moved to three other houses in the six years we were in Adelaide, and with every move, the plums came too. But I never allowed anyone to open them. Nor did I allow them to be thrown away.

'Tread softly because you might tread upon my plums,' I once said to a friend. But he hadn't read Yeats and he didn't know about the plums. He looked alarmed.

Those early Adelaide days had held many promises. I remember the time we went to a Sunday lunch party given by an Adelaide establishment family. It was the kind of party where everyone hid behind facades of charm, but every now and then flew paper darts with a cutting edge. The darts were thrown to see if you knew the code to deflect them. Are you, or are you not, one of us?

The sun shone. The sky was calm blue. There were grapes and figs and peaches growing in the garden. We played tennis and I fell. Jonathan also played tennis. He wore cream trousers and a white cricket shirt. The hostess came up afterwards and said how lucky I was to have such charming children, and how unusual to find a boy of seventeen so well-balanced, so intelligent, so delightful.

Many months later we were in a furniture shop, buying a second-hand wardrobe for Georgia. Jonathan had come back from Sydney, where he had been discharged from hospital. All joy had gone from his eyes. He wore stained jeans and a khaki jumper that had shrunk so his stomach was bare. His hair was greasy and he had no shoes. He walked behind me all the time, like a small boy afraid to go first. His head was bowed and he gazed at the ground. Just outside the shop he stopped by an old milk churn which was painted dark-green and red. It contained a couple of battered old tennis rackets. He picked one of them out and tried to stand it on end.

'Good party,' he said, as if it had been yesterday. Then he cocked his head even further to one side than usual. 'But I wasn't good.'

'You seemed good.'

'Not good. In pieces.' He banged his head with the racket.

'I didn't realise.'

'No.' He looked sombre. 'The pieces blew apart.'

He said it in a most matter-of-fact voice. It was the longest communication between us for weeks. But he was already shuffling out of the shop, his arms hanging stiffly by his side because the medication he was taking had caused his muscles to become rigid.

A young man who walked like a robot. A young man who said his mind had blown apart. How do you put the pieces together again? The question had an urgency about it, and I almost said it out aloud, but didn't because it had been engulfed by another question, one that terrified me.

What if the pieces *never* come together again?

Years later I talk with a young woman who had her first attack of mental illness when she was nineteen. She says, 'When I first had the breakdown, it was like dropping an egg on the kitchen floor. Part of the shell is still intact, but part of it's shattered, and my personality is the yolk, leaking away. And I can't get it back together again.'

But I digress. Two weeks after we first arrived in Adelaide, Jonathan decided to return to school. He had dropped out of school in Sydney one year earlier. His childhood up to the age of twelve had been reasonably uneventful. Then, as later, he often had difficulty sleeping, but a psychologist we consulted said that it was probably because he was highly strung – one of those vague terms that we all tend to use when a child has problems. His written work was chaotic (nowadays he would probably have been assessed as dyslexic) but in primary school he got away with it, because he was so advanced in his general knowledge. I used to be intrigued by how much he seemed to know about so many things – yet he did little formal study. From about the age of ten he had begun going to community art classes after school because he enjoyed them and he was good. He painted with surprising confidence, particularly as he was a timid boy.

He was twelve when he went to high school and into the top stream. At first, he had friends and an active social life. He was a good runner and swimmer, but he hated competition. He was the only boy who came back from football matches with his clothes still clean. If the ball ever came his way, he'd regard it with alarm, and get rid of it as if he had been thrown a grenade.

He was thirteen, and staying in the country when we came across a young horse that had caught its leg in a barbed-wire gate and was kicking in terror, so no one could get near. The farmer thought it might have to be destroyed. Jonathan calmed the frightened animal by touching and talking to it until it stood quite still, and slowly and gently he freed its leg.

But at high school, he began a dizzy spiral downwards. His writing became even more chaotic. He had problems concentrating and problems ordering his ideas. He seemed to find the environment of a big institution difficult to cope with. He found it hard to get up in the morning and was almost always running late. He became increasingly vague. He began to lose his friends, and he said that people were against him.

He wrote an essay that precipitated an urgent call from the school, to say they were very concerned because it sounded as if he were suffering from schizophrenia. In it, Jonathan had described hearing voices and walking along looking down at himself walking along. He said that time kept stretching, and that spaces moved. The school recommended one of the Education Department's psychologists, who called me 'mother' throughout the interview, and Jonathan 'son'. He wanted to know our major areas of disagreement. I said that Jonathan was currently wanting to go to the beaches at night with a group of much older boys, and I thought that at thirteen, he was too young. I said I thought they probably went to the beaches to smoke dope. Jonathan said I was being too protective, that I wouldn't give him his freedom. I said 'Too right.'

'I don't think your boy has any psychiatric problems, mother. I think you have communication problems,' said the psychologist. He recommended a parenting manual.

Just to make sure, Ellis and I took Jonathan to another psychologist who tested him and said he was fine. He may well have been. Who knows whether the essay was the product of a fertile imagination or whether indeed there were changes occurring in his perceptions of time and space? Who knows whether the world he saw was the same as the world the rest of us saw? Who knows whether those childhood times when he talked about faces changing into witches' faces were the beginnings of hallucinations?

At the beginning of his second year of high school, Jonathan was demoted to a bottom stream. He was distressed. He said he knew that he could do better and he thought he should leave. He wanted to try a boarding school, and asked to go to a small school just outside Sydney where two of his friends went. He enjoyed this new school and at the end of his first year, he came top in many of his exams. A smaller community and a structured environment seemed to suit him. This would be a recurring feature of his adult life. Give him structure and he did well. Put him into a situation of multiple choice or with lots of stimulation around him and he began to panic. His form master still remembers him vividly. 'He was such an interesting and intelligent boy.' But at the end of his first year Jonathan refused to return to the boarding school. He would give no reason.

He said he wanted to go back to the same high school as before. Once again, he started in the top stream but his descent was even more rapid than before.

This was still the 'seventies and the end of an era that had seen a generation or more of young people challenge institutionalised authority. Rebellion was fashionable, and Jonathan excelled.

He began to have big mood swings, from happy to depressed. His tolerance of any kind of frustration became minimal. He truanted. He rarely did his homework. He rebelled against the school uniform and took to wearing his father's old black tails, which swamped him. He had one ear pierced and insisted on wearing a sea-shell as an earring. The school refused to take him with the sea-shell. He refused to attend without it. I had visions of ringing round the schools of Sydney asking if they would take a boy wearing a sea-shell dangling from one ear. He kept disappearing. I kept hunting for him. He was smoking a lot of marijuana and was often stoned. He thought that people disliked him, or were plotting against him.

The only activity that he pursued with any regularity was his painting. He went to Life classes and came back with large canvases of joyful nudes. They were executed in charcoal with angelic faces, big breasts and even bigger thighs. His paintings were more allegorical, oranges and blues and mythical creatures soaring to the heavens.

Somehow or other he managed to get his School Certificate, and then announced that he intended to leave school and to get a job. He was sixteen. Both Ellis and I tried to dissuade him, but he wouldn't budge.

Ellis and I had separated earlier that year. Our marriage had been stormy for some time, but after we parted the fighting ceased. I hoped life would gradually revert to tranquillity and that Jonathan would settle. His relationship with Ellis had never been good. Ellis seemed to me impatient of Jonathan's dreaminess and always anticipating the worst. Jonathan was fearful of his father's unpredictability and so avoided him.

In January the following year, Jonathan worked for one day at a greengrocer who fired him when he knocked over a stack of fruit boxes, 'It was an accident,' he said irritably. He worked for a chemist and was sacked because he forgot to complete a delivery run. He didn't seem to know why he forgot. He tried selling household cleansers, door-to-door, but the only ones he sold were those bought by me. He began each new job with eagerness, like a young bird that flaps its wings ready to fly, but each time falls crumpled to the ground.

In March he contracted glandular fever and was ill for months. He become withdrawn and depressed, and I arranged for him to visit the psychiatric clinic for adolescents at a leading Sydney hospital. He went weekly for quite some time, and was then pronounced to be in no further need of counselling. The psychiatrist said he was a fine boy, who may have had some difficulties in his schooling, and in his relationship with his father, but who was now unusually emotionally mature, and should do well.

Jonathan had felt that Adelaide was an opportunity for a fresh start. He decided to return to school, and to select his own. I applauded his initiative. He found one that was strong in music and art and his first day went well. He spent most of dinner discussing his work. He sounded excited and positive.

Problems began to appear within two or three weeks. He said the school was stupid, the work was stupid, and he was stupid. He sat in front of his books with his head in his hands and you could tell that what was on the page wasn't reaching whatever was going on inside his head. He came home and paced up and down the kitchen, angrily telling me that people were scheming against him. Nobody liked him, he said. It was a familiar story.

He told me he was leaving. He said that he would go to Art School instead. Then he made an appointment to see the principal and said, politely but firmly, 'I have to leave.' I also made an appointment to see the principal and he said he was sorry, but there was nothing he could do. I don't suppose there was.

I forget the actual timing of incidents. There were so many. Had I been equipped with my present knowledge, it would have been clear that Jonathan had been heading for a breakdown for months, even years before it occurred. Maybe as you read this, you are also thinking that it was obvious. But I was grappling with that age-old parental dilemma of balancing the danger of being over-reactive with making sure that I was not guilty of benign neglect.

And then came Sunday, Sunday bloody Sunday, when Paul had brought Jonathan into the kitchen, and said, 'I think he's sick.' After that the days that followed were never quite the same.

As that autumn moved into winter, Jonathan seemed gradually to stabilise. He was no longer as angry or withdrawn. Although he occasionally giggled and talked to himself, it was possible to have normal conversations with him. He started painting again, and often went for walks down by the River Torrens, to the wild part that was overgrown with reeds. He said it gave him calm inside his head.

Early in May I was asked to go to Uganda to bring back magazine and television stories about life after Idi Amin and, after much agonising, I decided to accept. For some years I had been alternating working as a journalist, making documentary films and radio programs, with working on social justice issues for various government enquiries and organisations. I had given all this up when I moved to Adelaide, and had been trying to concentrate on writing film scripts, but life with Jonathan had been so distracting that I hadn't made much progress. Yet I was the sole income-earner for myself and the three children. The architect said, 'Go to Uganda', and one of his grown-up daughters moved in to help mind the house. The architect had three daughters by a marriage that had ended some years previously. Two were grown up and one was Joshua's age. The architect's daughters did not live with us; they were loving and lively, and we all got on well, which was remarkable considering the strains.

I flew to Uganda with an aid team from World Vision. Uganda had been liberated from Amin by Tanzania, and large tracts of the country had been destroyed in the fighting. There was a critical shortage of food, water, fuel and medicines. Many people were starving. Amin's eight-year regime had left the country in economic ruin.

For me, the overwhelming memory of Uganda was one of horror. Almost every person we met had someone in their family who had been killed, imprisoned, tortured or raped. I listened to stories of sickening similarity. I did not want to think about them because I could not bear to think about them.

We went to the headquarters of Amin's secret police, obscenely known as the State Research Bureau, where over two hundred people were murdered each night. It was a pale pink, modern building, set among trees, and looked like a small suburban hotel until we drove through the gates and saw corpses piled high against the compound walls. In the eight years of Amin's nightmare rule, up to half a million Ugandans were murdered. Amin operated with a network of some three thousand secret police who permeated every level of society; no one was safe.

Doomed prisoners were blindfolded, and led into the cellars of the State Research Bureau where their heads were hammered with a sledgehammer. Sometimes the guards would make the prisoners hammer each other. Women were not hammered; their throats were cut. Children were strangled. We had to use torches when we went into the cellars, and the smell of death was almost too much to bear. The walls and the floor were caked with blood, and at our feet lay pathetic pieces of clothing, a thong, a child's jumper, a woman's dress.

We drove into the country, past armed checkpoints, to stay with the Archbishop of Kampala, a lovely rotund man who was a fund of humour and goodness. His house and compound had been burned down by Amin's soldiers a few days before we arrived, and everyone was living in a cluster of army tents. We had a banquet on our first night together. We had Cadbury's Bournville Cocoa, and sweet potato, cooked seventeen different ways. It was the only food that remained.

I shared a tent with an evangelical journalist from the mid-west of America. Her name was Beverley. She had blonde corkscrew curls, freckles, white even teeth and a fervent handshake. She believed that a lady should look her best at all times, and had brought along her electric hair rollers and a pink nylon negligee. Before we went to bed, we were told that if we had to relieve ourselves, we should use a chamber-pot inside the tent, rather than squat down outside.

The land around the camp was mined. I could tell by the set of Beverley's jaw-line that she wasn't convinced, especially when she saw that the chamber-pot was a kerosene tin. She decided she would prefer landmines to tinkling tin. She put on her pink negligee and wandered off into the night. I prayed that the good Lord would reward her modesty by keeping her on safe ground.

The night before we left, a young trainee priest, who looked about the same age as Jonathan, and as dark as Jonathan was fair, came up to me and smiled sweetly.

'Sister Anne, Sister Anne, when were you saved?'

'Oh dear,' I mumbled, 'I don't think I have been saved.'

He smiled radiantly. 'Then do not worry, Sister Anne. I will pray for you and you will be saved.'

I hoped most fervently that he would be right.

When I arrived back in Adelaide, I found that Jonathan had been difficult while I was away. He had been harrassing everyone, particularly Georgia, and I felt upset and guilty. I was at the beginning of a pathway of conflicting demands: demands to earn the family income, demands to be a good mother, demands to work and keep my own sanity, demands of personal relationships and demands to act as if everything were normal – because that's my temperament, and it's both a strength and a failing. Until there came a time when I could pretend no longer.

At eleven o'clock one night in June, a few weeks after my return, Jonathan went into Joshua's bedroom, turned on the light, and began pulling books out of the shelves and onto the floor. Then he turned on Georgia's light and did the same. When we tried to stop him, he threw us across the room.

Then we were fighting in my bedroom. In between dodging blows, I was shouting 'Behave yourself!' like Miss Jean Brodie, decidedly out of her prime. Everyone seemed to be screaming. I hauled the other two children out of the room, and we huddled outside in the corridor, shaking with fright. Jonathan was still rampaging. I went back into my room and tried to hold him. He threw me out again. I rang a young woman psychiatrist whom I had recently met with mutual friends, and who already knew something of what had been happening. I sobbed out that evening's disaster. She listened, and then said clearly and firmly, 'Jonathan is crazy.'

This was the first time anyone had been so explicit.

'Crazy?'

'Jonathan almost certainly has schizophrenia.'

The impact was surprising. I felt a huge relief. Jonathan's rages, his strange behaviour, the bizarre delusions, all made sense within the context of not making sense. People can tackle almost any problem once they know what it is. She cautioned that, because she had never examined Jonathan, I was not to take this as a confirmed diagnosis, but that I should get him professionally assessed as soon as possible. She gave me the name of a doctor to contact at one of Adelaide's two major psychiatric hospitals and said that she would also speak to him.

By then, Jonathan had left the house, and Georgia and Joshua had gone to bed. I hunted through my books and pulled down a history of psychiatry. It said that the mentally ill had always been with us – to be feared, marvelled at, laughed at, pitied, or tortured, but all too seldom cured.

That wasn't much joy. I pulled down a family medical dictionary: *SCHIZOPHRENIA is a serious mental disorder marked by irrational thinking, disturbed emotions, and a breakdown in communicating with others. The cause is not known, although the possibility of a biochemical defect has been suggested. The name schizophrenia (from the Greek words 'schizos' – split, and 'phrenos' – the mind) was coined by the German psychiatrist Bleuler in 1911.*

My knowledge of schizophrenia was mostly limited to the movies. The last film I had seen was *One Flew Over the Cuckoo's Nest*, which had fascinated Jonathan so much that he had gone three times. In the film, the hero, Jack Nicholson, ends up with a lobotomy. Maybe Jonathan doesn't have schizophrenia, I thought hastily. But how the hell could I find out if Jonathan refused to go to the doctors and the doctors wouldn't come to him?

I went to the hospital psychiatrist, who said that he would willingly assess Jonathan, but that if Jonathan would not attend voluntarily, I would have to get him committed. This would not be possible unless it could be shown that he was a danger to himself or to others. Nobody would commit him, sight unseen. We were back to square one.

I decided the time was long overdue to enlist the help of the architect. Except for that first night of Jonathan's breakdown, the architect had tended, understandably, to think that Jonathan was bad not mad, so I had tried to keep Jonathan's exploits away from him. But one afternoon when Jonathan destroyed several of my favourite gramophone records and then threatened me, I thought, hell, if this is what life is really like, why try to hide it any more? Love me, love my children, I thought. The architect always found any kind of confrontation difficult, but he came round and tried to talk reasonably with Jonathan.

Jonathan told him he would break his records too, and stick a gorilla knife up his arse. *Jonathan*, I thought, *you are jeopardising my love life, my re-creation of happy families. Jonathan, don't do this to me, don't do it to us.*

Now I will move forward to one night in early July, when I am wakened by loud noises downstairs, feet, laughter, loud heavy music. I look at my watch. Three a.m. I go downstairs and find my living-room full of strangers, having a party. Jonathan is the only person I know, but he is slumped in an armchair with his feet sprawled in front of him. He is out to it. The men are all dressed in black leather, with boots and spurs. The smallest man has shaved his head and dyed his scalp a curious plum colour. All of them are heavily tattooed, but one man boasts a particularly rich profusion of serpents, starting from the tips of his fingers and coiling up to the tops of his arms. The women are also dressed in leather, tasselled, and they seem to have white or orange hair. There are beer cans everywhere. The strangers stare at me as if I'm the intruder, and I find my heart is thumping.

Plum Head swaggers up to me and pushes his face close to mine. He is hostile. 'Nice place you got, lady,' he says. He pushes me till I am backed up against the wall.

Serpent Arms says, 'What's upstairs?'

*Georgia and Joshua are upstairs*, I think in a panic. One of the girls turns up the music even louder, and knocks over a beer can.

It is like a B-grade movie, and I am caught in the middle of it. Intuitively, I become very formal. 'My name is Anne Deveson,' I say, 'and I am Jonathan's mother. How do you do?'

Plum Head backs off and looks discomforted.

Pulling my shrunken bath robe around me as if it were a gown of finest silk, I circle the room, shaking hands with all of them. I offer them tea. 'Milk?' I say. 'Sugar?' I invite Plum Head to help and he shuffles his feet in embarrassment. One of the girls jumps up and helps instead. She is called Cheryl and has nice legs.

When we have finished tea, I thank them all for coming and ask if they would mind leaving now because it is late and I am tired.

Plum Head shepherds them out, saying, 'Nice place you got, lady.'

I cover Jonathan with a rug, check all the safety locks on doors and windows and go up to bed. I am aching. I long for sweet dreams. *Please give me one, please God.* I dream I am a milk saucepan. A sturdily built, slightly battered saucepan that has been full of milk. The pan is on a gas jet that has been turned up much too high, and all the milk has boiled away. Any minute, it will burn.

After this incident, the weeks bucketed by, with one drama after another. And then I remembered Frank. Frank was a community psychiatrist in Adelaide who had impressed me by his common-sense when I was a commissioner with the Royal Commission into Human Relationships which the federal government had established some four years earlier. The Commission had been set up to inquire into the family, social, educational, legal and sexual aspects of male and female relationships, which was so broad a brief it required people of commonsense.

Frank was also a fine potter, a man with a lively, irreverent mind, and boundless energy. He greeted me cheerfully and leapt up the stairs ahead of me. He carried his keys dangling out of his pocket on a purple ribbon to make sure he did not forget them. He listened, and then proposed a plan of action. The plan included getting someone to visit Jonathan at home as a priority, and Frank being available for support whenever we needed it. This was the first time anyone had offered any practical assistance, and I felt like weeping with relief. If you are wounded and bleeding heavily, you don't want theoretical dissertations on the nature of the wounding. First you want to stop the bleeding.

Frank sent a colleague of his, a young woman who had worked extensively with disturbed adolescents. Sally arrived late one afternoon and Jonathan was home. He sat hunched up in a chair, peering at her through tousled hair. He would not speak. She came a couple of times, and on the second visit Jonathan talked, mostly about his painting. Sally felt it was possible he had been suffering from a drug-induced psychosis or period of madness, and that he might be pulling out of it. If he had another major flare-up we were to call for help immediately.

Jonathan's behaviour continued to be erratic over the next few weeks and then, one morning towards the end of September, he announced that he wanted to see his father, whose condition had deteriorated, and who had just been admitted to hospital.

I was not too happy about Jonathan going to Sydney as I felt he was still too unstable. This is codswallop: I was so exhausted that I would have sent Jonathan to the other side of the moon if it were possible. So I encouraged him to go and said I would pay his fare. I do not feel good about this revelation. Jonathan should not have been put on a plane to Sydney with only the most tenuous arrangements made for his arrival the other end, but I reckoned that something, anything, had to be done to change the status quo. If he were behaving badly because he was overly dependent upon me (one professional opinion), he would cease the drama once I was no longer around. He would survive. If the problem were drugs or schizophrenia or a combination (another professional opinion), then without my support, he would probably crash. But at least if he crashed, we could get help.

Jonathan said that he would stay at the home of an old school-friend (Ellis was too ill for Jenny to have Jonathan as well). I checked arrangements with the friend's parents and said that Jonathan had been unwell. I took him to the airport, feeling elated at the prospect of some respite, and miserable because I was worried about him. He was then eighteen.

Jonathan did not arrive at the friend's house, nor did he ring Jenny. He was missing for several days. We reported it to the police and I felt sick with guilt and fear. Late one night I had a phone-call from Jenny. Jonathan had turned up at her house, incoherent and ill. She had persuaded him to stay the night. Jenny was good with Jonathan. He liked and trusted her, and I will always be grateful for her gentleness and patience. Next morning I flew up to Sydney and we met round Jenny's dining-room table, Jonathan, Jenny and I, and Andy – a young community psychiatrist and friend of the family who was to take part in Jonathan's story several times over the next few years. Jonathan liked Andy, and when we were living in Sydney sometimes used to listen to jazz with him. Andy had the kind of laughter that made you feel good.

It was a round dining-room table, with a low hanging light, and Jonathan sat with his hands crossed on the table and his eyes downcast. He looked gaunt and hollow-eyed. Andy talked with him, gently.

Jonathan replied in a voice that was little more than a whisper.

'I'm all right.'

'You don't look all right.'

'They're following me.'

'Scared?'

'I reckon.'

'You'd be safer in hospital.'

'You reckon?'

'I reckon.'

Very late that night, Andy drove Jonathan to a city hospital where he was admitted as a voluntary patient and, a short while later diagnosed as having schizophrenia.

Looking back, I remember being relieved at having a firm diagnosis. At least it gave us something to work with. And, at that time I felt confident that Jonathan would pull out of the illness. I had no idea of what lay ahead.

In those days a certain shame surrounded mental illness; it was rarely discussed, and little information was available. Even today, the taboo remains, and schizophrenia is probably the most misunderstood of all illnesses, the most puzzling, and the most neglected. Yet we are dealing with a common condition which takes up more hospital beds than any other single illness, and which can happen to anyone, regardless of economic or social conditions, race or culture. Schizophrenia accounts for three-quarters of all mental disorders. One person in every hundred will develop the illness at some time in their lives: worldwide, that means 55 million people. Three-quarters of those will be young, between the ages of sixteen and twenty-five.

Although an equal number of males and females develop the illness, it occurs earlier, and in a more severe form, in males. One-quarter of people who develop schizophrenia will have one episode only, and then make a complete recovery. For the rest, it will be a lifetime's struggle against recurring attacks. Some may remain chronically ill, although later years tend to be less stormy than the youthful years. Some – from ten to fifteen per cent – will commit suicide because the struggle will have been too much to bear.

Although we still do not fully understand the causes of schizophrenia, and we do not know how to cure it, improved treatment means that it is no longer regarded as hopeless.

Back home in Adelaide, I resorted to reading medical textbooks in the library. The information I received was contradictory. The pendulum was still swinging between biological theories, which saw schizophrenia as a brain disease, and psychosocial theories, which saw it as a response to pressures of family or society. I oversimplify, but the confusion surrounding the illness at the time, and the tendency still to blame families were to have a profound effect on what would happen to us all. Very soon we realised that we not only had to deal with Jonathan's schizophrenia but with ignorance and fear. Some people thought he had a split personality, and that Jonathan the beautiful was turning into Jonathan the bad. Others thought that he was malingering. Or that his illness was due to his upbringing. Early on, I was told by a doctor that at first she had thought I was a noxious parent but had subsequently changed her mind. The psychiatrist who had been treating Jonathan in Sydney was more generous. He said, 'Jonathan has a wonderful smile. It's a sign of being much loved.' I was feeling so battered and defensive at the time that his words were quite magical. I wanted to hug him, and probably did.

Schizophrenia still presents medical research with one of its greatest challenges. Much about the illness remains a mystery, but gradually its complexities are being unlocked as advances in technology enable us to record activities of the brain in a variety of ways, and to identify specific differences in brain functioning between those who have the illness and those who do not. With schizophrenia, fundamental processes in the brain are disturbed, distorting the way a person thinks and experiences the world. Messages are channelled to the wrong responses, like an old-fashioned telephone switchboard making faulty connections. Information floods in, and overwhelms the brain.

Nobody is yet certain why this malfunctioning occurs. Some kind of vulnerability seems to be built into the system, which may be due to disturbances – genetic or environmental, or both – that affect the development of brain cells in pregnancy around the time of birth. It may be, for example, that a viral infection, or a shortage of oxygen in a difficult birth, or a developmental failure, creates this vulnerability, which is then triggered into malfunctioning later in life. Any number of factors may act as the triggers, ranging from environmental stress to drug abuse or hormonal changes. With schizophrenia, as in many illnesses, chemistry, genetics and environment intermingle in endlessly convoluted permutations.

Within the term 'schizophrenia' there is a whole range of manifestations and levels of severity. The more common type is indicatedby a gradual onset which does not become fully apparent until adolescence, the other main type by a sudden onset in adulthood. It is from the latter type that people can more often make a full recovery.

Now that I know more about the nature of the illness, it is easier for me in hindsight to understand much of Jonathan's bizarre behaviour.

Many of the more frightening symptoms may be a consequence of the mind trying to make sense of its inner turmoil. People may have delusions, like believing they are Jesus Christ, or that their neighbours have stolen their mind. They may have auditory hallucinations, hearing voices that tell them to behave or feel in certain ways. Sometimes the voices are friendly; often they are cruel and taunting. Visual hallucinations may bring about flashing lights or inexplicable images. Smells and taste may change, and so may perceptions of time and space. A minute may seem like a hundred years, and the face of a friend may suddenly disintegrate or distort into some horrifying form. Thoughts may become fragmented, and all sense of personal boundaries disappear, so that it may feel as if the world is invading body and mind, or that the person is spinning out into a black vortex, from which there will be no return.

Jonathan bangs his head against the wall and screams 'Leave me alone!' Jonathan gazes into the mirror, touches his face, touches the glass and sighs, 'Are you there, Joe?' Jonathan hears voices inside his head and outside; they tell him he will die if he doesn't put his left foot first when he climbs the stairs.

The illness has its active and passive stages, and these can overlap. Some of the more acute symptoms of schizophrenia, like delusions, hallucinations and thought disorders, occur in the active or psychotic stages of the illness ('psychotic' means an inability to distinguish reality from fantasy). In the passive phase of the illness, people seem to 'shut down', perhaps out of exhaustion, perhaps because this seems the only way to handle their anxieties. They become withdrawn and lacking in concentration. They look unwell. Like Jonathan, they might stay in bed most of the day, too drained and depressed to move.

A curious feature of the illness is that all over the world, symptoms are remarkably similar, which suggests a common biological disturbance. Research indicates that the breakdown is probably occurring within the limbic system, that part of the brain which acts like a filter, ordering and processing all the messages we receive, both internal and external. Explanations for people's symptoms will depend upon their cultural or educational backgrounds. A man in the rainforests of Nigeria says that the witchdoctor has stolen his mind. A woman in New York thinks that the television is broadcasting her most secret thoughts. Jonathan, sitting up in his hospital bed in Sydney, with his Walkman headphones plugged into his ears, believes that he is communing with Pink Floyd and journeying to the sun and the moon.

I could leave music for Jonathan to listen to, but I couldn't stay with him because I had the two younger children waiting in Adelaide. When I returned home, I found a message from the Australian Broadcasting Corporation asking me to make a six-part television series which would be screened during the International Year of the Disabled. Ironically, we were to film stories of people coping with disabilities. Some of the series was to be shot in Adelaide, but the rest would be mainly in Sydney, which would mean I could see more of Jonathan.

The first time I met Jonathan after the diagnosis he was wearing a white gown and lambswool boots. He had put on weight. His face was moon-shaped, his hair was blond and shining, and he walked with his arms held stiffly out each side.

'Hello Anne', he said, 'How are you today?' He kissed my cheek.

This was no longer the turbulent Jonathan. This was a docile Jonathan, robot-like, and different from any of the Jonathans I had ever known.

He kept repeating, 'I'll be a good boy, Mummy, I'll be a good boy.' He was eighteen years old and he sounded about three. But then he lit a cigarette, which wasn't the action of a three-year-old, and I saw the ash-trays overflowing with butts, and the fog of smoke that was to become so familiar in every psychiatric hospital I visited.

Jonathan's weight increase and his wooden appearance was partly due to the medication used to control the psychotic symptoms of his schizophrenia. For example, the night that he turned up at Jenny's, he believed that he was being followed by the secret police, and voices told him that he would be burned alive. He was in terror.

Medication took the edge off Jonathan's madness but it did not work as well as the doctors had hoped, and this was to be a recurring problem. Jonathan also seemed to have no insights into his illness. He kept saying that he was fine but everybody else was sick. When you suffer an illness that strips you of all sense of self, it is too terrifying to admit this vulnerability to the outside world.

My Sydney visits were depressing. I would have production meetings with the Australian Broadcasting Corporation in the morning, and in the afternoon see Jonathan, followed by Ellis. The hospitals were on opposite sides of the town. Though Ellis had lost a lot of weight and looked vulnerable and ill, he would sit up in bed and make prophetic statements like the Ancient Mariner. His silvery hair was thinning from the chemotherapy and he made valiant jokes about it. 'You will never forget me,' he said waving a gaunt finger.

I went to the other hospital to see Jonathan, who said, 'I want to come home, Mummy.'

My grief felt so raw that I often had a pain in my stomach. I would howl silently on the plane going back to Adelaide, my tears falling into the soggy sandwiches with their slices of pink rubbery meat and yellow rubbery cheese. I sometimes thought that if my seat belt weren't holding me in place, I'd have slithered in a crumpled heap onto the floor. Georgia and Joshua were angry when I returned, because they felt abandoned. The architect was angry because he felt abandoned. And I felt like a fruit tree whose branches had been pecked bare.

The time came when Jonathan was ready to leave hospital; he was no longer psychotic. His medication had been reduced although he still needed it. His general health had improved. I wanted him home, but I also did not want him home because I was terrified of more trauma. I had conversations with myself: *I hope he comes home ... I hope he doesn't come home ... He must come home, no matter what ... He may come home but only if I am guaranteed that we won't be terrorised again ... Come home, Jonathan, I want you home.*

Jonathan made the final decision. 'Adelaide's boring. Sydney's not. I'm not coming home.'

The doctor found Jonathan a hostel near the hospital and arranged to keep an eye on him. I didn't see him till he had been there for two or three weeks. He had changed from being Jonathan, the jolly young giant, to being Joe, *poor old Joe.* That was how he described himself. He must have lost all the clothes I had left for him. He wore three jumpers, shrunken and dirty. His jeans were obviously not his own because they were almost falling off him. He had hitched them up with a piece of string, and as he walked the cleft of his buttocks showed, white and vulnerable.

The hostel was primarily for people with alcohol and drug addiction. Nothing else suitable was available. There was, and still is, a gross shortage of accommodation for young people who are mentally ill. Most of the residents at this hostel were much older than Jonathan, and Jonathan was doing his best to get kicked out by bringing in bottles of beer.

The building was a gaunt Victorian mansion, with neither heart nor soul. The kitchen was plastered with notices about washing up, though one notice informed us that God loved us. The place was permeated with the smell of dank socks and stale ash-trays and sometimes of urine and vomit. It was not a place for an eighteen-year-old.

I went to Jonathan and said firmly that I wanted him to come home. Jonathan refused. We went out to get a meal. It was dusk and had been raining. We walked down a back laneway with unlit houses on either side. Jonathan began to drag behind me. I became anxious. The flow between us had vanished and in its place there was a scratchy tension. Jonathan began talking to himself. He spat on the ground several times, and then pissed in the street with a flourish that commanded attention. He swirled his urine up in the air, round and round like a Catherine wheel. I wanted to laugh; instead, I heard myself say in a squeaky voice, 'That's not a very nice thing to do.'

Jonathan said, 'Fuck off!'

'Fuck off yourself!' I stomped off till I hit the main highway with its harsh lights and screaming traffic. I stopped to look back. Jonathan was still standing in the laneway, a dark solitary figure, swaying from side to side. I walked back and slipped my arm through his. 'Let's go and eat.'

The next time I came up to Sydney, I called the hostel as usual. Jonathan was gone. The hostel manager didn't know where, nor did the hospital. I rang friends, other hospitals and the police. Nothing.

I returned to Adelaide feeling sick inside. *Jonathan missing, Jonathan missing.* Jonathan had often been missing.

Georgia said, 'Don't be silly, he'll turn up.' She sounded cross.

Four days later there was a phone-call at three in the morning from the mother of one of Jonathan's old school-friends. She had been woken by a noise in their kitchen and had found Jonathan at the fridge, helping himself to a ham bone, and giggling. He had broken a window at the back and climbed in. His hand was cut and bleeding but not severely. He was incoherent, thin and dirty. I flew to Sydney the following day.

The kitchen was white and bright and well ordered. Jonathan was still sleeping. He was lying on a bed, covered by a blue-and-white doona, his feet sticking out at the end. His hair was matted, his mouth slightly open. I arranged to come back later that night to have another go at getting him home. Jonathan had already left before I returned. I hung around for two or three days, trying to track him down, and then gave up and returned to Adelaide.

Two days later Jonathan arrived at the house of another friend in Sydney, lay down in the hallway and he refused to move. He lay there on and off for several days while I had long-distance phone-calls with him and with the new host family about the reasons why he couldn't go on sleeping in their hall. He said that if he slept north to south instead of south to north this would make it all right.

The mother of the family sounded distressed and the father

exasperated. The father said he felt he should call in the police, at least to try to get Jonathan to hospital. I agreed. I also decided to go back to Sydney once more to tackle the health services. But, again, Jonathan had left by the time the police arrived, and long before I arrived. He had become quite a powerful operator, the old Joe. He had me going back and forth between Sydney and Adelaide like a yo-yo. He had several households in Hunter's Hill torn between concern and anger at the way in which he kept disrupting their lives.

For several weeks, Jonathan flitted around the Sydney suburb where he grew up. Sometimes he was seen in the very early morning, striding along the main highway, holding animated conversations with himself. He had clung to his old grey Tibetan jacket, which by now was so dirt-encrusted it was tinged with brown.

God knows how much time elapsed. It seemed like weeks but probably was far less, when there was a telephone call from a stranger, a polite-sounding, anxious male who apologised for disturbing me. 'Your son is living in a cave at the bottom of my garden.'

'A cave?'

'By the river. I leave food out for him each day.'

'I'm grateful. I'm really grateful. Is he all right?'

'No, he's like an animal. Living in a cave.' The man finished on a rising inflection, waiting for me to respond with a neat and reassuring resolution.

I could not think of one. I was having to accept that I could no longer go on taking responsibility for Jonathan, and that his illness would not melt away.

I never found Jonathan living in the cave, and neither did Andy nor any of the friends I asked to look for him. By the time I was able to return to Sydney, he had moved on. I drove around his old haunts, and was about to give up when I spotted him padding through the streets, near the house where we used to live. At first I was distressed, and then I felt anger. He did not have to live like this: it had been his choice not to return home.

Anger was swept away by relief. We hugged each other and sat on a wall in the sun. He was wearing an old army greatcoat. His hair was long, and in a pony-tail. His feet were bare and covered in sores, but he looked quite well. He said that he was staying with various friends, and would come back to Adelaide soon, but not yet. He wouldn't mind a couple of dollars to buy some cigarettes. He took some money and hurried off down the road.

I found out he was getting social security, and this meant that theoretically he had enough money to eat. He also had friends. Even at his most distressed and distressing, Jonathan always had the capacity to get people to help him. They might have cursed him, be angered by him, be distraught and full of sorrow for him, but almost always they tried to help. Until the burden became too great; then they rang me.

By December it was clear that Ellis did not have long to live. When he was in his fifties he had sat up in bed with nightmares about dying. Death was something that would be beyond his control, and he could not cope well with anything he could not control. Now he had to find acceptance, and he did so with some amazement but with courage.

One day I went to the hospital and found Ellis had rallied. He had gathered all three of his wives around his bedside, with the same sense of occasion that had marked his living, as it now marked his dying. He spoke to us in turn and I have no doubt told each of us we were the best beloved. Perhaps we were; perhaps there can be many best beloveds. Another day, I managed to find Jonathan and he came with me to see his father in hospital. I would like to say they held hands and talked with deep meaning, but Jonathan sat with his eyes downcast, and Ellis looked bleak and exhausted. One late afternoon, shortly before Christmas, I went to see Ellis, and felt that it would be my last visit. In amongst the fake holly and the tinsel, and the trolleys that rumbled by laden with plastic food and fizzy drinks, we held hands and said we were sorry for the times we had hurt one another, and glad for the good times. And then we said goodbye. I did not find it easy to leave.

Back home in Adelaide, too, Christmas was approaching. The architect had a holiday place down the coast, near the sea. It was a square stone cottage with shuttered windows, surrounded by almond and olive trees, and large pine trees that dropped pine cones for winter fires and for those evenings when the ocean winds blew cold. In summer the grass was parched and tawny brown and laced with twisted, long-stalked pelargoniums, pink and red. The inside of the cottage was whitewashed and the big kitchen doubled as a family room with a long wooden table and a slate floor. From the cottage you could not see the ocean but you could smell it, and feel the salt on your body as you clambered between the thin white sheets which came from a chest that smelt of camphor.

We had arranged to spend Christmas at the cottage. Clare, who had worked with Ellis at the peak of his broadcasting days, also came to stay. Clare was Irish, pale-skinned and beautiful. Her father had just died and she was still mourning him. She wore a black-and-white caftan and often went to lie on the bed with her hands folded across her chest, or else sat meditating in the garden, her long red hair around her shoulders.

Every evening I went to the public phone-box at the end of the lane to find out about Ellis. Two days before Christmas when I rang, Jenny told me he had died. On the way home I tried to think back over the twenty or more years we had spent together but nothing would come. I felt barren of emotions, as if I had spent my soul's worth, and who knew if they would ever regenerate?

Clare kept telling us to cry. The architect said we had already cried. They argued about how much crying was the right crying, and I left them to go to the beach. I ran along the pale shining sand and into the water, so that surf frothed around my ankles and the salt air filled my lungs, and I shouted aloud so I could hear my voice. I felt wonder at the white gulls that soared overhead, and the small black crabs that scuttled in the rock pools, and I rejoiced in the current that tugged at my feet, and I shouted again. The salt spray became salt tears.

Christmas dinner was to be shared with the architect's family and our family and Clare. We decided not to alter our plans. We carried the long table outside to the back verandah, and the architect arranged that one end was to be vegetarian and one was to be for the turkey-eaters. We were the turkey-eaters. The architect's ex-wife of some years back, who was a person of warmth and sensibility, sat next to me and was concerned for us all, because Ellis had only just died. I sat at the other end of the table from Georgia and Joshua and was concerned at their concern, although they too were showing little emotion. Perhaps we were suffering from frozen grief. The architect's mother, a spirited woman in her seventies whose husband had just died, sat next to Clare and discussed death and dying with animation. Long before the meal was finished, the architect retired to bed, distressed because Christmas hadn't been as any of us had hoped. We were all so obsessed with our private miseries that nobody noticed he had gone.

On Boxing Day, I flew up to Sydney with Georgia and Joshua for Ellis's funeral. They were white-faced and strained. And Jonathan? Oh Jonathan. I found him the day before the funeral, and he came with his pants once again tied up with string and his feet bare. We had tried to get him to change his clothes but he became so angry and distressed that it seemed better to leave him alone.

The funeral service was held around the grave and it poured with rain. The mourners arrived in their best clothes and we waited patiently for the service to begin. The Australian Broadcasting Corporation, where Ellis had worked, had provided a chaplain who talked about his great qualities of patience and calm. I could think of many good things to say about Ellis but the last qualities I would have ascribed to him would be patience and calm. The chaplain called him Eric. Ellis would not have liked to be called Eric. The undertaker slipped a card to the chaplain, on which Ellis's name was printed in large letters. Perhaps undertakers always keep cards for such occasions.

When I die I want Mozart's Great Mass in C Minor, and 'God be in My Head', and something irreverent that I have yet to decide. But you can't have music when the funeral is outside. Jonathan provided the accompaniment. He giggled. His giggles grew louder and louder, and it was hard to ignore them. As we looked down at the coffin, topped with the bluest of cornflowers, it seemed to me that while we were hovering on the edges of death, Jonathan's giggles took us to the edges of somewhere else, somewhere that was out of my reach, and just as beyond my understanding.

Three
# *The House by the Sea*

*Far and few, far and few,*
*Are the lands where the Jumblies live;*
*Their heads are green, and their hands are blue,*
*And they went to sea in a sieve.*

EDWARD LEAR

*January 1980*   I was sitting on a pile of green garbage bags on the Adelaide sea-front, thinking all this was a big mistake. The garbage bags were stuffed full of cushions and clothes but one of them was leaking a thin trickle of sour-smelling liquid. We were in the middle of house-moving. Jonathan was then eighteen, Georgia fifteen, and Joshua eleven.

After Ellis's death, Jonathan, Georgia, Joshua and I had returned to Adelaide where the architect and I had bought a house together. Which is why, on this blistering-hot summer day, all our worldly possessions were scattered along the pavement and stacked up by the side of the road. Correction. The architect had not brought along all his worldly possessions: he had chosen only to move his work tables and a couple of pictures. 'Cautious bugger,' I muttered sourly, and then had to admit that, in view of Jonathan's illness, for a careful man the architect was actually being quite reckless. He had just disappeared underneath a large wardrobe which he and the two removal men were trying to heave up two flights of stairs, while Georgia and Joshua carried cases and armfuls of books, and Jonathan had wandered off somewhere down the road.

Jonathan seemed much better, and I was deliberately leaving him as much space as possible. So why was I being so scratchy? Perhaps because I had just poked around and found that the leaking garbage bag was the one that contained my jumpers, or perhaps because the architect had just remarked crisply, 'You do have a *lot* of possessions.' Perhaps I was just tired. I heaved myself off the bags and

43

looked up at the splendour of our new home.

Halfway through the year before, the architect and I had begun looking at houses to buy together, but there had always been something wrong with them. Some were too big, some too small, some faced north, some south, some had gardens, some didn't. I had just about decided that maybe this was telling us something about our wish to live together, when we went for a drive along the coast, and spotted the house by the sea. It was so splendid, so architecturally impeccable, so reasonable in price, that neither of us was able to find an excuse for not buying it.

The house was one of ten bluestone terraces known as The Marines, which dominated the coastline because of their size and architectural grandeur. The Marines had been built in the 1880s, at a seaside suburb called Grange, and were one of Adelaide's first examples of speculative development. Grange was to be the Monte Carlo of the south. The developers ran out of money, and the suburb became a mixture of unfashionable boarding houses and terraces that teetered into disrepair.

During the time we lived at Grange, The Marines were mainly let as flats or rooms, but three of them had been converted back into private houses and ours was one of these. The houses were four storeys high, including a large basement. Each floor above ground-level had a full-length wide verandah, with ornate cast-iron railings and columns, painted a dramatic Venetian red. Pairs of French doors opened on to the verandahs. Inside, the houses had sweeping mahogany staircases, and vast rooms with marble fire-places. These were houses that made demands upon their occupants; you couldn't curl up in a corner reading comic strips and eating toffees, not in these houses.

We found that there were some days when we might all be at home together – Georgia, Joshua, Jonathan, the architect and I – but never see one another except to pass on the stairs. The kitchen was at the back of the house, and was cold and uncomfortable. The living-room was a drawing-room in the Victorian sense of the word, and demanded respect. Our bedroom was on the top floor and was over ten metres long. One agent described it as a billiard-room and another as a ball room. In this room we would lie in bed gazing at the sea, which would change colours throughout the year, from softest grey to brilliant greens and blues. There was nothing to interrupt our view except the red railing of the verandah, so we could pretend we were on an ocean liner, sailing up the coast, or into the Mediterranean or, if we were feeling reckless, around Cape Horn – except then we had to imagine the waves. These were gulf waters so there was no surf.

The beaches were long and straight and you could see for ever up the coast. Every so often the sea's emptiness was punctuated by an extraordinarily long timber jetty, as if the coastline had been neatly divided into grids. The jetties were built on timber uprights which storm and tide had battered into strange shapes. They were functional jetties, where people promenaded at dusk and in the early morning, and where small groups would gather to fish, with faded rucksacks and small parcels of bait. Many of them were Greek and Italian families. It was homely fishing, and I rarely saw anyone catch anything of any size. But it was ritual to peer into the plastic buckets and admire the wriggling tiddlers. Once Joshua caught a respectable fish and I cooked it for breakfast – at least, I think Joshua caught a respectable-sized-fish – or is this one of my fantasies of how I would have liked life to be?

The Grange beach kiosk was built of liver-red brick. It sold pies and pasties, cool drinks and icecreams. Coloured plastic ribbons flapped from its doorway. The lifesavers wore red and orange bathers and caps, and in summer drilled all available small boys into running races and practising mouth-to-mouth resuscitation. In winter the beaches were deserted, but the lifesavers would heave their boats into the water and row around, shouting instructions at each other.

In early mornings, when the sea and the sky were oyster-grey and shining, we would run along the sand, and horses would gallop towards us in the morning mist. When days were calm, I liked to think they were Aurora's horses but sometimes, after nights of terror, they became the Four Horses of the Apocalypse, give or take one or two. On other more mundane mornings, they were horses from the stables up the road, on their early morning training run. They would gallop past the boldly painted beach signs:

WELCOME TO GRANGE BEACH

HAVE A GOOD DAY

BALL GAMES PROHIBITED

NO HORSES

NO DOGS

NO FIRES

NO LITTER

NO BIKES

I wanted to paint underneath: NO PEOPLE.

Grange had a sense of being at the end of the world. Flat, so flat you could fall off if you waded out too far, or ran too fast. Innocent too. A place that had a Rip van Winkle air about it, so that small boys still fished with bent pins, and women wore floral bathers with built-in plastic cones. It was a place where there weren't many trannies on the beach, and not much anointing with oil, and where bare breasts would have sent the councillors into a dither. How to deal with bare breasts on a painted sign?

In summer or winter, whenever the winds blew, great coils of seaweed would pile high on the beach and the air would be rich with the smell of iodine. Sometimes I leapt into the seaweed and hoped that if I lay there long enough I would emerge reborn. Sometimes I thought of hiding there, forever.

The scale of the house was daunting. I turned the smallest room into my study because this was the only room where I felt secure. This room was once a dressing-room and had just enough space for my table, one upright chair and a few books. I sat and wrote here and, when I went downstairs to make coffee, by the time I returned the sand had blown through the windows and covered my papers with a fine yellow film. I felt as if I were caught in some gigantic hour-glass, and that someone else was measuring my time. Or was it theirs and was I the intruder? You see how easily I drifted into fantasy. Often I felt as if our lives had become unreal and that we were playing someone else's part. Sometimes when I stood at the window, feeling that terrible loneliness, I would chant *The Lady of Shalott.*

But there were no long fields of barley and of rye, only the grey sea, and winds that blew the hamburger wrappings into the air and the sand into your eyes. That's what it was like in winter. That's what it was like when you needed two people to open the front door because the sea winds were so fierce. But in summer, the summer when we arrived, the days were blue and golden, and once more we thought we were beginning anew.

The architect had kept his own house as an office and a bolt-hole, but he lived in the seaside house, more or less full-time, and led a local battle concerned with sea-front development. Georgia and Joshua had returned to school, and said they liked the new house and the beach. And together we were beginning to enjoy the minutiae of domesticity – like sweeping the front verandah free of the sand, and going to the markets together, and even working out uneasy rosters about who would do the cooking and when. We swam before breakfast, and sometimes at lunch-time and often at night. Night swims were mysterious. The sea looked black and foreboding, but when we dived in, the blackness splintered into phosphorescence, and I would feel exultant.

Jonathan had decided that he wanted to go to art school. He took a portfolio of work along, and was admitted. I felt optimistic. And then an old friend of ours from England, a wonderful woman in her seventies who was still active as a journalist, came to stay. Barbara had known the children since they were little. Jonathan gave her an enormous hug, and she thought how well he looked. But one morning she came to me and said, 'Ducky, have you noticed how Jonathan keeps laughing when there isn't anything to laugh about?' I had noticed, though I had tried not to. Barbara had also noticed that Jonathan was putting his face very close to people when he became agitated, as if he had no judgement of space. I had a sudden sharp memory of Jonathan at the age of thirteen, wearing a green school jumper and shouting at Barbara with his face almost touching hers. It had seemed like strangely hostile behaviour for a boy who was normally gentle. One of the manifestations of schizophrenia is sensory distortion. Sounds may seem louder or sharper, colours brighter, touch unexpected, smells more pungent. Sometimes objects become distorted and frightening. The steering wheel of a car might seem to turn into a snake. There might be a growing sensation that everyone is watching you. Noises might follow you. Time can seem to disappear, slow down or speed up.

The problem was that Jonathan had stopped taking his medication and, slowly, all the old symptoms were beginning to reappear. Today, a range of powerful drugs, known as anti-psychotics or major tranquillizers, are the main medications used in the treatment of schizophrenia. The drugs do not cure the illness but, in about seventy per cent of cases, they help reduce some of its psychotic symptoms, such as hallucinations and delusions, enabling people to have some control over their illness. The drugs are far less useful in the treatment of the chronic symptoms of the illness – the withdrawal and loss of drive. It is not fully understood how these drugs work, but it is related to the blocking of dopamine, a chemical in the brain which transmits information between nerve cells. It is believed that people with schizophrenia may have an excess of dopamine.

The drugs are marketed under many different brand names, and may be given as tablets, syrup, or intra-muscular injection. Every individual reacts differently to the drugs, and it can take quite a long period to find out the drug and dosage that is most effective, particularly as the drugs often have neurological side-effects, which I was only to discover later. Many people will need to continue indefinitely on medication if they wish to keep their psychotic symptoms under control.

Before the 1950s, when the drugs were developed, there was no effective treatment of schizophrenia. Most people who became ill went on a one-way ticket to an asylum, with little chance of ever being able to return to the outside world. I went to one of these institutions in the days before medication was known, and I still have memories of people tormented by their psychoses, and with nothing to bring them relief. They howled, they rocked, they laughed and talked to themselves and to anyone who would listen. Some gesticulated, some screamed, some lay curled up in dejected bundles on the green linoleum floor. The building smelled of urine, faeces, disinfectant and despair.

The history of mental illness helps to explain the weight of oppression that people with the illness have inherited, and still struggle against. It also lets us see how the way we view an illness affects the way we treat it, and how, in turn, this affects its outcome.

In the Middle Ages, when mental illness was seen as a mark of the Devil, people were burned as witches, or cast out to wander the countryside. They were consigned aboard a 'ship of fools' to sail the canals of Europe on never-ending journeys of despair. At London's Bethlehem Hospital (known as 'Bedlam'), up until 1770, the general public could pay a penny admittance to view the patients who were chained to cells, in galleries, like caged animals in a zoo.

In Victorian times, treatment was based on the belief that mental illness was usually a degenerative condition brought about by weakness of character. The majority of mentally ill people were now consigned to asylums, and although treatment was sometimes humane, many endured cruelty, filth and starvation. The recovery rate in some places was estimated to be less than three per cent.

Hospitals remained the primary place of care for most mentally ill people until the 1950s. The Victorian treatments of purging, flogging and drenching – perhaps attempts to 'shock' people out of their madness – were now replaced by insulin, shock treatment and even lobotomies, reflecting a savage desperation to find some kind of cure.

Then, in the 1920s and 1930s, psychoanalysts began questioning whether the basis of schizophrenia was physical, or was caused by traumatic childhood experiences or bad parenting. These theories were further developed in the 1950s and 1960s, when the anti-psychiatry movement saw schizophrenia as a label for scapegoating people who were eccentric or difficult to live with. None of these beliefs was substantiated by valid research, and they have since been discredited, but for a long time they led to cruel criticism of families of people with schizophrenia.

The discovery of the anti-psychotic drugs in the 1950s at last enabled people who were mentally ill to manage their illness and to live in the community. Although these drugs are not a cure for schizophrenia, the outcome with them has steadily improved so that, today, some sixty per cent of people who were diagnosed schizophrenic thirty years ago will either have recovered completely or be much improved.

John Ellard, a Sydney psychiatrist who first saw the disorder 'en masse' at army psychiatric hospitals during the Second World War, says that people used to come in wild, bedraggled, rubbing faeces in their hair – mad. 'That was the standard method of presentation.

Now they come in and say, 'I haven't been thinking straight and I've been to the library and I've read it up and I think I've got schizophrenia.' Ellard is among many psychiatrists who not only believe that schizophrenia is becoming less frequent, but also that it is less severe in presentation and has an improved outlook.

It has long been known that the recovery rates for schizophrenia in different types of society are extraordinarily different. Multinational studies by the World Health Organization, extending over two decades, show that people who have schizophrenia in developing countries have significantly higher chances of improvement or even recovery than those who live in the industrialised world. The reasons why have not yet been fully explained, except that, as schizophrenia is a universal illness, it is almost certainly the environment that is influencing these results, although medication remains the primary means for dealing with psychoses.

So whenever I baulked at the need for people to take medication, I would make myself remember what it had been like before they were available. But now, my immediate problem was that Jonathan was deteriorating, and I had been given no information about his medication: what it was, how much he should take, and if he didn't take it, what might be the consequences.

I rang Frank who obtained this information for me, and suggested that I should bring Jonathan to his clinic each week so that he might monitor Jonathan's medication. Jonathan agreed, and at first improved. For my part, I promised to cease clucking over Jonathan. He must learn to become independent, and therefore he was not to live at home, although he would be welcome to visit at any time. I was to help him find a place to live near art school which he could share with fellow students, and we were to trial these arrangements for six months.

Jonathan said this sounded good, and he and I went house-hunting. We looked around a student area in a suburb called Prospect, one of the oldest parts of Adelaide. Prospect had streets called Myrtle, Beatrice, Olive and Azalea. The houses were mostly cottages with corrugated-iron roofs, bull-nosed verandahs and neat gardens, or they were larger bluestone villas of passing prosperity. The shops were jumbled together and cheerfully unfashionable. Not long ago I went back there to rekindle memories. I passed a junk shop with old radiators, a basket full of yellow-and-black knitted gloves, shelves of cheap glasses, streaked with dust, and, on the pavement, chrome and red chairs and a rack full of old-fashioned clothes. The florist next door had its window crammed full of plastic flowers and bridal displays.

I remembered walking by these shops with Jonathan and diving in to see what treasures we could find. A fierce-looking Alsatian from one of the junk stores rushed out at us, barking loudly. Jonathan dropped on all fours and barked back. The dog licked his face. Jonathan looked up at me and gave a broad smile. 'I want Toby!' he said.

Toby was one of the two dogs we had brought from Sydney. The other dog was an Australian terrier called Liza. Toby was an even smaller terrier, with buck teeth and one ear that stood upright and one that flopped. Toby had come to us after another of our dogs had been run over. We had bought him from a department store where he sat in a cage labelled 'Poodle' and didn't fool anyone. He came before we were really ready for a replacement and so we resented him. Toby behaved accordingly. He peed on dustbins and trouser legs, bit little old ladies, and yapped at children.

Toby moved in with Jonathan quite happily. By then it was March, and Adelaide Festival time. It was a good Festival that year and included a splendid performance by the Spanish puppet group La Clacca which used giant masks painted by Miro. I went twice, the second time with Jonathan because I thought he would enjoy the Miro masks. He became intensely involved, angry when the baddies were winning, cheering when they were losing. I was curious because he seemed fully aware of the political background of Spain. As a child Jonathan had read a great deal, but now he scarcely ever read because he was unable to concentrate. He didn't watch much television. He listened only to music on the radio. But as if by osmosis from the world around him, he seemed to amass a huge amount of random information which he would blurt out at high speed and, just as suddenly, retreat into silence.

Early in April the architect made a national television appearance, talking about the need to preserve the quality of urban environments. He was good. By now, we were both of us working from the seaside house. I wrote on the second floor; the architect used the third floor. I had also become involved in various government and university committees. I wanted to feel I belonged.

Jonathan was keeping his regular appointments with Frank at St Corantyn. St Corantyn was a community mental-health centre specialising in sexual disorders. It was housed in a beautiful white-painted Victorian mansion, surrounded by trees and herbaceous borders. I usually waited for Jonathan in the top hallway, and there I had regular conversations with Mr Klapeas, who had a luxuriant moustache and paced the floor almost as restlessly as Jonathan, up and down, up and down.

'You married?'

'No.'

'Where your husband?'

'He's dead.'

'You sure you not married?'

'Yes.'

'Then marry me.'

I collected proposals for several months. Mr Klapeas never varied the tone of his proposal, nor did he ever seem to want a reply.

In spite of the well-intentioned theory that Jonathan should be living a separate life from the rest of us, particularly from me, the reality proved different. Jonathan only went to art school three or four times. Again, he said that people were against him. He still seemed to gather friends around him, including one or two faithfuls from the short time he had spent at high school the year before, but no one would live with him for more than a few days. They said he was too chaotic.

Sometimes, people ripped him off. They would move in, pay no rent, and move out, stealing most of his things. As I had to stake Jonathan's bond money, landladies and estate agents knew where to find me. I wince at the remembrance of angry phone-calls because Jonathan had chucked his garbage outside, or left the lights on all night and the doors and windows open wide, or wakened the neighbourhood with the howl of Pink Floyd. He was supposed to be paying his own rent out of the sickness benefit payment he received, but he would lose his cheques or spend them. Sometimes payments would inexplicably lapse. The Department of Social Security would apologise for computer or postal errors, Jonathan would giggle, and I would write endless letters of complaint.

Friends would scold me for intervening. Frank would reiterate that Jonathan must learn to be independent. So next time round I would do nothing, Jonathan would be evicted for non-payment of rent, his possessions would disappear, and he would return to us like a homing pigeon, usually in the middle of the night. The same thing happened with cleaning. If it were left to Jonathan, half-eaten food would be left strewn around his house, and maggots would be crawling on the floor. Jonathan was feeding neither himself properly, nor Toby. We tried other arrangements with cleaners and social workers calling in, but the cleaners never stayed and Jonathan closed the door on the social workers. By the end of June he had been ejected from three cottages and from three boarding houses, including one run by the Department of Health. Frank said sadly, 'He's deteriorating again.'

A major reason for Jonathan's slide was that he had again stopped taking his medication. Some people with schizophrenia forget to take their medication. Others will not accept their illness or their need for drugs, or else they think that they are better. Many stop because they are experiencing unpleasant side-effects. Once people stop their medication, the symptoms of schizophrenia reappear. But the mind that is malfunctioning is the same mind that has to know it needs help. People may have some years of repeated episodes of schizophrenia before they accept that they have an illness needing ongoing management.

At this stage the only way to get Jonathan back onto medication would have been to enforce it. But he was not psychotic enough to be involuntarily committed, and this has been a major flaw in mental-health legislation – or its administration – around the world. You watch someone you love becoming psychotic, but you can do nothing until they are so ill that they are judged to be a danger to themselves or others. I used to wonder how society would react if we took the same approach with a physical illness. If someone had an infected leg, for instance, what would happen if we made them wait until it were gangrenous before giving any medical help?

Mental-health laws vary from country to country and from state to state. Some are better than others. All depend upon the willingness of doctors and lawyers to implement them. It is true that there have been terrible abuses of people with mental illness, and that lawyers helped prosecute those abuses. But in our zeal to protect people's rights, we have created a climate in which mentally ill people sometimes keep their freedom but lose their mind, and in which the civil-liberties argument is sometimes used as an excuse for neglect.

Meantime, I was again going broke. Running two homes, one for us and one for Jonathan, was financially demanding. Jonathan was always losing everything – clothes, money, even furniture. Stocks had constantly to be replenished. So I accepted an assignment in Somalia for a documentary film on refugees. It would be shown on one of the commercial networks later in the year. When I write it down like this it sounds easy: *I accepted an assignment in Somalia* – but the decision was difficult. The architect was still at home. So were Georgia and Joshua. Jonathan wasn't. But, given the unpredictability of his illness, anything could go wrong. Could I afford to go? Could I afford not to? I went.

Our documentary film crew travelled to the Ogaden desert, the same region we had visited five years earlier when we recorded famine in Ethiopia. Somalia and Ethiopia share a common boundary, somewhere in the middle of the Ogaden, and they had been fighting for many years. The fights would have remained tribal skirmishes if America and Russia had not supplied massive military assistance, including napalm. Fighting by proxy is the most obscene kind of warfare. People are slaughtered and homelands devastated in the name of political ideologies that mask greed, power and fear. The casualties were the nomadic people of the desert region whose waterholes had been poisoned, and who were dying in their thousands from starvation and disease. Now they no longer drifted from waterhole to waterhole, but from one refugee camp to the next. Refugees provided an opportune way of attracting international aid. Ironically, some of the families we filmed had been the same families we had filmed on the Ethiopian side of the border five years earlier. We recognised each other.

We filmed mainly at one of the largest refugee camps, Las Dure, in northern Somalia. It looked like the hell I had imagined in my childhood nightmares. We had a three-hour drive each day from our base camp to the refugee camp, and would set out at dawn to get as much done as we could before the heat overcame us. Our jeeps would crest a small hill and look down at a vast sprawl of tents and humpies, each one roofed in black plastic. As far as the eye could see was barren: every tree, every scrubby bush, had long ago been chopped down for shelter and firewood. By eleven in the morning the heat was so searing that speaking became painful. Our mouths were dry and cracked. Even the grease in the cameras had dried.

At first, I commented that the children looked better than I had expected. I was told that others were hidden in the tents. The mothers were ashamed to show the condition of their children. I spent time with one young woman whose baby was dying. I nursed her child. He felt so frail that I was fearful of crushing him. I stroked his cheek, hot with fever, and felt, *if only I could give him my strength, please God let it pass through my hands.* I looked at the woman and she looked back at me, gravely, and with such despair. We touched hands. There were no words.

We filmed a young Chinese doctor from Hong Kong who worked for hours in the searing heat, moving from tent to tent. Twenty or thirty children were dying each day from malnutrition, dysentery and measles. He had no drugs. He turned to us and said, 'I've never felt so helpless in my life.'

I found these African filming expeditions distressing, but getting away from the drama at home to a drama of such epic size helped bring an acceptance of the beauty and cruelty of life. We will never rid ourselves of suffering, but the fact that we cannot does not mean we do nothing. We do not turn away from the child who is starving, or the villages that have been burnt, or the people who are dying. Or the son who has lost his mind. 'Where would you find a mind?' I said despondently, when I returned to find a note from Jonathan: *Gone to get a mermaid. No worries. Must control your youth.*

At the beginning of July Jonathan disappeared. I went round to the cottage several times and there was no sign of him. Toby sat bright-eyed on one of the mattresses, his head cocked to one side. Then I had a phone-call from Sydney. Jonathan had hitch-hiked there, and was sleeping on the floor of an apartment belonging to the mother of one of his old school friends. This was someone new he hadn't tried before. I arranged to fly up. The mother of the friend said she would appreciate this. She couldn't keep Jonathan forever, she said.

It was clear that both Jonathan and Toby had to come home. My decision was not popular:

'He's not coming back, is he?'

'It's his home too.'

'Then I'm leaving.'

'You can't leave, you're too young,' and grimaced at my cliché.

And there was the architect, oh patient man who had promised to move in his furniture but never did. 'I'm not sure I can manage living with Jonathan,' he said apologetically. He left his toothbrush and some of his gear but for the rest of our time together hovered in a state of transition, gradually withdrawing his belongings, and always referring to 'your house', never 'our house'.

Toby moved back first. Within three days he had nipped the ankles of two lifesavers and bitten an old lady who was walking home with her husband. The husband wrote me a letter: *My wife was attacked by a small dog which was barking ferociously and seemed highly dangerous. I fended it off with my umbrella. Your animal is not safe. Kindly remove same or I will prosecute.*

I inserted an anthropomorphic advertisement in the newspaper: *Toby Wants a Home.* The phone began ringing at six in the morning and I spent most of the day listening to lonely people telling me why they so desperately needed a pet. The first person who rang was a woman who lived in a wealthy suburb and who arrived in a Mercedes. She had a diamanté collar for Toby. He drove off on a velvet cushion.

Two days later I drove past Jonathan's old cottage to make sure the Salvation Army had picked up his furniture which I had left outside. Probably I'd soon be buying it back again. As I turned the corner, I saw the mattresses still piled up on the pavement, waiting for collection. Toby was perched on top of them. He leered at me, and wagged his tail. He had found the way from his new owner to the cottage without ever having travelled that particular route. The new owner told me the local school-children had been saying Ave Marias for Toby. She begged to have a second try. Once more Toby was driven off in the Mercedes, and this time he stayed. If we had been able to give Jonathan the equivalent of diamanté collars and unending devotion would all have been well? I knew it wasn't like that. Families get engulfed in guilt, and the guilt gets worse as you deal with conflicting emotions of love and hate. I loved Jonathan, as strongly as ever. But at times I was beginning to hate him, and I had not yet learned to disentangle Jonathan from the illness and Jonathan from his behaviour.

When I flew to Sydney to get Jonathan, he did a repeat performance of saying he did not want to come home. I sat with his friend's mother, trying to get him to see that he wasn't looking after himself. He said that he wanted to sit on the pavement and be a happy hippy. There will be several times when he will say he wants to be a happy hippy and several people who will believe him. They will think that his ambitious middle-class mother is ashamed of him, and that this is the major cause of his problem. I wish it were as simple.

'Be a happy hippy,' I shrieked. 'But look at the sores on your feet. The sores on your face. The fact you have no money. That you can't stay here sleeping on the floor.'

The mother of the friend was calmer. 'You're not well, Joe. You should go home.'

Jonathan examined the sores on his feet and said nothing. Twice I tried to get him to the airport. Twice he disappeared. Finally we made it. Jonathan came home. I want to write that the others hated me for it, but this is melodramatic. I don't know that the others hated me for it because I avoided asking them. I hadn't yet learned that to acknowledge everyone's feelings, however painful, is better than pretending they don't exist.

Joshua retreated into his sport, Georgia retreated into her studies. The architect retreated back to his ordered villa. Once I heard Georgia and Joshua talking together. 'Get a hit man,' said one. 'But he's our brother!' said the other.

The cleaning lady, Bernadette, who had been with us since the beginning of the year was the most accepting, but then she wasn't living with us. 'He's a lovely boy,' she said. Bernadette had a pragmatic philosophy of life that you made the best of it, no matter what. In her case, making the best of it included accepting the fact that her only daughter was intellectually handicapped and almost blind.

I fitted up the basement as a bedroom for Jonathan. Sometimes he lived there, sometimes he disappeared to friends or to squats. He seemed unable to settle in one place for more than a few nights at a stretch. He still wasn't taking any medication, and I had given up fighting him about it. He refused to return to Frank and said all psychiatrists were mad. Frank said dryly, 'He's right.'

Sometimes I was fearful that Jonathan would burn the house down. He smoked heavily, and we would find cigarettes stubbed out on the floor, on tables, smouldering in his bed. He brought friends in, and sometimes they would stay the night.

The basement people wore odd, ill-matched clothes, and were usually dirty. Their hair hadn't been combed or washed in days. They had blank eyes, with lids at half-mast. And they smelled, a dank smell that began to permeate the whole house. Some of them were drug addicted, some weren't. All of them were mentally ill. I worried about the other children with such a strange population drifting in and out, but it was Jonathan's home and they were his friends.

Georgia said, 'One of the saddest things is when you come to accept it all as normal,' and then she wrote a poem about one of them. She was fifteen.

*MARTIN*

*I smelt him before I saw him,*
*Stale sweat and smoke*
*Invading every crevice and corner of the house,*
*And I cringed*
*Because I knew he was another one:*
*Eighteen or nineteen, no home,*
*No job, no future, and so much time*
*In which to do so little.*
*He would be around for a month, maybe more,*
*At any time, the knock on the door*
*Will make our stomachs sink just slightly*
*As we get up and show him in.*
*Or, more often than not, make excuses,*
*Jonathan's out, he's sleeping, I'm sorry,*
*Come back soon,*
*Carefully arranged smile and the door slams shut.*

*But it's too late,*
*He's filtered through the house anyway,*
*Just little reminders here and there;*
*A smell, a cigarette butt, a few words,*
*And no matter how hard we try*
*We can't wipe out his existence,*
*Because he's a person,*
*And when he gradually fades into oblivion*
*There will be another to take his place;*
*And another . . .*

Martin came from New Zealand. He was twenty-five and had been a physics student before he had a breakdown and was told he had paranoid schizophrenia. He was a thin, delicate young man with parchment white skin, dark auburn hair to his shoulders and a long straggly red beard. Often he wore only a loin cloth. I never managed to have a coherent conversation with Martin. He would dart nervously into the kitchen carrying scrolls of graph paper under his arm, and he would spread these out on the kitchen bench and begin filling in the squares, in alternate patterns of red and blue. He did this for hours. It was important to Martin that someone would look at the squares and tell him that he was doing good work. When I asked him what it meant, these red and blue patterns, he would peer very closely at the paper and say 'It's my life.'

Somewhere, someplace, Martin's mother was probably grieving over him, aching as I ached over Jonathan. I wished that I knew Martin's address so that I could write to her, but if ever I asked him he would shake his head and scuttle out of the room.

Then there was Simon. Simon the street poet was sixteen but looked more like seventy. He was a small, resourceful-looking boy who wore a Mao hat pulled down over his eyes, and always carried a canvas rucksack bulging with papers. Simon looked perpetually ill. His teeth were already blackened from drugs, and he smoked rollies incessantly, so you could hear Simon's coughing long before he would drift upstairs. Simon put out a weekly broadsheet of poetry which he gave away on street corners:

*PUBLISH YOUR OWN POEMS, FREE TODAY HEY! POST-A-POEM*
*Real friends are good people without them I cry*
*They're people that help me*
*To try to get by*

The person I remember best was Clayton Pring. Clayton Pring wore purple socks and a purple beret. He was a good-looking man in his late twenties who talked about poetry and philosophy with such fluency that it took some time before you realised that much of what he was saying didn't make sense. Clayton's eyes were the deepest blue, and he could stare at you with mesmeric intensity as he told you that Atlantis would rise again next Sunday.

Clayton had written and published a book with an orange-and-black cover which he called *Saint Vitus' Confusion.* He gave us a copy and wrote inside: *To Joe and Mum. Love and Peace.*

The book had four dedications:

*Dedication I:*    *The Abolition of Compulsory Drug Treatment in Australian Mental Hospitals.*

*Dedication II:*    *The Allowance of an Eight Hour in Cell Time in Australian Jails.*

*Dedication III:*    *To the success of the Down to Earth Movement in Land Separatism.*

*Dedication IV:*    *To the success of the Aboriginal Government of the NW Quarter of Australia, or, the NW Quarter Split.*

There was an Author's Note:

*The way in which this book is written is on a level of new Australian English, not that of only, but, combined British, English and American English, thusly new Australian English. This may sound all Greek to some. It is no wonder.*

Clayton's book began with these words:

*I am wrapped up in a cocoon of my own ego, an ego that has transcended beyond the level of earth, into the eternal horizons of heavenly flight. The cocoon is there to hope that I will angel myself from human without death, yet death is everything's conquerer, yet, it is defeated by itself, for even death faces death. Upon its tombstone is engraved eternal life. This is a fact of one that has been Christ Tried in Elect Trick City.*

Clayton said that he was brought up in the then avant-garde school of dirty socks and hard knocks called hippydom. He wrote about himself:

*By those that ally with him he has been praised as Messiah and Australia's greatest genius, but, in equal manner, has been just as condemned by those that are against him.*

He said that in India he once faced stonings, was beaten unconscious with sticks and almost hanged by a wild mob. Then he found deep friendship at the Shirdi Sai Baba Village, where he was annunciated. He returned to Australia to found the Christalite Reformation of the Aeschaeton, which he said was highly persecuted by the secret police.

One day Clayton came marching into the kitchen, made some tea in our battered blue teapot, and asked if I would give the Christalite Reformation Society some money to send him to India.

'No, I don't have that kind of money, Clayton.'

Clayton twirled the teapot round and round so it became a spinning top. He picked up his beret and set it on his head. His nostrils flared. He was fire dragon, looking for a sacrificial lamb. He leapt onto the nearest kitchen chair and proclaimed: 'I, Clayton Pring declare war on Anne Deveson. My cannons will be trained on your house. My guns will be trained on you. To the death, ma'am.'

He jumped down from the table, grabbed the broom, draped a tea towel over it like a flag, and marched out.

That night I thought nervously of Clayton's cannon. Supposing Clayton really did have a cannon, hiding under the raspberry canes and the grapevines, trained to blast us through the roof, up and over the moon and into the dark night sea?

Unlike the rest of the basement people, Clayton was well-dressed. But Clayton wasn't a regular. Much of the time he lorded it over a squat in North Adelaide, where a drifting population lived in a derelict but splendid old house.

One afternoon in early winter, Martin was at the kitchen bench filling in red and blue squares on graph paper and Jonathan arrived, leaving the front door open so it swung in the wind, and the smell of the sea filled the house, which was just as well. Jonathan was high. Jonathan was higher than I had seen him for a long time. He was rushing round and round the kitchen, picking up and putting things down.

'God's a chrysanthemum, and I am a chrysanthemum, yellow all round and fantastically powerful. I can do anything. I am the sun and the moon. I am everything. Bright red blood is falling everywhere, and God is grave. And then suddenly, everywhere there are stars, and I am the chrysanthemum and I am God.'

Jonathan had begun leaving notes all round the house, strange secret messages which we could not decipher. He wrote them in thick black texta, and decorated them with the same suffering faces I had seen him draw in his bedoom a year earlier: *If you want my four leaf clover hat, look under Georgia's tartan dress.* Scraps of paper everywhere, bits torn out of telephone directories, books, bus timetables, left in strange places, Jonathan's injunctions to himself or to others: *Avoid the mirror. Tell them you are a mind without a metronome. I have lost the glue in my brain. Don't close your right eye.*

When someone with schizophrenia is psychotic, their thoughts can lose their logical procession and fail to connect with language. Sometimes the language sounds nonsensical, and is known as a word salad. 'Gumble-fish-thumb', said Jonathan one day, and I said 'Yes,' and wrote it down. Sometimes the language reflects opposites in thinking. Sometimes there is a tenuous connection between the ideas or between the sounds, but it is only tenuous so that you are left feeling something is a little odd. 'I have a dumb tongue. I have to get a ruler to teach it to talk,' said Jonathan angrily one day, walking on the beach.

Jonathan took to attacking Georgia, following her round the house, calling her 'moll' and 'dyke'. She tried to avoid him but he seemed to have an uncanny ability to taunt her. Yet when they were little they had been very close. Our family albums are full of snapshots showing them playing together, two very blond small children, one with brown eyes, one with blue. Jonathan was three years older and although they had obviously had their normal share of sibling squabbles, he had been protective towards Georgia and had led the way in childhood adventures. I have a picture taken when he was about eight and she was five. They are both in their dressing gowns, he has his arm around her, and she is looking up at him and beaming. I often thought that it must be really difficult for her to cope with the fact that the brother she loved could now appear so malevolent and hurtful.

She developed an astringent sense of humour and wore it as protective armour. She was getting breakfast in the kitchen and said, 'Shall I get an egg for Jonathan?'

'Yes,' I said. 'Treat people as you want to be treated yourself and they'll respond.'

'Oh sure, give him an egg and he'll stop being crazy.'

Joshua was also suffering. Joshua was six years younger than Jonathan and had looked up to him as his older brother who played cricket with him and read to him. Only the year before, when we had just arrived in Adelaide, Jonathan had tried to teach Joshua to swim. The friend whose swimming pool we were using had watched the two boys playing together, and had remarked on Jonathan's gentleness. 'He is a very loving young man,' she said. 'You are lucky.'

Jonathan moved into the North Adelaide squats and Clayton told me he would make him well. Clayton would stride up and down the yardway and in and out the rooms, talking about the power of loving, and because I too believe in the power of loving I willed myself to think that everyone at the squats would one day arise phoenix-like from the ashes. You might ask why they needed to arise. Why weren't they happy as they were, 'just bein', just lyin' around developin',' as a young person once suggested to me at an alternative school? I guess I thought they needed to arise in some shape or form because most of them looked pretty sick and miserable the way they were.

The rooms at the squats were dark and littered with strange shapes. Bodies curled like foetuses, so it was hard to distinguish a hand from a foot, a leg from an arm, male from female. Many were on drugs and some were mentally ill. Mattresses were lumpy and stained and sometimes heaped on top of one another. Clothing was scattered across the floors – jeans, T-shirts, matted jumpers, sandals, rags.

I wrestled over the drug issue, particularly with those people who would wipe their hands of Jonathan, saying, 'He's a drug addict, what can you expect?' Or when hospitals refused to take him because he smuggled dope into the wards. Most mental health services will not take mentally ill people if they have a drug problem, and most drug and alcohol services will not take mentally ill people. 'They

...kins, people who are docile and amenable to cure,' said ...er, a wise friend and who is a professor of community ...and generous-minded, works voluntarily one day a week at one of the refuges for homeless men.

Yet people with schizophrenia quite often drift to street drugs because this is one way of handling their illness. Dr E. Fuller Torrey, a clinical and research psychiatrist in Washington and one of the world's outstanding authorities on schizophrenia, writes in his book *Surviving Schizophrenia*:

*Hearing voices for the first time in your life, for example, is a very frightening experience; if you then begin using hashish, Phencyclidine (PCP) or some similar drug, it provides you with a persuasive reason for hearing the voices. Drug use can put off the uncomfortable confrontation with yourself that tells you something is going wrong – very wrong – with your mind. You are, quite literally, losing it. Drugs and alcohol as well, may also partially relieve the symptoms. In these cases, persons can be said to be medicating themselves.*

Drugs (including medications, alcohol, tobacco and street drugs) themselves do not cause schizophrenia. But many mind-altering drugs, incuding marijuana, can make psychotic symptoms worse if a person already has schizophrenia, and they can undo the benefits of anti-psychotic medication. Mind-altering drugs may also produce symptoms that are similar to schizophrenia. Amphetamines (speed), and Lysergic Acid Diethylamide (LSD) and Phencyclidine (PCP) can produce hallucinations, delusions and disorders of thinking. So can marijuana, especially if its use is prolonged.

I knew that Jonathan smoked marijuana. I also knew he took sedatives and cough mixture (for its morphine content). One day he wandered into the house, with his lips pursed, and said, 'Ever taken heroin? I just did and I saw God the Father and God the Son and God the Holy Ghost. And all these rings came in concentric circles, and I felt exultant. And I thought I heard from God, so I packed everything into a backpack, and went into the desert. I only lasted two days. I got my nervous breakdown. My revelation was that I was being a stupid idiot.' As he spoke, he paced around the room.

Jonathan was going through a period of restless energy, as if hounded by a Greek fury. He went on insisting that he was a heroin addict. I could not tell where his reality ended and his fantasy began.

By then I had become so conditioned to his exploits that most things had lost their shock value. Jonathan had twice been tested for heroin while in hospital, and on both occasions the results were negative.

'Why did you say you were into heroin?' I asked. I was washing-up and my back was turned towards him.

He came and dabbled his hands in the water, then said loudly in my ear, 'Junkies are cool; schizos are rejects.'

'Roses are red, violets are blue, I'm a schizophrenic and I'm one too,' yell children in a playground. 'The only good schizo is a dead one,' says the joking voice on the radio. 'The Illness that Breeds Killers' is the headline in a best-selling magazine. And a city hoarding boasts,

> CINEMA OF THE INSANE . . . *Nymphomaniacs, Firebugs, Serial Killers, Foot-fetishists, Obsession, Schizophrenia . . . A Festival of the Dark, Disturbed and Deranged.*

We live in a society that is ignorant of mental illness and treats it with contempt. Yet, for a while, I romanticised it. I wanted to believe that, even amid the squalor of the squats, there was fellowship in this community of drifters, that they accepted and looked after each other. I took along vegetable seedlings which we planted in the wild old garden. But as no one ever watered them they died. Sometimes I brought food. Sometimes I went with Jonathan and Clayton to the markets. The markets were in the centre of Adelaide. They were a meeting place, a place of good smells and brilliant sights: mounds of fresh vegetables and fruit, stalls loaded with German sausage and sweet dark breads, barrels of black and green olives and sacks of rice, the strong smell of roasted coffee and handmade chocolates. And we always liked the stalls around the fringes of the market, which sold Indian clothes and jewellery, sandals and silver, second-hand books and pots of fresh herbs.

After the markets, Jonathan would come home and hover, sometimes moving from one foot to the other, sometimes nodding, sometimes talking, sometimes lying flat on his back in the hall, in the living-room, on the verandah by the few straggly geraniums and the red iron gate which would never properly close.

He said he felt stressed. The voices gave him little peace. They taunted, cajoled and threatened, *Your brain is shrinking Jonathan*

*Joe . . . your    brain    is    cancerous . . . rotting    away . . . you're
evil . . . worthless . . . you'll    die    if    you    don't    put    your    left    foot
first . . . now, put your left foot first.* Sometimes they told jokes and
he would giggle. He rarely spoke about his voices, mostly he denied
hearing them. He had learned that they were associated with
madness.

*'And I am not mad!'* He pounded the table so hard that the cutlery
scattered and we all jumped.

It is hard to comprehend the fathomless terror of being psychotic,
we who live in a world that has its road maps, recognisable to us
all. We look at the faces of those we love, and know that they will
not disintegrate in front of our eyes. We reach out for a glass and
it is where we expect that it will be. We do not have voices telling
us to kill ourselves. We do not believe that the television is
broadcasting our most secret thoughts. We look at our children, and
their faces do not distort into the faces of wickedness. We do not
believe that everyone in the world is plotting against us.

Jonathan looked for supernatural explanations for what he was
experiencing. He tried tarot readings, astrology, runes and clairvoy-
ants. He wanted to know everyone's birth sign. He asked to have
his palms read. He pulled down the Bible from the bookshelves
and hunted through its pages. His poring over the Bible surprised
me at first, because no one in our home was committed to formal
religion and our church-going was limited to weddings, christenings
and sometimes Easter and Christmas. Jonathan's knowledge of religion came from school scripture classes and his reading. Jonathan
hoped that God might speak to him and this seemed to excite him.
Some psychotic experiences, especially in their initial stages, bring
euphoria and a sense of heightened awareness. Some people experience this as being touched by God; others turn to God in attempts
to find salvation.

God did not seem to be responding, and Jonathan looked for
other ways to calm his mind. He said he would like to learn
meditation, and asked me to go with him. He said it would be good
for me too. I booked both of us into two sessions at the Trans-
cendental Meditation Centre.

The Centre was in a bluestone villa in one of Adelaide's best
suburbs. It smelt agreeably of incense. At the first session we sat

with about twenty other people in a large room, which was bare except for a picture of the Maharishi. We sat cross-legged, including Jonathan, who spent most of the time examining his feet, picking off large flakes of dry skin. When the young woman who was taking the session told us that the divine spirit would shine through us all, Jonathan nodded and looked pleased.

The following day, we had a second session. Jonathan and I had arranged to meet there but he didn't arrive until halfway through. He walked in, dragging his feet, wearing sandals that were tied to his feet with string. His jeans were held up by an old tie and he trailed a cloth bag on the ground. He lay on the floor, full-length, and promptly went to sleep. The devotee told me that Jonathan was highly sensitive and needed a lot of encouragement. She urged me to keep trying and to book another appointment as soon as possible.

'Who's responsible for me, Anne?' said Jonathan one week later, when he was in better shape.

'You are.'

'I am? I'm sorry I hassle you, Anne.'

Jonathan was not getting any better. I decided to see if counselling would be of any help and booked into two therapists called Graham and Susan. I went to Susan first, who said she would be willing to see Jonathan. Jonathan agreed, but only because she did not take a medical approach. He sat peering at her in much the same way he had peered at Sally some months earlier, talked in monosyllables, thanked her at the end of the session, and then refused to return.

Even if Jonathan had rejected help, I needed every bit of assistance I could muster. I booked myself in for a session of intensive therapy with Susan and Graham, known as a marathon. The marathon consisted of two days where everybody poured out their innermost problems and hoped they could stuff them back in again by Sunday night at 5 pm. Graham and Susan were, and are, outstanding psychotherapists of many years' experience so they knew what they were doing. Emotionally cathartic therapy is only risky when the therapist isn't skilled.

We met in a room full of brown velvet beanbags and cuddly toys. I leered at a giant panda and sat as far away as possible. There were about twenty of us, a mixed assortment. We all had conversations with our mothers, our fathers, our grandparents, and anyone else in our lives with whom we had unfinished business, and in between we hugged each other. Two people regressed to having two-year-old tantrums as part of their therapy, and everyone said how beautiful they were. Then we had a general anger workout, the moment I had been waiting for. Several people came forth and beat beanbags with padded clubs, screaming at their husband, their wife, their lover, their boss, and any other motherfucker who might be troubling them, either now or from the past.

'I have trouble expressing my anger,' I said, always anxious to please.

'Wait till you've been doing therapy longer,' someone counselled.

I hesitated, then decided I wasn't going to miss out, even though at that particular moment any anger I might have felt was swallowed up in stage-fright and Anglo-Saxon embarrassment.

I aimed for the beanbag with a tentative swipe. I was angry at my feeble effort. Come on, you can do better: aim, swing, hit!

There was a yelp of pain. I had hit the therapist instead of the beanbag.

A chorus of voices told me that subconsciously I had intended this to happen; that deep down I was a malicious child, wanting to release repressed rage. I protested, red with embarrassment, and crept out at the end of the session.

I was not going to return, but my own behaviour was alarming me. I found I was driving my car without knowing where I was going or even from where I had come. I would start crying and be unable to stop. Once I parked on the edge of the beach, closed all the windows and screamed until I had to stop because my throat was too sore to continue. My car had become my safe place, the place where I could let go of my feelings. One afternoon I was driving to Joshua's school and nearly had a head-on collision with a bus. I was on the wrong side of the road.

I returned to Susan and Graham because I believed they could help me, and they did. Going to weekly group therapy sessions was the best investment in sanity and friendship I could have made. They took Jonathan's condition seriously, and advised me to get him to Bangalore, in India, where an American psychotherapist, called Jacqui Schiff, was running an international centre for young people with schizophrenia. Her methods were radical but the results were supposed to be good.

I wrote to Jacqui Schiff and filed the notion of taking Jonathan to India in the back of my mind. My brain had become a card index, stuffed full of information about schizophrenia, both conventional and alternative – of doctors, therapists, homeopaths and acupuncturists, of priests and spiritualists, astrologers and shamans. I had lists of youth centres and youth refuges, of caravan parks and boarding houses, of schemes for unemployed youth, of half-way houses and centres for living skills. I collected books and medical journals, articles and tapes. All these were my life-line to hope. Each time I tried something new, and it did not provide the miracle cure, I would replace it with the next idea, and the next. I said that I would never give up.

Somewhere around this time I received a letter from two young friends of mine in Sydney called Anne and Andrew. Andrew had known a young man with schizophrenia who had killed himself and he felt he could help Jonathan. He and Anne had just bought some land two hours' drive from Sydney. They wanted Jonathan to come and live with them:

*The clue is to channel mental energy into physical energy. The idea would be to get Jonathan with people he trusts and perhaps involved in the creation of our farm. Maybe we are dreaming, but we would like to try.*

I showed Jonathan Anne's letter and he said that sounded pretty good. I wrote to Anne:

*Perhaps the best plan would be for Jonathan to come over with me on one of my Sydney visits and then come down to you on a fairly casual basis, so that if it doesn't work out, there are no hard feelings. If he feels this is a plan to fix him up, he will get agitated and set himself up to fail.*

Anne replied:

*I think all that we can do is offer ourselves and our place, and Jonathan can decide for himself how far he wants to take it. Maybe a shelter of his own on the other side of the creek, with his own vegetable patch and animals will be all he wants – maybe more. He will have to let us know to some extent. Also, now you will have a place in the country to come to!*

Jonathan never made it to Anne and Andrew, but this story is one of many where people tried all manner of creative ideas in an attempt to find a cure.

The year continued in crises as Jonathan progressively deteriorated. Each crisis was punctuated by attempts to get him into hospital. Each one failed. Frank could only commit him if he saw him when he was crazy. But when Jonathan was crazy, he slipped in and out of our lives like a will o' the wisp. Now you see him, now you don't. At the first hint of a suggestion that he might need help, he would flee. It was the same pattern as the year before, when he first became ill. Once, when he said he was ill and frightened, I even persuaded him to come as far as the hospital gates. But then he crossed his arms and said, 'Take me back. I want to go home. Take me back. I want to go home. Take me –'

'Okay,' I said, 'I'll take you back.'

I believe Jonathan's rejection of hospitals was partly because even the best of them tended to be authoritarian institutions, run to suit the system rather than the patient; and partly because his sense of self was so fragile that he dared not commit himself to anyone or to any place that might take over the last vestiges of his autonomy. He said he did not want to be swallowed up, to disappear forever into the black hole.

He was leading a peripatetic lifestyle, always staying at different places, sometimes the squats, sometimes the park, sometimes home. Often he came in the middle of the night; whether he stayed or left, he almost always left the front-door open. Sometimes he used the tall windows that fronted the ocean, and he left them open too.

Once, at about two in the morning when I heard a banging noise downstairs, I came down to find a strange man in a raincoat climbing in through the window. The moonlight on the water was moving in long cold ripples.

'What do you want?' I said in a voice that had risen at least an octave.

The man looked startled. 'I'm looking for Eric.'

'Eric doesn't live here,' I said. My heart was pounding and I felt afraid.

'They said he did.'

'They are wrong. Please leave.' He did.

Life with Jonathan, whether he lived in the house or out of it, was therefore an ongoing hazard: with front doors being left open, stoves turned on and burning all night, showers running till they flooded the house. I gave up trying to get Jonathan to knock on the door before he walked in. I gave up on policing keys. He would take mine off my key-ring and lose it. Anyway, he would always find a way to enter: if necessary, jemmying open a window or even breaking a pane of glass.

We were all strained. Georgia gave me a poem she had just written which I found beautiful and disturbing.

*DAUGHTER TO MOTHER*

*I*
*Often you look at me,*
*With a hint of worry in your eyes.*
*Then you ask me questions about myself.*
*I can't explain why I can't answer and*
*Why the real me is buried so far inside.*
*But I can say that I love you,*
*And just because I don't talk doesn't mean I don't feel.*
*Remember, that I am part of you,*
*And that all of me,*
*Which you say you can never find,*
*Is within yourself.*

*II*
*Sometimes I wonder*
*How our roles became so reversed.*
*You cry and I cry.*
*You laugh and I laugh.*
*Yet, you tell me your problems*
*And I keep mine to myself.*

*You are my mother,*
*And I am your daughter.*
*Yet I feel so maternal*
*Towards you*

*When you pour out your heart*
*Like water into my hands.*

*I know I should do the same to you,*
*But I'm so scared;*
*The gaps between your fingers*
*Will be too wide and I'll trickle away,*
*Dissolving like water into the dust;*
*Losing myself for ever.*

All during this time I was filming the ABC television series on people with disabilities. One story was about a young woman who was intellectually disabled, another about a group of young people who were quadriplegic, a third about a man with crippling cerebral palsy. All these were people who had learned to accept their disabilities. Until then I had never really thought of schizophrenia as a disability because I had not yet accepted the reality of the illness. It was something that would go away. Jonathan would get better. But now I was having to confront the possibility that this illness was more likely to stay than go, and unless we could find better ways of coping so would the drama and anguish that accompanied it.

On Friday, 14 November, Jonathan was arrested overnight and appeared in court the following day, charged with a number of stealing offences. The police required cash bail of $500 and $400 surety, and the case was adjourned until Monday, 15 December.

Jonathan was described in the police records as being of medium build, with fair hair, wearing a black jumper, a fawn beanie and yellow rubber gloves. He had been picked up for stealing a Sara Lee Danish Apple Cake and five dollars in change from a house near where he lived.

Police records show that at the police station he had said to the interviewing officer: *Can I talk to you man to man? I would like to tell you about some breaks I have done that go back to July.'*

Jonathan claimed that he had stolen a dozen eggs, thirteen records, a clock-radio, and six bottles of vintage port. *The vintage port has been drunk, and the clock-radio is in the River Torrens behind Channel Ten. I ate the Sara Lee Danish Apple and the dozen eggs, and I spent the money.*

When I bailed Jonathan out of prison I felt awkward and ashamed. By the time I got him home I was angry because he had stolen when there was no need. But Jonathan wasn't the slightest bit contrite. He recounted what had happened as if he were a child describing stealing a Violet Crumble bar. Jonathan's emotional age had seemed much younger than his chronological age ever since he had been ill.

He walked up and down the front room, waving his arms, and talking at high speed. 'It's like this, Anne. I'm at the window slashing the fly screen with my knife. It's my fishing knife. And I climb inside, but I don't disturb anything, right. There's lots of things I could have taken – jewellery, valuables – but that's not my scene, right?

'Then I find this money in a piggy bank. I put on your yellow washing-up gloves so I won't leave any fingerprints, and I take the money from the piggy bank and an Apple Danish from the fridge, and I climb back out. But I have a feeling the police might be watching me. They are. And they chase me. So I dive round the corner and down this lane, and I hide in a drain.

'And then I get this good idea. I'm wearing a blue jumper and underneath that two other jumpers. So I take off my blue jumper and I'm in a brown one. That means I'm in disguise. The police keep following, so I take off the brown jumper and now I'm in a grey jumper and that's another disguise. And all the time I'm running and swerving, but they come up behind me, and say, "We got you." '

'So I put my hands up, and I say "Okay, I'll come quiet." '

'And they say, "You're a housebreaker, son." '

'And I say, "No I'm not a housebreaker." '

' "Listen, you're a housebreaker." '

' "No, I'm not a housebreaker." '

' "Listen, see that car? There's two more guys in there, and we're going to throw you in the ditch and kick your guts out, 'cos you're a housebreaker." '

' "Okay I'm a housebreaker." '

' "Good boy, son." '

'And when we get to the station one of the cops says, "I'll come with you to the detectives 'cos they could beat shit out of you, 'cos you're a housebreaker, right?" '

' "Right," I say. "I'm a housebreaker." ' '

*God,* I thought after I had listened to him, *instead of committing crime, he should turn to a career of writing about it.*

On 21 November Jonathan was charged again, this time with stealing six empty soft-drink bottles. He was clearly not popular with the police. By the time we arrived at the Adelaide Magistrates' Court he had already pleaded guilty. He was bound over for three years in the sum of $100, on condition that he be of good behaviour, that he be under the supervision of a probation officer, and that he obey that officer's lawful directions. This was where we acquired Brenda. Brenda became Jonathan's probation officer. Brenda scooped up Jonathan after the court case, and scooped up me as well. She said wryly that the property had been recovered, and then read Jonathan the terms of his bond.

He was wandering up and down, talking to himself and appearing not to listen.

She tapped him on the shoulder. 'Jonathan, this is important.'

Jonathan giggled. 'I reckon.'

'Okay, so listen.'

'I have,' he said irritably, his eyes skeetering around the room. He then sat down, spread his long legs straight in front of him and recited, word for word, the entire terms of the bond. He spoke without pausing and without any inflections in his voice. I marvelled as I heard him; only years later did I realise that this was a manifestation of his illness. When someone with schizophrenia is psychotic, their senses not only become razor sharp, in tune with everyone and everything, every decibel of noise, every flicker of movement, every nuance in conversation, but at the same time that their brain is being bombarded with all these messages, their own thoughts are also cascading into their mind. No wonder Jonathan sometimes said, 'I have three brains, sometimes four.' When he would suddenly speak at a furious speed, it was probably because he was trying to catch up with the racing activity inside his head.

Brenda was equally astounded at Jonathan's performance. 'Quiz kid, are you, Joe?' she said.

And Joe giggled, 'Yair, but where's my prize?'

Brenda was one of the kindest, most helpful people I met during Jonathan's illness, and I owe her an immense debt. She was English-born, dark-haired, lively, and with a splendidly dry sense of humour.

You could rob five banks, marry an alcoholic, and vomit on Brenda's doorstep, and she would still have time for you. Years later, when I first began writing this book, I went to Adelaide, and Brenda and I met in a fast-food dump on the Great North Road, and together looked back into the past:

*Remember when it was as hot as this, and Jonathan insisted on wearing an Army great-coat, and three jumpers underneath? . . . how we used to keep a stock of belts and string for him because his trousers were always at half mast? . . . and the police once arrested him for showing his bum? . . . Remember searching for him in the squats? All you had to do was ask for Joe. They all knew Joe . . . Remember your saying, 'Thank you Anne, thank you for letting me know he's nearby and probably off his trolley'. . . Remember . . . ?*

I had engaged a solicitor to appear for Jonathan on the November charge – another Andrew. On 28 November Andrew saw Jonathan, and recorded that Jonathan did not want to use medical evidence as grounds for defence:

*He says is not in need of psychiatric assistance and feels that that is simply something that his mother has arranged as it suits her purposes. He simply wants it to be said that on the occasions that he has broken in he has done so because he has been hungry, he has not had any money, his efforts to obtain money have not been successful and he has been forced into breaking in to obtain money and that is why he has done it.*

When I read these notes I felt angry. Jonathan was on social security and also had open access to home. Often I gave him extra money.

On 5 December Brenda wrote:

*Made a home visit to Jonathan at the commune. He was still in bed at 11 a.m., which consisted of a mattress on the floor and a sleeping bag. The room was dark and I could not see Jonathan's eyes to see if he was stoned but he was not making a great deal of sense. However, he did know who I was and why I was there and he does not want to go into hospital. Any further conversation was futile.*

In preparation for the case, the solicitor wrote to Frank asking whether or not any useful treatment could be given to Jonathan if he were to admit himself to psychiatric hospital. Jonathan had since changed his mind about hospital, but not about accepting drugs.

On 11 December Frank replied:

*When I saw Jonathan today I talked to him for about three-quarters of an hour. During the early part of that he sounded tolerably rational, although his ideas were rather unrealistic and idealistic.*

*Towards the end however it became clear that he was quite disordered in his thoughts and he admitted to auditory hallucinations.*

*His mother tells me that at times he is far more disturbed, laughing and muttering to himself, strangely grimacing in the window or wandering restlessly about her house at night time. She also reports that at times he is grossly deluded and talks about himself being in charge of the world and suchlike things. He may, of course, deny these because he can pull himself together by an intellectual effort and then appears not to display these disordered thoughts.*

*In anyone's language Jonathan is at present psychotic and the history would suggest that he has been continuously or intermittently for several years. He has had psychiatric treatment on a voluntary basis in Sydney but although some improvement may have occurred with drugs administered there, he refused to continue on them and there seems to have been no general improvement from that admission.*

*Jonathan would not voluntarily go to Glenside [hospital] unless it were an alternative to prison. He would accept it then on the basis that it might improve his physical health by giving him rest and food and shelter. I do not believe that he would accept any medical treatment at all and very likely his behaviour would be such that he would not be acceptable and he would be discharged or he would voluntarily discharge himself.*

*Jonathan tends to be very angry at anybody trying to regulate or control his life in any way and demands that he be given a free hand to do exactly what he likes. Then when he gets into any difficulties he calls for help from his mother who puts herself out considerably to try and save him from the disaster he has got to the brink of. Once he has been saved from that he then demands the right to go back and do exactly as he likes again.*

*In my opinion, Jonathan is clearly certifiable in his present state and if someone requested that I certify him I would be prepared*

*to do so. His mother does not request that since she is concerned
about her relationship with him. He is very hostile to her despite all
her help and he is sometimes violent towards her.*

*I do not feel it would be well for Jonathan to be imprisoned. He
is very sensitive to pressures and resents any authority. He would
quickly get into serious difficulties and his abnormal mental state
might not be recognised by those about him since he can cover it
up intellectually at times, and then he might be subject to vicious
or hostile action from several sources.*

So now I knew that Frank would be willing to certify Jonathan,
why didn't I ask him to go ahead? Because I did not feel strong
enough to face Jonathan's anger, and because the only way to get
Jonathan to hospital against his will would be by calling the police
which seemed such a hostile thing to do. If Jonathan had appen-
dicitis, he would have been taken to hospital by ambulance. Only
the mentally ill are treated as if they have committed a crime. Physical
illness is met with sympathy, mental illness with shame.

**15 December**   The day of the magistrate's hearing. We had a bad
night. Jonathan did not sleep and neither did we. He roamed the
house, saying that his eyes were hanging out of his head. He wrote
several notes saying: *Do not kill Jonathan, signed Joe Blow.* He told
me that my head had cracked open and that he could see my brains
pouring onto the floor. Eventually he went to bed, but it wasn't until
about four in the morning. Georgia and Joshua went to school, and
I rang Brenda at nine and burst into tears with strain and exhaustion.
I woke Jonathan half an hour later, as he had to be at the court by
11 o'clock. He came into the kitchen in his filthiest of clothes. On
his feet were blackened and smelly sandshoes. The soles flapped
as he walked.

'How about changing?'

'Nuh.'

'Okay. But if you go the way you are, the magistrate might think
you don't look after yourself and don't care.'

'Yeah?'

'If you put on good clothes he might think – there's someone who
wants to get himself back together again.'

'Yeah.' He liked the idea of that, and chuckled.

He wandered into the kitchen half an hour later wearing the new clothes but with bare feet.

'Shoes?'

'Nuh.' He wandered up and down the kitchen. From where we stood, we could look down the hallway and through the open front door see the sea and the sky, blue and shining and dancing with light.

'Do you feel paranoid in Adelaide, Anne? Do you feel the violence? I think I'll tell the judge I need a nice quiet place and a long rest.'

I hoped that Jonathan meant hospital, but this seemed too good to be true.

Jonathan went to court carrying his old clothes in a plastic bag which he would not let anyone touch. His old clothes were his chosen identity, not these new ones that I had bought and which he understandably resented.

Outside the court Jonathan put on his new shoes. A friend called Marl had come with me. For some time now, Marl had been a stalwart help, funny, loving, and generous with her time. We had a running joke that she was my foul-weather friend. Brenda had also arrived. We were gathered together in a small group just inside the entrance to the court building when I became aware that Jonathan was lying full-length on the floor, blocking the entrance to the courtroom so that people had to step over him.

'My mother won't let her little boy be a happy hippy.'

I glanced down at Jonathan's feet as he lay sprawled in front of me. His new shoes had been slashed from side to side. He must have done this just before leaving. I thought, *Good old Joe, at least you're consistent.*

He sat up suddenly and said he was going to get some cigarettes. Marl went racing after him. They came back together and this time he lay on the floor in a foetal position. When his name was called, Brenda nudged him with her foot and said cheerfully, 'Get up Joe, you're on.'

'Stand up, stand up for Jesus,' he said. And stood up.

The magistrate found that there was a case to answer, and Jonathan was committed for trial in the Central District Criminal Court. Bail was allowed on Jonathan's recognisances – again, of $500 with a surety of $400. The case would come up in the new year, probably towards the end of the month.

In December the Somalia film was shown on Channel Nine. Just before its screening I was interviewed by the *Australian Women's Weekly*. I read the article now and note that in answer to a question about parenthood I had priggishly replied:

*Everyone has a basic desire to be a good parent. But people expect too much. They are too hard on themselves. Guilt? I've none, really, I don't think being a parent is easy at any time but I think it can be fun. The more you learn from your children and vice versa, the more everyone will grow.*

Oh, brave front! My guilt was growing rampant like weeds in a summer garden, and as fast as I rooted out one shoot, a thousand more grew in its place.

Just before the close of this most troubled year, Jonathan wandered into my study, and looked out across the sea. I noticed he was wearing the old Tibetan jacket. The sun sparkled on the water. A dog was racing up and down the beach. During this moment of innocence, Jonathan stood in silence, still gazing out of the window. Then he turned. He looked and sounded like a child again, a small boy of six or seven, grave and polite.

'Please Mummy, give me a certificate of sanity. I want a certificate of sanity.'

Four
# The Search for a Cure

*Go, and catch a falling star,*
*Get with child a mandrake root,*
*Tell me, where all past years are,*
*Or who cleft the Devil's foot.*
                              JOHN DONNE

**January 1981**  A time of expansiveness, when friends of all ages
drifted in and out of the house, and for the first time it was filled
with people in the way large houses need to be filled. January was
swimming; it was sitting in companionable silence on the verandah
gazing at sunsets spreading orange and pink streamers into the sea.
And January was when we first met Tom, who lived in a boarding
house just up the road, and took the local dogs for a walk on the
beach at dusk every day. Tom was eighty. He was bow-legged and
strong and he wore a battered hat on the back of his head. He'd
walk with the dogs tied together with pieces of string until they
reached the sand when he would let them go, carolling 'Off you
go, my darlings.' He used to return our dog last of all. Every night
he would knock on our door and stand there, cradling Liza and
singing, 'I'll Take You Home Again Kathleen'.

He did not always sing. Sometimes he just said, 'Here's Kathleen.'
Tom was important. He never failed to call, and so for me he became
one of the few vestiges of stability in my life.

Jonathan also took to the beaches, and would sit on the sand,
wearing his many jumpers. Sometimes he would come walking with
me, his eyes downcast, occasionally venturing near the water and
then stepping backwards in fright. He was nineteen, and thin and
pale.

He was due to appear in the Central District Criminal Court on
19 January. Brenda and I wanted Jonathan's schizophrenia to be
raised in court because we hoped the judge would issue a treatment

order. But Jonathan did not want this. He said he wasn't ill, and Jonathan – as a legal adult – was the one who instructed his solicitor.

Years earlier, when I had a daily radio program, I would argue long and hard about issues of civil liberties and mental illness. I would have been appalled at the notion of using a court-case to try to compel someone to have treatment. But Jonathan was progressively deteriorating and I was desperate.

**15 January**   Brenda recorded:
*It seems as if everyone has ethical reasons why they are not going to mention Jon's psychiatric problems in court. Jon has requested that the matter not be brought up. It looks as if it leaves me to do the dirty work if I can sort out where my responsibilities lie. I came to the conclusion that if no one else will bring the matter to the judge's attention then I will do so in the form of a Probation Officer's Report.*

Jonathan did not want Brenda's report to be tabled, and the magistrate did not ask for it. Why should he? It seemed to be a relatively minor offence and he would have had no more idea of Jonathan's medical history than of any other stranger's in the court. Jonathan was released on an unsupervised bond of twelve month's duration. Legally, this was a good result.

That night, Jonathan was psychotic and began checking himself out again in the bathroom mirror. 'Good boy Joe. Are you sure it's Joe? Yes it's Joe.'

When he saw me looking at him he stopped. I felt like an intruder on someone's private conversation. I think I even said, 'Sorry.'

**20 January**   Andrew, the solicitor, said that he felt badly about the results. He realised Jonathan needed treatment. He thought that maybe he had better not act for Jonathan in the future because, as a friend of the family, there was a conflict of interests. I wrote in my diary, *This legalism is absurd. Surely it is in Jonathan's interest, even more than mine, that he gets better?*

**21 January**   Jonathan told Georgia she was a maggot, and that I was a capitalist toadstool. Dinner was tense. The architect was present but left after dinner. In some ways this was a relief as it meant one less person to worry about. Margaret, another stalwart, new-found friend turned up for coffee while Jonathan was racing up and down the stairs, cursing us whenever we appeared. We played him some music and eventually he went to bed, but got up again in the middle of the night. I decided that I would ring Frank the following day.

**22 January**   Frank was away. Jonathan seemed calmer. He left at midday saying he was going to visit some friends. At the end of the afternoon I was driving through North Adelaide when I spotted him walking along the middle of the road. He waved at me to stop. He asked me for a milkshake so we went into a cafe, and talked for a few minutes before he began glowering at me, and muttering. The tension of the past few weeks, waiting for the trial, was bound to erupt sometime. It erupted over me.

One minute Jonathan was blowing into his chocolate-malted. The next, he had thrown the milkshake at my face, followed by the pepper and salt, upturned the table, and chucked a chair at me. People gasped, the waiter came running and Jonathan shot off, out the door and up the street.

I shook the milk off me and tried to rub the pepper out of my eyes, which made it worse. The waiter hovered, hoping for an explanation. I couldn't think of one that wouldn't take half an hour, so I paid the bill and left.

Brenda and Margaret thought I should charge Jonathan with assault. They said I had to set limits. The idea appalled me. But I did feel angry: angry with Jonathan for hurting me, angry with the system for not helping him, angry with the illness. The hardest anger to deal with was the anger with Jonathan, because of its paradox. Can you be angry with someone if it is their illness that makes them so destructive? But I *was* angry, so angry that I felt like thumping anyone and everyone, so angry that I had to belt my rage out on some cushions, and even then could not assuage it because I felt so powerless.

**23 January**   As Jonathan hadn't called to see Brenda, she went looking for him. She called round to the commune, and wrote in her report:

*Jonathan was lying half on and half off his mattress. He did not respond when I spoke to him and the radio was blaring away. He looked very pale and at first I thought he was dead but was very relieved to find he was breathing. There was no evidence that he had taken anything and I understand that he does become almost unconscious when he is having psychotic episodes. So I left. The room was in its usual grotty state with a shower of bus tickets around the place.*

**24 January**  Jonathan arrived home in the middle of the night by forcing one of the windows. He was psychotic, laughing and talking to himself, going into high-pitched giggles, and racing up and down the stairs. At one stage he pulled down all the medical books, followed by the Bible. I sat on the floor with him and tried to get him to talk about what was happening, but he ignored me and raced through the pages like a fast-track film sequence, reading aloud made-up words, and scrumpling the pages as he turned them. I phoned the crisis centre but they told me to phone the police. I phoned the police but, by the time they arrived, two hours later, Jonathan had left.

Early next morning I went out to my car and found Jonathan slumped over the driving wheel. He looked as if he were unconscious or dead. He was neither. When I got in the car, he took my finger and bit it so hard that I yelled in pain. He forced my head back against the seat, so that I began to choke, while his teeth kept gripping my finger. He giggled. Then he let go of my finger and my throat, suddenly, and leapt out of the car and ran down the road. I sat in the car for about five minutes, hugging my finger and crying, and then dragged myself into the house. I felt sick and desolate.

It seemed as if I were the one who mainly precipitated the violent outbursts. When Jonathan was psychotic, he incorporated me into his delusions and he would hear voices commanding him to hurt me. His internal conflicts must have been terrible. He had written on the blotched and mouldy walls of his squat a large message in black texta: *Don't harm Anne.* Over the years I would find scraps of paper on which he had scrawled similar injunctions. The more psychotic Jonathan became, the greater his terror, and the stronger his need to protect himself. Once, he said that God had told him

I was the Devil and should be destroyed. Perhaps, as he looked at me my face was distorting so greatly that, to him, I looked like the Devil.

At this stage, our whole family was like a ship engulfed in a terrible storm. As we were swept from one crisis to another, Georgia and Joshua must have felt in danger of being overwhelmed. Georgia was now sixteen and Joshua twelve. If they tried to include Jonathan in their social engagements, he invariably behaved grossly, in what seemed like deliberate attempts to sabotage their acceptance of him. He would urinate in the garden, belch and fart, and attack Georgia with the crudest language he could muster. If they excluded him, then his absence hung in heavy reproach. They had to deal with their own paradox of anger and grief: anger with Jonathan for how he behaved towards them, grief because they had lost the brother they loved. They also had to deal with their anger towards me, and with the indignation they must have felt that the one who was misbehaving was getting all the attention.

Ami Brodoff, a young writer, expresses these conflicting experiences and emotions in a US *Schizophrenia Bulletin*. She describes what happened when her older brother Andy developed schizophrenia:

*As our family privately lurched from one emergency to another involving my brother, and the ebb and flow of his moods became the main focus of each day, I began to feel neglected for being healthy. My own concerns were often dwarfed by Andy's larger problems, while my joys and successes seemed even more trivial. I craved more attention and recognition from my parents, but felt guilty about these longings since Andy was obviously so much more needy. In bitter moments, I felt that the only way I could win my parents' affection was by becoming sick too. Yet I knew that mental illness was far too high a price to pay – even for love.*

Josh's cricket continued to be his escape. He wielded imaginary cricket bats in the supermarket. He made up ingenious cricket games with a card index system, and spent hours putting dots on the cards, each dot representing a score.

Georgia wrote more poetry.

They knew, these younger children of mine, who lived in the front line but showed no visible wounds, that, given the circumstances, I did the best I could. They knew that I would have given anything for this not to have happened. They knew that I loved them. But knowing is different from feeling, and for a long time within the knowing child was also the yearning child.

And the architect? The times we spent together became less frequent and they were always overshadowed by the sense that at any time Jonathan might erupt on the scene. The support I needed was too great for any one person to provide and what was happening would have tested the staunchest of relationships, even longstanding ones. Ours was new and quite vulnerable.

Jonathan suffered the worst torment of all. He had to bear the terror of his illness, the loss of his promise, the loss of himself.

**2 February**   I wake to hear Jonathan's voice downstairs. I lie there trying to hear only the sea. *Please God, if I close my eyes and am very good, perhaps he will go away, because I am tired, so tired, and I do not feel I have the strength to go downstairs.*

Jonathan is walking up and down the hall, talking to himself. 'Noddy Noddy, Noddy,' he says, 'Noddy, Noddy. Don't hurt yourself, Noddy. Noddy, mustn't sleep, Noddy Noddy.'

I go downstairs in bare feet, slowly at first and then running because I am frightened that he has in fact hurt himself. Josh and Georgia are awake and their doors are open.

Jonathan is banging his head against the wall, shouting, 'Don't hurt yourself' over and over again. He pushes past me and runs into the bathroom and stares at his face in the mirror. He holds his head to one side and then the other. He giggles. I put my arms around him, but he pushes me away and says, 'Who are you lady? You're the Devil, aren't you, lady? Make her go away, Mummy, make her go away.'

He has his old boy-scout's knife in his hand. He fingers the blade, and I nearly say 'Don't be melodramatic,' but then don't quite have the nerve. Abruptly he pushes past me to the kitchen where he picks up a large black texta and writes on the wall, 'Fuck off Noddy'.

Now he is banging his head again and is screaming. I say, 'Jonathan, I won't let anyone hurt you.'

But he shouts at me, 'I'm mad Anne, Noddy Noddy. There's my

heart. All bright red blood on the floor, Anne, all mixed up with yours, Anne. Noddy Noddy. What's it like to know you're mad, Noddy Noddy? Poor Joe's head is falling apart.'

I seem to remember shouting, 'Then dear God, let's get some help!'

'Leave me alone.' He shoves at me.

I go upstairs. My study is next to Joshua's room. Joshua is awake and lying there rigid. He whispers, 'What's going on?'

I tell him, and tell Georgia, and then ring the hospital. The hospital tells me to ring Crisis Care. Brenda has already spoken with the people at Crisis Care but the voice the other end tells me to ring my doctor. I ring Frank. There is a recorded message to say he is away. The screaming is continuing, so I ring Crisis Care again and the young man says, 'We don't take house calls if someone is psychotic. Ring the police.'

I ring the police. The police tell me to ring Crisis Care.

I am afraid that Jonathan will hear the telephone and run away like he has in the past. He is in the living-room, downstairs. He has pushed the furniture to one side of the room and has the family photograph albums and the Bible spread out on the floor. But when I enter he is staring into the big mirror that hangs above the fireplace. He is tracing the contours of his face with his fingers. His face is very close to the glass.

'Jesus was snow white, Snow White and Dopey. And you're the wicked witch.' He rushes down to the basement.

My fingers are shaking as I ring the police again. 'You have *got* to come,' I demand.

'Righto, lady, we'll call by.'

'When?'

'About four.'

'That's two hours away!' I am sounding hysterical. I am feeling hysterical.

'We'll make it earlier if we can.'

I go down to the basement which is in darkness. Jonathan is pressed against the wall and he is howling. It is a dark primitive sound. It is summer but I am shivering and I can feel the hairs on my arms standing on end. I have taken to wearing an old Ethiopian silver cross because I figure that this might persuade him I am not the Devil. I hold up the cross.

'Go away,' he says. 'Go away, Devil.'

'Jonathan, I am not the Devil. This is God's love and God says "Go in peace".'

My words seem to calm Jonathan. I take him by the hand and lead him upstairs to the kitchen. I make sure he can't block my access to the door and I do not turn my back on him. I am frightened. I make some tea and suggest we listen to some music in the front room. I put on some Mozart. He sits on the floor hugging his knees, and I sit in one of the big armchairs, and then I must have drifted off to sleep because I wake to find the music has stopped, and a strong wind is making the carpet lift and fall. Jonathan is still on the floor, his head between his knees, silent.

The phone rings. It is the police. They want to know whether Jonathan will recover as soon as they arrive. They are being wary. They have had the experience of taking psychotic people to hospital, only to find they become quite sane as soon as the doctor appears. This period of sanity is usually brief, but long enough to make an inexperienced doctor believe that nothing is wrong. When I have seen Jonathan do this, it's as if fear has given him a surge of energy to gather up the fragments of his mind again.

I tell the police that I don't know what will happen with Jonathan, but I will hold them responsible if they don't come and something happens to me.

When I return to Jonathan, I feel like a Judas. Why don't I tell him I have called the police? Because if I do he will pad off into the night. About an hour drifts by. The door-bell rings, a small sound after the other noises we have experienced, but it seems very loud. I tell Jonathan it is the police and why I have called them. He says nothing. There are tears in his eyes.

Three police officers enter the house, two large men and one young woman who carries a torch. Jonathan's face is chalk-white and his hands shake. 'I am very sorry, sir, I didn't mean to frighten my mother and my brother and my sister, sir. I am very sorry, sir.' There is a whine in his voice and his eyes are downcast. I can smell his fear. The older policeman takes me on one side and says he doesn't doubt what has been happening but there is no way they can take Jonathan to hospital while he is apparently behaving and talking quite rationally.

'The doctor will say, "He's not crazy. He's okay".'

'He's not okay,' I say through clenched teeth.

The policeman pats my hand. 'I know.'

He goes to the kitchen and tells Jonathan that he needs help, and would be better in hospital.

'No thank you sir, no thank you.'

'Sooner or later we'll have to take you because you're not well, son. You go outside and have a walk around and think about it.'

Jonathan goes out to the laundry and shuts the door. There is silence. Maybe he's gone out the laundry door, out the back gate, and away? But minutes later he returns.

'I'll go.'

The policeman rings the hospital. I can hear a voice the other end, a crackly sound. The policeman relays the medical message: 'Doctor says, Why can't he stay with his mum and come in tomorrow morning?'

I am dumbfounded.

The policeman answers for me: 'Because he's been frightening his mum and acting strange.'

The phone goes crackle crackle. The policeman says: 'Doctor asks, "What's wrong?" '

'Schizophrenia.'

'Schizophrenia,' says the policeman. He listens. 'Doctor says, "There's no such thing as schizophrenia." '

I think of the long night and the fear and the anguish of Jonathan. I grab the phone from the policeman and begin talking, and don't stop until I have convinced this idiot, this cretin, this man with his absurd textbook theories, that unless he does something there will be hell to pay. He gives in. Perhaps he decides he would rather face Jonathan than me.

The kitchen is cold and the tea is cold and I am cold. Jonathan is pacing up and down talking to himself. The two other police officers are sitting with straight backs on the two tall stools as if they are participating in some formal function. They stare ahead, embarrassed perhaps.

The older policeman says to Jonathan, 'Now you go with your

mum, and don't give her any trouble because we'll be following behind.'

When we get to the hospital, Jonathan says 'I'm sorry, sir,' to the doctor and I feel a sinking sensation as the doctor raises his eyebrows and says, 'Seems all right to me.' It's Mr Smarty-pants No-such-thing-as schizophrenia, but I am too tired for a fight. I put my head in my hands, and then I hear Jonathan.

'I think you've put me in here to punish me for my sins. Do not electrocute me, sir.' His voice trails away into a sigh.

I should have felt relieved. Instead I am unutterably sad.

When I get home from the hospital it is nearly dawn. I look out across the sea which is grey like a stone and then, like Jonathan, I turn to the mirror. *The mirror crack'd from side to side; 'The curse is come upon me,' cried The Lady of Shalott.*

But the mirror wasn't cracked. I was. As I peered into the glass I could make no connection between my face and my feelings inside. My face was familiar, my feelings indescribable. I felt as if this was some monstrous endurance test, which would never end.

The next morning I went to visit Jonathan and to bring him a change of clothes. The hospital looked like a motel on the outside, and an airport departure-lounge on the inside. I met Jonathan in the day room, which had muzak, over-full metal ash-trays and imitation leather chairs. The room was full of people who were either sitting and smoking, or shuffling round and smoking. Some were in dressing-gowns and plastic slippers, others were in day clothes.

Jonathan hugged me with arms outstretched and stiff, like tea-towel racks. 'What's wrong with me?'

Later the doctor said cheerfully, 'You can take your boy home this afternoon.'

My head throbbed from no sleep. I found it hard to believe what I was hearing. 'But you haven't examined him,' I said. 'You've no idea what's been happening. And you certainly haven't had time to give him proper treatment.'

The doctor looked awkward. 'Come and see me later.' I did. I told him the long saga. 'In that case he'd better not come home yet.' The doctor's voice was precise. He had already confirmed the diagnosis that Jonathan had schizophrenia. He now switched dramatically from the injunction that I should take Jonathan home to agreeing to keep him in hospital. I was beginning to discover that, unless relatives insist on it, doctors often don't listen to families. When I pressed him about my fear of Jonathan's rages continuing, his solution was that I might have to consider moving interstate.

I saw a social worker, who said in a syrupy voice, 'I know you are a very busy woman, but try to love your son.'

How dare she! I wanted to hit her. 'I do love my son. God! I do love my son.' And now my anger is being drowned by tears. Later, the social worker tells Brenda that it is obvious Jonathan missed out on affection as a child and that I loved the other two children more. Not long after that, another professional tells me that perhaps I have been overly involved with Jonathan – 'smother-love' it is called.

This is a no-win situation. I have lost the son I knew. My two other children are living under a fearful strain. My relationship with the architect is fast disappearing. I am cursed and alone. I feel pain howling through every part of me. The doctor is walking past me in the corridor. 'You all right?' he says. He sounds surprised.

The doctor sent me to a psychiatrist who had brown hair, a brown office, smoked a brown pipe and sat in a brown leather armchair. He was pleasant and listened attentively. He asked me about my mother, my father, my childhood, my marriage and the architect. At the end of two hours he said that he thought he could work with me, but that analysis required weekly visits and that it might take some time to work through my depression.

I said, 'Thank you.'

On my way home I began to feel cheated and angry. I did not need analysis. I needed practical help. I was depressed because there was abundant reason for depression. Tears ran down my cheeks and I had to stop the car. I pulled up by a telephone box, and in desperation rang the social worker who had thought me loveless.

'Are there any support groups? People like me I can talk with?'

'I haven't heard of any.' She sounded almost disapproving.

'I'm desperate.'

'I'll make some enquiries. If you don't hear from me you'll know there aren't any.'

'Come to my funeral,' I shouted, but I had already put down the phone.

Jonathan tried to run away from the open ward so he was moved to Anderson House, the locked ward. It was a red-brick building, set among roses and pepper trees. The locks were discreet. The linoleum was shiny red. I waited in the waiting-room and Jonathan appeared with his hair brushed forward and plastered smooth. He was wearing someone else's clothes. His jeans were too small and his blue jumper too short.

'Hallo,' he said. 'Hallo. I am looking at you.'

'Why?'

'To see how sad you are. I am sorry if I have made you sad.'

I hugged him.

'Keep hugging me. I'm so cold. Did you put me in here because I hurt you?'

'No, no.'

'I want to go home.'

'I want you to come home too. But not till you're better.'

Jonathan hung his head and shuffled away a few paces, and then returned. 'How are you?'

'Okay. And you?'

'Stoned. Stoned on Stelazine. Do you think I will get better?'

'Yes. You will get better.'

'My throat's so dry. I feel terrible.'

'Poor old love.'

'Do you think there is anything wrong with my heart? It is aching. I think it is broken.'

'Let me give you a cuddle.'

'All I want is a simple life,' he said sadly.

The doctor said Jonathon was not responding well to the medication. It didn't seem to clear his thinking much, and he was withdrawn and depressed.

'You won't give him ECT, will you?'

The doctor looked surprised. 'ECT isn't normally given for schizophrenia.'

'Well, don't, without letting me know what's going on.'

I had asked about ECT because I knew Jonathan was frightened of it. He had come across it in movies like *Frances* and *One Flew*

*Over the Cuckoo's Nest.* In the past, ECT (electro-convulsive therapy) was sometimes brutally administered and over-prescribed, and indeed has been a controversial issue in psychiatry since its introduction in the late thirties. It is now mainly used, under anaesthetic, in the treatment of severe depression, where it can provide relief, although the reasons why are still not fully understood.

The next time I visited Jonathan he was back in the open ward. 'They say I will be here another four weeks. Anne, why did you put me in here, just because I wanted to have a sandwich and was hungry? I'm only a simple boy. I want some girl-friends and some fun.'

A boy about sixteen wandered up to us. He had a punk hair-cut and heavily tattooed arms. 'You Joe's mum? I'm Rambo.' He giggled. Jonathan giggled.

We were sitting in one of the plastic armchairs, an ash-tray between us. Jonathan was holding an orange. His hands were shaking from the medication and when he tried to peel the orange, he found it hard. It dropped in his lap and then rolled away, between the plastic-slippered feet.

Georgia wrote:

### VISIT TO HILLCREST

*They've stolen you from within yourself.*
*I saw it in the long dark corridor*
*And the overheated sitting room*
*Where they sat.*
*Shiftless stares, mumbles and robot movements,*
*Occasional laugh*
*And a freshly starched nurse*
*Puts oranges on the table.*
*Your hand shakes*
*As you try to peel it;*
*The broken-down shell of a body*
*Won't let your last vestige of self-respect*
*Escape through its uncontrolled shivering.*
*Frozen eyes with no hint of past or future,*

*There's no exit, just listen to the rain*
*If you can hear it,*
*Above the drone of the radio*
*And the footsteps on the lino.*
*My mind has left and I chase after it*
*Down the hall*
*And on to the grass where the children are playing.*
*You follow me,*
*And as you step out of the door*
*I can see that you understand, and in that understanding,*
*A glimmer of hope.*

That night there was a phone call from Jonathan. His voice was flat. The sea outside was dark red from the setting sun.

'Anne, how long have I been here? They say they want me to stay four weeks. Do you reckon I'm sick? They say my voice doesn't connect with my thoughts. Is my voice dead?'

'No, not dead. But tired. How are you?'

'Scared.'

'Why scared?'

'In case I get ill again, or they hurt me, or I hurt you.'

'No one will get hurt.'

Next evening there was a news item about the hospital, and I only caught the end of it. A patient called Jonathan had strangled another patient in the shower. I put my hand to my mouth as I heard the announcement. I think I stopped breathing. And then let go when I heard it was another Jonathan.

On 12 February Brenda visited Jonathan and reported that he seemed depressed. He had been hitting his head against the wall because he felt so confused. He said he could not face life any more.

'Why me, why me, why me?' he asked, and all the while I was asking 'Why Jonathan, why Jonathan?' I may as well have asked why there is a moon in the sky and stars at night, and floods and fire and pestilence. I was learning acceptance, which is different from resignation.

Jonathan's condition changed very little. He still did not respond well to medication, and he escaped from hospital at regular intervals. Once, at three in the morning, the phone rang and a laconic voice said he was the sergeant from a country police station, several hundred kilometres away. 'We have your son here. Says he is a mental patient. Says he has escaped. Wants you to come and get him.'

'Now?'

'I reckon.'

'First thing in the morning?'

'I guess.'

I started to doze off to sleep. The phone rang again.

'Lady, he says he knows Jane Fonda. Does he know Jane Fonda?'

Before my journey with Jonathan is ended I will have become so used to those early-morning crisis calls that they become built into my patterns of waking and sleeping. Even now, if I get woken unexpectedly, my heart races and I think, 'Jonathan'.

A few days later I was in Sydney when I rang the Adelaide hospital to check Jonathan's progress and spoke to a young nurse who said brightly, 'He's all ready for his procedure tomorrow.'

'What procedure?'

'ECT.'

I threatened the wrath of God before I got a promise that ECT would not be given until I had discussed it with the doctor, as he had promised.

I cut short my film shoot and flew back the following morning. The doctor said that Jonathan was no longer psychotic, but was now severely depressed. ECT was almost a last resort. I said I thought the reason for Jonathan's depression might be because he felt sad about being ill, sad about being in hospital, and hated taking the medication that was supposed to improve his condition. In those circumstances, I thought I would also feel depressed.

I do know that Jonathan feared hospital and was convinced that sooner or later, the straitjacket and the padded cell would be used. Images carry their weight of legend, and Jonathan had seen plenty of films about madness which coloured his apprehensions. He found the medication so deadening that he resisted taking it, and would flush it down the lavatory. He could not sleep at nights and he walked up and down the wards waking people up. He played his music too loud, and he refused to conform to hospital regime.

Several years later, I spent some time with the famous Scottish psychiatrist R. D. Laing, who asked me in an exasperated voice, 'Why can't our hospitals be more hospitable?' In hospital, he said, people are stripped of almost all responsibility for their lives from the moment of waking to the moment of sleeping. A lot of medication may be required to keep up this regimentation. For example, with many psychotic illnesses a person's bio-rhythms operate in reverse from the norm. There is nothing intrinsically pathological about being awake at night and sleeping during the day, but there is no possibility of that in our psychiatric wards. 'Where in the world are lunatics allowed to bathe naked in the moonlight?' said Laing.

Laing had been part of the anti-psychiatry movement of the 'sixties whose other well-known members included Thomas Szasz and David Cooper. The movement rejected notions of biochemical abnormality in schizophrenia, and viewed mental illness in political terms as a means of expanding the power of psychiatry and psychiatrists, and as a label for scapegoating people whom society found difficult, or who had alternative views.

The anti-psychiatry movement grew out of the psychoanalytic school of the 1920s and 1930s, when psychoanalysts began questioning the medical basis of schizophrenia. The illness was said to be the result of traumatic early childhood experiences, particularly those of cold and rejecting mothers, who were then given the label 'schizophrenogenic' (which means causing schizophrenia). Families were described as 'toxic' or 'noxious'. Psychoanalytic theories were followed by family interaction theories, which held that abnormal and destructive communication within families could lead to the development of schizophrenia. The phrase, 'double-bind' became common jargon in psychiatry; it was said to occur when parents sent their children 'heads-I-win, tails-you-lose' messages.

The advent of a spokesperson as brilliant and witty as Ronny Laing clinched the anti-psychiatry movement. Generations of young health professionals marched forth to liberate the mentally ill from the cruel oppression of their parents. Not only did parents have to deal with the problems of their child's illness, they also had to cope with persistent and quite cruel scapegoating. These family interaction theories were rejected in the absence of any convincing evidence, but traces of blame lingered for many years. I was often confronted by such attitudes and, in moments of wretchedness, would partly believe them.

Jonathan had now twice been diagnosed as having schizophrenia. With each attack he had deteriorated. Doctors kept stating that his particular form of schizophrenia did not respond well to medication and was hard to control. They said there was nothing more they could do for him, now that I had rejected the idea of ECT. I decided I must search for alternatives.

I thought again about the international clinic in India which I had learned about from Susan and Graham, the two Adelaide therapists. The clinic was run by an American psychotherapist, Jacqui Schiff, and was regarded as innovative and controversial. It catered for young people between the ages of seventeen and thirty-five who suffered from schizophrenia.

Jacqui Schiff's first major involvement with schizophrenia came in the 'sixties when she was living at Charlottesville, Virginia, in the United States. She and her husband Morris were social workers at the medical school of the university. In 1965 they took into their home a very disturbed young man who had been diagnosed paranoid schizophrenic. Dennis, who was later adopted by Jacqui and became Aaron, was described by her as an 'exceptionally large and powerful boy with a stupid, slack face; he was incredibly dirty and had a severe scalp rash.' Within a few months the Schiffs had a whole household of severely disturbed youngsters, mostly with schizophrenia. There was then a growing demand to find alternatives to drugs and hospital.

Jacqui Schiff believed that schizophrenia had its beginnings in early family situations and that people needed to regress back to those initial traumatic experiences before they could recover. Regression might mean regression into infancy, and therapists sometimes found themselves putting on nappies and giving bottles to enormous 'infants', who could be bigger than themselves. After regression came growing-up time again, but within the warmth of a therapeutic community and with new 'adopted parents'. In this way people could develop new patterns of behaviour and of relating to others.

In 1972, a year after Jacqui and Morris separated, Jacqui helped form a non-profit educational corporation, Cathexis Institute, to research and develop innovative approaches to the treatment of

psychosis. The parent organisation, Cathexis, still contin[...]
in California, but in the 'seventies Jacqui moved to India t[...]
a residential community where living would be che[...]
possibly because there she would be subject to less interference.
The community was called Athma Shakti Vidyalaya.

Earlier in the year, in January, I had received a letter from a
member of the Athma Shakti community:

*I think that you have probably read enough about Reparenting to
know that part of the treatment usually involves patients choosing
new parents from among the staff and identifying with them. One
of the consequences, which you need to recognise, is that quite often
kids no longer wish to identify with their families of origin.*

*Here we are much more like a large family than an institution
and is the only place I know where people suffering from schizophrenia can get their needs met and get treatment without being
put down or made not okay. Demands are made on the kids here
to function normally and this is stressful. However, we have
accumulated a lot of solid evidence that our treatment works and
that people get cured.*

How would I feel about Jonathan abandoning me as his mother,
and adopting Jacqui or one of the other therapists as part of getting
better? I knew how I would feel. I sent a reply to Jacqui:

*I realise that Jonathan might wish to have nothing more to do with
us at the end of his stay, and yes, it would hurt, so I hope it will
not happen. But I'd rather have him well than tied to us in pain.*

Jacqui also wrote to Jonathan:

*Dear Jonathan,*

*We have a letter from your mother about the possibility of your
coming here. I know that the idea of coming to India must be
overwhelming, especially for anyone who is having difficulties
anyway. It is always hard for people with emotional problems to give
up environments which are familiar even if things aren't working
very well.*

*Anyway, people do get well here and I want to reassure you that
you can get well. A lot of people have, and if you're willing to work
and understand that you will have to face some hard things, you
can do it too.*

*Best wishes to you in whatever you decide to do.*

Jacqui asked Jonathan to write to her when he came out of hospital, but his hands were shaky from the medication, so we sat on the floor in the big front room and recorded a tape. You can see the difference that five weeks in hospital and medication had made to Jonathan – even though he wasn't particularly responsive to it. Before he went into hospital, he had sounded crazy and chaotic. Now, on this tape, he was thoughtful and coherent and, perhaps for the first time, acknowledged his need of help, and the kind of help he wanted.

*I'm just interested in getting more information about your place. Information about how big it is, whether I'd be locked in, what sort of system it is. I gather it's not run like a big institution. I want to know how long I'll be there for, and more news about the way you work for my particular illness, if you can call it that.*

*I do feel encouraged by the letter. It's made me feel that some things are available for me, particularly help without drugs, which is good, because I don't like taking the medical drugs given to me in hospital.*

ANNE: *How do you feel about the idea of going there?*

JONATHAN: *Oh, I want to get better. I feel very uptight and worried a lot of the time and, oh I don't know, I do have some sort of nervous problem. They say I'm schizophrenic, but, I mean, what is 'schizophrenic'? They don't know. But I feel the pressure on my head, a lot of pain in my head. I've felt that for quite a while. Just out of step with reality.*

ANNE: *How do you mean?*

JONATHAN: *I feel an anger against society for putting labels on me which I don't feel I necessarily deserve. I feel as if there's a lot of tears to be shed. I feel like a volatile thing that's just sitting there, that could go off at any moment.*

ANNE: *How do you want to be helped?*

JONATHAN: *With a lot of love and understanding. And a lot of talking with people. No drugs and no punishment. I am a reasonable person and I am prepared to be reasonable in most things. I'll talk about it with the people. I'd like to thank them for the letter. I appreciate it very much, and I hope I will see them soon.*

Because the Indian option was not yet secure, I decided to have a blitz on other possible alternatives. My second option was the headquarters of Cathexis in California, but it became clear that it would be difficult for Jonathan to get an American visa. A third option was a community in London known as the Arbours, which harked back to the days of R. D. Laing and which I discarded because of the visa problem, but also because it would have been too expensive. I tried a community in Queensland run by an alternative psychiatrist, but the main problem here was that I could see Jonathan hitching down to Sydney or Adelaide within a matter of days. For the same reason I rejected a therapeutic community in the mountains just near Sydney, who, anyway, did not feel able to manage people with psychoses.

Then there were the Adelaide charismatics, who offered to ex-punge Jonathan of the Devil, but Jonathan said he liked the Devil and didn't wish his presence to be expunged.

I took afternoon tea in the sedate hills of Adelaide with Dr Kenneth McAll, a 74-year-old visiting missionary psychiatrist who treated mental illness with exorcism rather than medication. He had worked all his life in China. He said many illnesses were the manifestations of tormented souls, ghosts in the ancestral family tree. His technique was to identify these 'outcasts' whose sins had never been expiated, and put them to rest with prayer and communion.

Dr McAll was a conventionally qualified medical practitioner, who had trained at Edinburgh University. He was on a world tour, meeting medical and lay groups. He was a balding shy man, who wore a grey woolly cardigan and politely offered me tea and scones, which he seemed to enjoy preparing. It would be easy to dismiss him as a religious crank, but he came across as a serious-minded man. He agreed that much of mental illness has physical origins, but firmly believed that for some illnesses, especially those which didn't respond to treatment, the causes were spiritual.

'Perhaps you had someone in your family?' Doctor McAll's voice was gentle, apologetic.

I tried to think of some tormented souls on my side of the family tree but I failed. So I dobbed in Ellis's. 'How about a hanging judge who had lots of children and then eloped with a sixteen-year-old when he was in his seventies?'

'Maybe.'

'Then he had hundreds more children.'

Dr McAll smiled, a faint dry smile.

'So he could still be hanging around?' I paused. 'Sorry about the pun.'

Dr McAll forgave the pun and said, 'Who knows who might be hanging around? Shall we pray?'

Another possibility I tried was the orthomolecular, or nutritional approach. Orthomolecular psychiatrists believe that schizophrenia is caused in large part by mineral and vitamin deficiencies. Orthomolecular psychiatry is dismissed by mainstream psychiatrists on the basis that research does not substantiate its claims. Other nutritional theories about schizophrenia are also unsubstantiated. But as mainstream psychiatry once backed psychoanalytic and family-interaction theories, which also had no research basis, the dismissal of nutritional theories as mere fads is ironic. I met a young school teacher in South Australia who firmly believed that her schizophrenia was controlled by dietary means. She adopted a way of living which nurtured and sustained her, so that she glowed with good health. She still became psychotic occasionally, and would admit herself to hospital, where she would have to battle the administration to be allowed to maintain her diet. Yet if a person is managing her life valiantly and well, and believes in a particular approach, then as long as that approach is not harmful, then who are we to deny it?

The trouble with trying to give Jonathan healthy food, let alone combinations of vitamins and minerals, proven or unproven, was that his lifestyle precluded healthy living. He was peripatetic, so that he often ate his food on the run, and never at regular hours. He had a craving for junk food, which included Coke, Jaffas and potato crisps. I would try and combat these with a battery of health-food supplements which I would secrete in his food. I pushed vitamins into sandwiches, ground them up into powder and stirred them into stews and, when Jonathan decided that the only food he wanted to eat was Mars Bars, I stuffed Mars Bars with vitamin pills. Josh complained that even the salt tasted funny and he was probably right.

Years later when I was talking to a friend about my hunt for alternatives, she reminded me of the story of a man who went around selling pills in an earthquake. He kept shouting, 'Pills to cure the earthquake.' Someone came up and said to the old man, 'You can't cure an earthquake with pills.' 'I know,' said the old man, 'but what's your alternative?'

We are part of a culture that believes in the notion of cure. So when we cannot cure those we love, we embark with them on odysseys of hope. I would not have it otherwise; nor would I ever scoff at other people's quests, however strange I might find them. Even if the goal is not achieved, the quest will have brought hope.

Meantime, Jonathan was still refusing medication. He said he wasn't ill, and that the drugs gave him bad side-effects. Often, further drugs are required to counter these side-effects, which can pack quite a wallop, including involuntary movements of muscles, slowing down of speech and thought processes, blurred vision, weight gain, dryness of the mouth, muscle fatigue, rigidity, and the development of a mask-like facial expression. Some of the neurological side-effects may be irreversible. Young people with schizophrenia joke about 'the Mellaril mumbles' and 'the Stelazine stomps', and this is another reason many of them chuck their medication down the sink.

Once, in the second year of his illness, Jonathan came to my bedroom with his face twisted into a fearsome grimace, and his neck wrenched around so his head looked as if it had been stuck on backwards. He was choking and pointed desperately to his mouth. His tongue was swollen and protruding. I thought he was dying. All his muscles seemed to be in spasm. I tried to help him down the three flights of stairs but he fell and I fell, and, half-carrying each other, we managed to get into my car. I raced upstairs to tell Georgia and Joshua where we were going.

*Oh God, please let him be all right,* I chanted inside my head like a mantra, and *What if he chokes to death before I arrive?*

Jonathan didn't choke to death. He had experienced a severe reaction to his medication, and hadn't taken the drug to counteract the side-effects of the other drug. No one had thought to tell me about it.

In the middle of the night the hospital was dark and silent and empty. A nurse hurried Jonathan away to give him an injection to end the spasm. The young doctor who eventually returned with Jonathan said to him gently, 'It must be rotten.'

Tears welled up in Jonathan's eyes and splashed on the arm of his chair.

Professional acknowledgment that someone is having a torrid time is such a little thing to give but means so much. When a doctor says 'It must be rotten', this is an emotional response which carries its own healing. It doesn't happen enough. Simon, a young painter who has struggled with schizophrenia for nearly fifteen years says, 'Doctors rarely talk to us or look at us as if we're human. All they ever say is "How's your medication?" But I'm not a chemical tablet. I'm a soul, and psychiatrists never use the word "soul". They never use the word "love". Some even say we cannot love.'

Ray, an inventor, who also has had a lifetime dealing with schizophrenia says: 'I know what medication suits me and what doesn't. But I go to the doctor (a new doctor, it's always a new doctor) and he writes a script and I say "That doesn't work for me". So he gets his notes and writes down, *Patient obstreperous. Won't co-operate.* And doubles the dose.'

Great passions are inflamed by the issue of drug treatment in mental illness. Some critics believe enforced medication is an assault on the person's civil liberties; that it acts like a chemical straitjacket, designed to ensure obedience to the medical regime. They believe doctors are 'trigger happy' in prescribing medications and are dismissive of side-effects. Others, usually family members, tell stories of doctors reluctant to prescribe the anti-psychotic drugs, or of being unrealistic in expecting all patients to look after their own medication, and of not giving families any information about dosage and side-effects. At Syracuse in the United States, where I attended a conference on schizophrenia, numbers of parents talked in exasperation about muddled messages from doctors: 'I'm not telling you not to take your medication, but I'm not insisting that you do take it.'

Improvements in medication have been relatively few, and people with schizophrenia sometimes become angry at the crudity of the drugs. People can be discharged with insufficient time to find the best kind of medication for their illness, or the correct maintenance dose. Over-medication can be a problem. On many occasions doctors fail to investigate the reasons for a new episode of the illness, and respond by simply increasing the dosage. Perhaps this stems from the time when people with schizophrenia were considered incapable of having feelings. In fact, the reverse is true. The extreme sensitivity of people with schiophrenia to so much in their environment means that their painfully raw feelings can trigger psychotic behaviour, or else they might 'shut off' and retreat into catatonia.

Studies now show that if medication is accompanied by giving more information about the illness and about its management to people with schiophrenia, and to their families, hospital re-admissions can be significantly reduced.

**12 March** Brenda wrote:
*Although Anne is no longer under tremendous strain. I felt there was something wrong as she sounded tired and flat. She admitted that, now she was no longer living on adrenalin, she felt almost less able to cope than when she was in the crisis situation. In fact, she does feel slightly depressed but is aware of what is happening to her, and says that she is getting adequate support. The whole family is . beginning to show signs of great strain.*

I was giving Georgia driving lessons which we abandoned when she knocked over a dustbin and I screamed at her. I was far too nervy to be giving anyone lessons.

She said wistfully, 'I wish we were a white sliced-bread family.'

'How d'you mean?'

'White bread sandwiches, cut in triangles, home-made cake, cut in squares, and a bunch of grapes. Instead of which we're a hunk of Vogel bread, a lump of cheese and a bruised apple.'

She was still writing poetry which she put under my bedroom door.

### SCHIZOPHRENIA

*Your knife clatters,*
*And lies abandoned on the table.*
*All eyes stare*
*As your long fingers pick their way through the food*
*And total oblivion seems to shroud you.*
*Only animal hunger and a perplexed solitude*

*Gape through the matted hair.*
*You laugh,*
*Yellow teeth and a complete break from reality*
*Cause pain and perhaps*
*Just the smallest touch of disgust*
*To flicker through our eyes.*
*Still staring,*
*Conversation stilted,*
*And I watch the tears form in her eyes,*
*For she is the only one*
*Who really understands his aching mind*
*Or is it her own that makes her cry?*
*It's hard to separate a mother from her son.*

Managing work and home had become an excruciatingly difficult balancing act. Without work there was no money. I made increasingly intricate arrangements to make sure someone reliable was at home in my absence. Sometimes I had to fly back to Adelaide in the middle of a shoot because some crisis had erupted.

The extent of my strain began to penetrate my dreams. One night I dreamt I was walking along a road with the three children and we came to a house where people were drinking tea. The room was warm, the guests were well dressed. A big man came into the room clutching a sack on his back. He was powerful and overwhelming. He picked up all the precious things in the room and stuffed them in his sack. Then he took the food. No one tried to stop him, but after he had gone we felt bleak and hungry.

Next we were on board a ship in the middle of a fierce storm. The boat was heaving and shuddering, yet the children and I were sitting on deck-chairs pretending that everything was calm. When the waves become so great that they broke over the side, drenching us, I put Joshua on my back, and my arms around Georgia and Jonathan, and we tried to climb to the top deck where the waves could not reach us. The deck was rotten and full of holes and the sea was boiling beneath our feet. The stairs to the top deck were also rotten and part gave way. I was gasping for breath and I could feel the children slipping from my grasp. I was frightened but I was also determined that I would not let go.

Then we were walking along a steep and rocky mountain path. A tall man was walking by my side and one arm was outstretched as if trying to shield us from falling into the gorge below. The three children were walking behind me, and we were linked together by a rope. The man gave me a sense of security. Suddenly, a giant boulder fell from above us, and sent him hurtling to his death.

In the fourth and final scene of the dream I had almost reached the top of a steep climb. I was alone. A person came to join me and walked by my side, without touching me. I did not know whether it was a man or a woman. I climbed the hill and found strength from the presence of my companion. At the top of the hill I found myself on lush green plains, with people playing musical instruments, and children laughing. It was like a colour plate in a child's guide to the Bible. I felt happier than I had ever known. Could I dream Jonathan into the same kind of sweet content? No, you can only dream your own dreams; you cannot dream for other souls.

**11 March**  Jonathan agreed to go to a general practitioner who tried to persuade him to look after his health. Jonathan said he would run on the beach. I said I would run on the beach. The doctor looked at me and said, 'I think you'd better walk.'

**22 March**  Jonathan was arrested again, this time for offences he had committed in July the previous year. He had stolen a portable radio and ten dollars. This threatened to scuttle the Indian plans. If the court proceeded as normal, the case would not be heard until May which would be too late for him to be accepted in India. Jacqui was returning to the United States at the beginning of May and had said that Jonathan must arrive before the end of April. Andrew made an impassioned plea to get the case heard early, and succeeded.

**2 April**  The day of the trial. After all Jonathan's misdemeanours, it was possible that he would get a prison sentence. At one point, the judge stated that even with the most favourable medical evidence, the court might still have to say 'Well, so be it.'

Andrew, the solicitor, argued for a bond so that Jonathan could go to India. Andrew looked like pictures of a young Lenin, with his steel-rimmed spectacles and balding head. He was tenacious. He pointed out the futility of imprisonment, and said, 'We are dealing with a most adventurous move by a parent . . . It has only come about because she has already tried unsuccessfully every possible option she can think of to find treatment for her lad.'

Brenda went into the box next: 'I have been very concerned for this young lad, for his family, and for the community . . . I think every avenue of treatment should be explored and that he should be given the opportunity to go to India. I also ask your honour to take into account the almost herculean efforts of his mother to try to find some viable treatment, and I ask your honour to impose a penalty that will enable him to take advantage of that treatment.'

His honour remarked dryly that one could use quite lavish language to describe the efforts that had been made to help Jonathan.

Jonathan was required to be of good behaviour for a period of three years. This meant he would be free to travel to India. Should he not go to India, he was required to be under the supervision of his probation officer.

The judge told Jonathan: 'Treatment is only as effective as the person is willing to receive that treatment . If you are willing, there is some hope that things will come good. If you are not willing, I suspect it is not going to do you much good.'

Jonathan said 'Yes sir', and left the court, shoulders bowed, head down, nodding.

**7 April** I flew with Jonathan to Melbourne to see a therapist nominated by Jacqui who was to assess his suitability for the Indian community. The therapist that Jonathan would benefit greatly.

Jonathan had not wanted to see the therapist. On the way back, we had to wait for a train and he walked off down the platform, shouting, 'Call yourself the bloody Human Relations Commissioner, turning your own son out of home. D'you hear, everyone? Anne Deveson, the fucking Human Relationships Commissioner, sends her son to India to get rid of him.'

I gazed up at the sky, down at the railway lines, and looked around me, trying to spot this cruel woman who was abandoning her son.

**13 April** The hospital reported that Jonathan was claiming that he was a heroin addict. He was tested and was definitely not an addict. He wandered up and down the house mumbling: 'I'm on a health kick. I'm smoking sixty cigarettes a day.'

*14 April*   I was getting nervous that Jonathan would commit another offence, or run away, or have a psychotic attack before we could get to Bangalore. I decided that I had to get him out of South Australia as quickly as possible. I made arrangements to fly to Western Australia the following day and stay on a friend's property for the week before our flight departed.

*15 April*   Jonathan disappeared. He hitchhiked up to a folk festival in Whyalla.

*16 April*   Joshua came back with the afternoon papers, which reported that there was a domestic airline strike. Jonathan was still away.

*22 April*   Jonathan returned from the folk festival. He said he was now glad to be going to India. Brenda said wryly that Jonathan must have decided that five years in India would be a mystical experience compared with five months in prison.

International airlines joined the strike. The let-down was difficult for everyone. Jonathan headed off next morning to meet his friends and Brenda spotted him squatting in the gutter making frog noises. I decided that strike or no strike, we had to leave. We would drive either to Perth as originally planned, or to Melbourne, and wait there for the first available plane to India. Brenda and Frank advised against Perth. They feared that Jonathan might become psychotic during the long drive across the desert.

*24 April*   We had a farewell gathering. I still have snapshots. Jonathan looks unwell, but I remember it as a happy evening. I felt full of optimism.

*25 April*   The drive to Melbourne took two days. Twice on the way Jonathan became frightened and started thumping my arm. Once the car veered off the road. In the motel, we had dinner in the public dining-room and he turned on one of his belching and scratching acts.

The second day's drive was better as we played childhood games. We played 'Spot a white horse'. The white horse would bring us joy. We found a splendid white horse just as the sun was setting.

In Melbourne we stayed with Eva. Eva was then heading the Human Resources Centre at La Trobe University. She is a tiny woman, with masses of dark curly hair and immense vitality and warmth. When we arrived Eva was taking non-stop telephone calls, finishing a research paper, cooking dinner, and soon delighting Jonathan with stories about India as well. Our next ten days, waiting for the strike to end, were spent in trying to persuade Jonathan not to hitch back to Adelaide. We took it in shifts to be with him. Once Eva was only just in time to stop him picking up a lift. She said she would miss him if he left, so he picked her up and carried her home, loping along the road with his fair hair over his eyes and his disarming grin.

A couple of days later we were out shopping when Jonathan decided to have a haircut. I went to have a cup of coffee. When I returned, Jonathan was talking animatedly with the hairdresser who had pink stubble hair, and safety pins dangling from his ears. Pink Hair was telling Jonathan that when he was fourteen he used to stick safety pins through his nipples, and that he was a hooker and on heroin. 'Jesus,' he said, 'you don't have to go to India to go tripping, man: I can take you to some real good places right here, I can, man.' Pink Hair also told Jonathan that all hospitals were jails, all doctors psychopaths, and all medication was poison.

I groaned. Of all the hairdressers in Melbourne, we had to pick this one. Jonathan walked out, announcing that he would catch the next bus to Adelaide. 'There aren't any buses to Adelaide,' I wailed, but it was too late. Jonathan had leapt onto a passing bus. All we could do was hope that somehow or other he would remember Eva's address and return.

We drank black coffee. At about ten o'clock, Jonathan walked in looking cheerful and said that the sun was his heart.

Eva said, 'Just now you're looking over my head. What at?'

'I'm looking at that boy.' (This was a framed photograph).

'That's my son.'

'He's quite a straight guy. Interesting and intelligent. He seems to like me. Oh, there's this woman on the cover of your record, Eva, and I'm talking to her at the same time. She likes me too.'

He walked up and down and there was a glitter about his energy. 'I communicate with the spirit of the sky, and I feel like a cloud evaporating, blue energy and white, sprinkle sprinkle. All my tensions disappear. I've seen this picture of a guy called Sunflower and he lived with me for a while. And the other night I got in contact with a space creature called Zolar and he was magic. He had wings like an arrow, with a little ball on the end of each arrow. They're all shaped like that and they attach themselves to flying saucers. They're part of the cosmos. Sometimes bulk numbers attach themselves to me, and I can feel incredible power flowing through my body. I listened to Beethoven one night and I got such a high that I nearly fell off the chair. And sometimes I'm waltzing in beautiful woods in Vienna, and my legs become the waltzing, and at the same time I'm riding for hundreds of miles along a smooth endless highway. I am this beautiful girl with long fair hair, clean of spirit, just zapping along an endless highway.' He stopped talking almost as abruptly as he had begun.

Finally, the strike was over. On the last night Jonathan packed his bag including some new music cassettes, a Pink Floyd record, and Tolkein's *Lord of the Rings* which he took with him wherever he went. I still have his copy. When he had finished packing, he kicked the bag and declared: 'I'm not going to India. I'm going back to Adelaide because I'm going to fight the police, yeah.'

'Don't fight the police, Joe,' said Eva. 'You might get hurt.'

'Well then, I'm going to build a tent city. I've got work to do, man.'

Eva said, 'I wish I were going to India, man.'

Jonathan laughed, not giggled. He gave Eva a piggy-back around the room. He looked happy. His moods changed quickly. One moment he would flare into paranoia, the next he would be laughing uproariously at some private joke. That night he went to bed with hot milk and slept peacefully.

*1 May* Eva came to the airport to wave us goodbye. During the flight Jonathan spent long periods of time in the lavatory. What was he doing? Gazing into the mirror, talking to himself? Gazing into the mirror, not talking but peering, to reassure himself he was really there? Or had he baled out ? Was he catapulting to earth where he would have a miraculous landing and the shock would cure him? Miracles are like spiders' webs, beautiful to spin.

Jonathan emerged from the lavatory. 'When I get to India I'm going to buy me a whopper bike and ride around and meet some girls and some holy men. Can I have another Coke?'

*2 May*   Bombay airport was dangerous. The air was hot and heavy. People crushed into us. Small boys like piranhas darted in and out, grabbing at our legs, our arms, our bags.

'Hey mister, you want nice hashish, mister? Cocaine?'

'Yeah, yeah.'

'Jonathan come back, Jonathan!'

Jonathan gave all his money to a beggar. 'What's the most you've given to a beggar, Anne?'

We had a few hours to wait before the plane to Bangalore so I booked a taxi to the Taj Mahal Hotel. It would be safe there, ordered, cool. At the entrance to the Taj, Jonathan took off. The piranhas had reappeared.

'Cheap hash, sir, very cheap very good hash, sir.'

I followed. *Oh Jesus! I'm going to lose him!* I surged my way through the crowds. I slipped. My sandal broke. I butted past a large woman dressed in a white sari and I grabbed hold of Jonathan's sleeve. We had a tug of war. The small boys were yanking at Jonathan. I was also yanking. I won. Jonathan giggled. I felt more like crying. Jonathan said, 'When I have my motor-bike I'll take you riding, round India and back again.'

We spent our short time in Bombay safely inside the Taj Mahal Hotel. We sat in the foyer pretending we were waiting for someone. We went to the coffee shop, then to a bar for a cool drink, then back to the coffee shop and the other shops, and up and down in the lifts. We talked about spirits and holy men, about the smells of cooking, about seeing the insides of people as well as their outsides, and about the book *Zen and the Art of Motor Cycle Maintenance*. Jonathan promised not to run off on our way back to the airport.

The flight to Bangalore left at 4 pm. The plane was full, mostly with men, some wore dark-coloured suits and carried shiny brief-cases; others were in dhotis, and carried their goods in baskets and in their arms. Jonathan and I were seated somewhere in the middle of the plane.

Just before we landed at Bangalore Jonathan became agitated. 'You fucking turd, I don't want to go to this fucking place. I'd like to bite your ear off.'

I took his hand and said 'It'll be okay.' It wouldn't be okay if he bit my ear off but I felt reasonably safe that he wouldn't. Suddenly I felt excruciating pain. Jonathan was punching me on the head. One, two, three blows, and I was reeling and yelling 'Stop!' The hostess came running. In my dazed state it seemed as if the men in the plane were all Peter Sellers, wagging their fingers at Jonathan and chanting, 'You must not hit your mommy in the head.'

'You hurt me'.

'I'm sorry.' He grabbed my head. 'Here, I'll make it better.' He started crushing my head. I jabbed him in the stomach and he let go.

'Why are you doing this?'

'Because I've got a head problem.' He giggled.

'Thanks. Now I've got it.' I rubbed my bruised and throbbing head and the side of my face which he had also clipped. I was sore and angry. When we got out of the plane at Bangalore, I had a fixed grin on my face, and I was still shaking.

A young woman with lots of curly brown hair, dressed in jeans and T-shirt, met us, and said she was Sharon. 'I'm staff. Mom's at home.'

Jonathan was smoking. Sharon said, 'Jonathan, you won't be al-lowed to smoke at Athma Shakti so you'd better put that out.'

'I'm addicted.'

'It doesn't matter. You won't be allowed to smoke.'

"I'm addicted."

'It doesn't matter. You won't be allowed to smoke.'

'But I'm addicted.'

'Put it out.'

'Can't I go outside and have a last smoke?'

'No, if you're going to give it up, the best time is now. And take your cigarette out of your mouth when you talk to me.'

We drove to Athma Shakti. Bangalore is a pleasant city, high up, with a lingering sense of the British Raj. All the roads are signposted, but deeply pot-holed, so the car threw up clouds of white dust. The traffic was horrendous. My throat was aching and so was my head. I had red marks down the side of my face. I wondered if I would have a black eye.

The car pulled up outside a two-storey white building, with ornate iron bars at the windows, blue shutters and faded blue mosaics. There were a few wispy trees, and scattered up the road were more cubed houses, like a dry and dusty toy-town. I was feeling scared. Jonathan must also be scared. I squeezed his hand and said 'Courage.' Sharon led us through the wide open doors.

At the time of our visit, the residential community consisted of about forty people. Twenty-five of these were clients, or 'kids'. The majority were from the United States and England. Others came from India, Japan, Jugoslavia, Sweden, Italy, Israel and France. Most were in their late twenties and early thirties.

Therapists and trainees included psychiatrists, psychologists, psychotherapists and general practitioners. They too came from all over the world. Jacqui's deputy, Hank, was an American Jesuit priest who had worked with the rag-pickers in India before joining the community.

Sharon led us through an entrance hall into the main living-room, a big room with marble floors. A large group of people of all ages were seated cross-legged on the floor in a big circle. A few were seated behind the circle on chairs. Some were Indians; some were Europeans. A group discussion was in process.

A very short woman dressed in black cotton baggy pants and tunic came forward to greet us – Jacqui. Her jawline was determined. Her light-grey eyes had a hypnotic quality. This was not a person to be taken lightly. She was built square but soft. She had grey softly waved hair, wore no make-up, and had the fine skin of a very young woman even though she must have been nearly in her fifties. Her voice was surprisingly high and squeaky, a little-girl voice that did not match her presence. She said 'Welcome', and introduced us to the group.

Jonathan pulled out a cigarette, stuck it in his mouth, and lit up.

'We do not smoke here, Jonathan. Put out your cigarette,' Jacqui said.

Jonathan ignored her. He dragged deeply on his cigarette. Everyone in the room was watching.

'Put out your cigarette.'

'Fucking old tart,' said Jonathan. He shoved her with his free hand.

Jacqui bounced back. 'Put out your cigarette. Immediately.' Jonathan threw her across the room. Jacqui rolled over and over like one of those googly dolls that bob back whichever way you push them. She came up smiling and unhurt. Was she used to this? Was this a regular event?

'I was an acrobat when I was young,' she squeaked, dusting herself off.

Meantime, what had happened to Jonathan? Jonathan was struggling beneath a mass of bodies. The other residents – the 'kids' – had thrown him to the ground and now they were holding him as he kicked, spat and yelled. The rest of the people in the room calmly observed the mêlée.

Jackie took my arm and said in a confidential voice, 'They'll hold him there until he deals with what was really going on.'

'How long will they hold him?'

'As long as it's necessary.' She steered me up some stairs into another room which seemed to be full of beds. 'They'll take it in shifts. The kids don't like anyone hurting their Mom.'

I thought *What if they smother him?* She guessed what I was thinking. 'They won't,' she said. 'Scrabble?' The last thing I wanted to do was play Scrabble. I played Scrabble. I lost. Someone came and took me to my bed. It was in a room with a therapist from Sweden and a young woman from Jugoslavia who had arrived the day before, accompanying her brother.

As I passed the heap of bodies on the floor, Jonathan was still letting out the occasional curse. I did not sleep well.

The following morning, breakfast was at eight: fruit and yoghurt, cereal and breads. Jonathan was still on the floor. I could see a leg, an arm, and a huddle of three or four people on top of him.

'Surely he's been there long enough?'

'He hasn't levelled yet.'

'Jonathan, it's Anne. Say you're sorry. Say what was going on.'

'Fuck off.'

'Oh God, Jonathan, why must you always make things so hard for yourself?'

I spent the morning with Jacqui talking about Jonathan. She did not seem the slightest bit interested in the fact that he had a cerebral haemorrhage at birth. Given that her theory emphasised the influence of early childhood experiences, I would have thought that to be put in an incubator, with needles in your spine and tubes up your nose, would have been a significantly frightening start to any life. She was more interested in whether I breast-fed him, how often, how I felt about it, and what age he went onto solids. We sat very close, side by side on cushions on the floor, and all the while Jacqui talked in a confidential whisper. She reminded me of Tenniel's illustrations of the White Queen in *Alice in Wonderland.* I shook out our family history for her and felt gutted.

Jonathan capitulated at about two in the afternoon. He said he was sorry and that his underlying feelings were those of fear. The kids believed he meant it and they let him go. He was taken off for a shower and something to eat.

When he returned he was weeping. He had become very polite and his eyes were downcast. He said, 'Mummy Mummy, I want to go home,' and his voice was little, like a four-year-old's.

*Oh Mummy Mummy, I want my Mummy too, I thought, and I want to go home. Are we at some mad-house run by a crazy woman who has everyone in her thrall, a bizarre mix of Mary Poppins and Genghis Khan? Perhaps we should escape while yet there is time.*

I went outside and paced up and down. I reminded myself of Jonathan's behaviour, of his distress, of the threat of jail. I recalled that in hospital in Australia he used to say 'Mummy Mummy, I want to go home.' What's more, he wasn't four years old: he was nineteen. I prodded the ground angrily with a stick, and marched back in.

Jacqui caught me for another game of Scrabble. She ate chocolate violet creams.

By the following day I had sorted out the layout of the place, and begun to make better sense of what was going on. Most of the activity took place in 'The Living Room', which was also the name given to stage one of the program. The Living Room was a large room with a bare floor, mattresses and bean bags, a piano, a blackboard, an old-fashioned radiogram, a couple of low tables and some books and magazines in a rickety bookcase. There were two yellow ceiling fans. Off the Living Room there was a dining-room, and a long kitchen opening up to a dusty yard where a group of Indian children were playing.

Upstairs was Jacqui's room, known as Mom's Room. Jacqui's room contained Jacqui's double bed, which was a mattress on the floor, several other mattresses and a large cot, a cupboard and an old armchair. Kids who were regressing or going through a hard time, as well as trainees who were having problems, would sometimes sleep in Jacqui's room. Off Jacqui's room was a terrace (probably it was the roof of the garage) and Jacqui had made this into a roof garden. Jacqui had two or three splendid Weimaraner dogs, which she bred, and these used to sleep upstairs with her, usually on the roof. Both the Living Room and Jacqui's room were in the main house where all the females lived. Males lived in an adjoining house.

Group therapy was held every morning after breakfast at 9.30. Throughout the day other work included yoga, problem-solving exercises, a group for those who wanted to regress, another for those with poor motor co-ordination, and individual sessions with individual therapists.

It is important to distinguish insight-oriented psychotherapy and psychoanalysis from what is popularly known as supportive psychotherapy. In the first two the focus is on exploring childhood experiences and then restructuring the patient's personality, while supportive psychotherapy concentrates on teaching living skills and how to cope with the symptoms and problems of the illness. Many psychiatrists now tend to believe that, while supportive psychotherapy is helpful, insight-oriented therapies are of limited value in the case of schizophrenia, and a number of research studies seem to substantiate this. Jacqui used a mixture of therapeutic techniques at Athma Shakti.

Newcomers were under the care of a 'Responsible Person'. A Responsible Person was someone who had made progress, and had been voted by the community as able to take responsibility for the care and safety for another. Newcomers had to keep the Living Room tidy, and to learn to interact with others in a sociable and responsible way. They were not allowed to get their own meals; they had to ask a Responsible Person to get it for them. If they did not ask nicely, or had been behaving unpleasantly, the Responsible Person mightn't feel like helping them. The Responsible Person might say 'Get nicked.' Anyone who went without food was given a milk food supplement. It came in orange and blue plastic mugs. I remember, because Jonathan had lots of it in the first three or four days. After that, he asked for his food in the most charming way.

Newcomers also had to get someone to accompany them to the toilet. Again, the same rules of politeness applied. Only Responsible People were allowed to move independently; others always had to be under surveillance. This was because they had been weaned off their medication, and were therefore vulnerable to becoming psychotic. For this reason no knives or forks were available in the Living Room; everyone ate with spoons.

People who had just arrived were put straight onto the Living Room stage of the program. Some were on restraints, which were coloured webbing leads or handcuffs. The leads were either tied to the wall or held by a Responsible Person. People who were catatonic were on leads which would be jerked every time they went into a stupor. Before bedtime each night, some people were put in handcuffs to stop them from harming themselves or others, and to prevent them from running away. The handcuffs were fastened to rings on the wall just above the beds.

The aim of the community was to get people well by making them accept responsibility for themselves. In this way, they were no longer allowed to use mental illness as an excuse for not functioning reasonably. Jacqui believed that all behaviour stems from the way people learn to adapt to their particular circumstances of life. The behaviours of mental illness were seen as maladaptive responses, brought about by some disturbance in development at an early age, but not fully apparent until adolescence. Treatment was therefore bases on learning more appropriate behaviour.

Jacqui also believed that by determining a person's particular kind of schizophrenia, she could assess the approximate stage at which the problems first occurred. During the last half of the nineteenth century, different sub-types of schizophrenia were described as separate diseases. These sub-types were known as 'paranoid', 'hebephrenic', 'catatonic' and 'simple'. But, as few people fall cleanly into one sub-type or another, the use of sub-typing has largely been discarded. Jacqui, however, stuck to sub-typing. She would first assess the patient's sub-type from a battery of diagnostic tests, and then make pronouncements about their early development. For example, if a person tested as hebephrenic, to Jacqui this would mean that some kind of trauma had occurred at the age of nine months.

Jacqui made people confront their craziness. She would not countenance any abnormal behaviour, and neither would the community. She would say that, although societies know so much about brainwashing techniques, they were always used in negative ways; she was using these techniques for positive purposes. All feelings were okay; they had to be acknowledged and not suppressed. Positive behaviour was rewarded; negative behaviour was punished.

Rules and regulations were few, but had to be obeyed. People were required to participate actively in their own treatment and that of others. They were expected to be sociable, helpful and well mannered. They were to fulfil their responsibilities. Alcohol, drugs, sex and cigarettes were out of bounds. Physical violence was not tolerated.

Rewards came by way of positive affirmations and physical stroking or hugging from the community. Sanctions included confrontation, withdrawal of privileges, containment by holding people down or standing them in the corner, expressions of disapproval, shame, even physical pain through slapping.

Gradually people learned to give and receive clear communications, and to give and accept responsibility. Students who were getting better were involved in various aspects of planning and managing the community. Peer-group pressure and responsibility were widely used. The community decided when someone was ready to be promoted to a position of responsibility. The community decided on sanctions and rewards. But ultimate responsibility and power always remained with Jacqui or senior staff. Once a month the residents rated each other in terms of behaviour and progress, on a scale of one to ten. Any kind of bizarre or unseemly behaviour was confronted immediately, and the Living Room was often like bedlam. People shouted at each other, challenged, wept.

'I do not like what you are doing, Matthew.'

'Stop agitating, Greg.'

'That was really disgusting, Greg – what you just did.' (As I read my diary, I wonder just what the hapless Greg had done that was so disgusting.)

'Nina, get yourself cared for without shifting your agitation onto someone else.'

'Jane, it's easier to say you hate someone than to say you love them.'

'Arvind, I really hate your icky-sick pose.'

I was sitting on the floor, along with everyone else, when suddenly I heard my name being called. 'Anne Deveson!'

'Anne Deveson? Who? Me? *Me*?'

'Anne Deveson, you are showing your knickers.'

I jumped. I pulled down my skirt. I blushed. I have never shown my knickers in public again.

Nita, an Indian woman in her late thirties, was in nappies, tied to the wall. She was incontinent and soiled herself. She kept putting on her glasses and taking them off again. She also kept trying to untie herself but without much energy or application. Nobody liked Nita. The 'kids' felt her passivity was deliberately aggressive, and that as she was not getting any better, she should be discharged.

A few of the 'kids' were playing basketball outside the Living Room. Some were playing chess inside. Recreation consisted of ball-games outside, other games inside, country dancing and sing-songs at night and at weekends. There was a television set and a video but neither was used very much. All books and films were heavily censored by Jacqui. Most were of *The Sound of Music* vintage.

This was a well-behaved community. Say please and thank you, or you won't get what you want. Behave well, and there will be treats, like candy from home. Dress well, or you will be sent back to your dormitory again. Once a week, the 'kids' participated in 'the Game', which meant they all gathered together in one large room. They sat on chairs, in any order or direction they wished. For one hour they could say exactly what they wanted, all the anger, all the sadness, all the fantasy, all the sexuality. Nothing was barred. There was only one rule: no physical violence.

The days passed and I hovered half downstairs, half upstairs.

Jacqui had tested Jonathan. She called me upstairs to tell me the results. The first test showed Jonathan as normal, the second test as paranoid schizophrenic, the third as manic depressive. 'He is paranoid schizophrenic,' said Jacqui, 'I am hardly ever wrong. He must have felt rejected when he was nine months old and decided from then on there was something wrong with him. That's why he acts out.'

Downstairs Jonathan spent much of his time playing chess with the Jugoslav boy. He was meek and quietly spoken by now. His eyes were downcast. I felt miserable to see him so cowed. If I went anywhere near him he immediately became the manipulative child. 'Take me home, take me home, take me home.'

Perhaps I'd be doing the same if I were in his position, especially stripped of all avenues of escape. Again, I had to keep reminding myself of what had been happening before he came, of the terrible chaos of his life.

In one of the group sessions I decided to be courageous and, as a parent, to confront my feelings of alienation within the community. 'Natural parents,' we were called, as if natural parents were unnatural, the progenitors of all trouble.

'Maybe I am being paranoid,' I fumbled, 'but it's how I'm feeling.' The group was interested but I felt no warmth. I remembered the period in Adelaide, when I went through therapy and had a hate-my-mother-hate-my-father period. So what was the difference here? I came full circle back to my parents: I didn't go through an adoption process. Why should I let this woman Jacqui – player of Scrabble and eater of violet chocolate creams – why should I let her become mother to my son?

'I don't want another mother. Fuck you! You're all mad. I've got a mother,' yelled Jonathan. I felt like smirking, and probably did.

Later, many years later, Hank, Jacqui's deputy (who is now running Athma Shakti), wrote me a letter in which he said that he still believed in the need of the person with schizophrenia to be out of his or her natural family for some time: *The kid has got to come to the realization that he cannot blame everything on his parents and that he has to accept them for what they are and take responsibility for himself.* This makes sense. When someone has a mental illness, all too often the whole family becomes involved in manipulative behaviour and new ways of relating need to be learned – on both sides.

On the fifth day, Jonathan and the Jugoslav boy disappeared and relays of people went searching the streets. The two runaways were brought back by the police some three hours later. Everyone was angry with them. Angry because they had been worried about their disappearance. Angry because they had to go out in the heat searching for them. Angry because now they had to expend further energy on dealing with them.

The community decided to put them in the corner: one in one corner, one in the other. They had to stand on tiptoes. I protested. Jacqui said this kind of discomfort was necessary to break their pattern of running away whenever things were difficult. 'When people have a high tolerance to discomfort because they live in discomfort all the time, you have to create an even higher level to break through their distorted thinking. It's a great motivator to thinking about what you did and felt and what you need.'

Jonathan roared, the Jugoslav boy roared. I went outside feeling sick. Susan, a young woman from Australia, came out to talk with me. She said that when she had first arrived at the community, she found such treatment difficult to accept, but she too had been put in the corner, on tiptoe, and the pain quickly brought her to her senses and made her deal with what was really going on.

I reflected that in Australia I *had* imposed limits and sanctions on Jonathan which had caused discomfort. When he became crazy and threatened me, ultimately I would call the police. When he had refused to take medication, and therefore became psychotic again, I tried to get him locked up in hospital so that he would be compelled to receive treatment.

In both these instances, as in the corner punishment at Athma Shakti, the ultimate goal was recovery. Susan, who is now back in Australia says, 'The issue was that you had to decide what you would accept in order to get sane, within that definition. I look back and I think, *My God, we did some strong things to people*, but most of them came out of it sane.' Susan is better, but she questions that she ever had schizophrenia; she believes her problem was probably manic depression – which had been Jacqui's diagnosis for her.

That is the challenge of dealing with insanity. You are continually confronted with paradox. Do ends ever justify means? Whose liberty? Whose sanity? When I chaired a committee to recommend new mental health laws, and I argued vehemently for the right to commit someone involuntarily, I argued not from the position of their right to liberty, but from that of their right to treatment and getting well. I accepted what happened at Athma Shakti because it came from a position of caring, but it could easily have been abused.

My contract with Jacqui was that I was to leave Athma Shakti ten days after our arrival. The day before my departure I spent most of the time outside wondering if I was doing the right thing to leave Jonathan behind. On the one hand I realised that I was a sucker as far as my emotions were concerned, Jonathan only had to say 'please Mummy' and I went to water. On the *other* hand, I said as I paced up and down, this place can give him a chance of getting better. So bid him goodbye and quit. I did not go to say goodbye until I was really clear about what I was doing, and only then was I able to say, 'I find it really hard leaving you, but I want you to stay because I believe if you do, you can get better.'

'I want to go with you.'

'I know. And I shall miss you.'

'I want to go with you.'

I stroked his head and then I hugged him. 'I love you. Please stay.' I fled up the path and did not look back. I howled in the cab as I howl now, sitting in my study in Sydney, because the memory is such a painful one.

As I had taken a special excursion ticket to India, I still had several days to fill in before I could go home without forfeiting my cheap fare. I had planned to go to Darjeeling, but at Bombay airport I suddenly changed my mind and decided to go to Kashmir. I had been in Kashmir some fifteen years earlier and had found it beautiful. I needed a place that would give me balm and I took the next plane there. At Srinagar airport, passengers were greeted by Kashmiris carrying posies of fresh field flowers – poppies and daisies, cornflowers and wild roses. I asked for a houseboat at the travel counter and they gave me one called Shalimar Rose.

Kashmir used to be the playground of the British Raj. Waterways, orchards and gardens nestle in a valley cradled by snow-capped mountains. Gentian and primula and edelweiss grow there. The lakes are fringed with willows and in the orchards you can see cherries, peaches, mulberries, walnuts and chenar trees. The houses are tall and made of mud-brick and stone rubble. They have carved wooden balconies and lofts full of sweet hay.

The British Raj brought houseboats to Kashmir and moored them along the banks of the lakes. The lakes are busy with boats; long wood boats, grain and cargo boats, and small boats bearing fruit and vegetables, shawls and rugs, precious stones, embroideries and wood carvings.

The small boats are called 'shikaras'. Merchant shikaras fly over the water after each new tourist arrives.

'You buy very bootiful jewels, moddom. Is bootiful, is marvellous. Is wonderful. Is exquees.'

Taxi shikaras have embroidered curtains and cushions, and names like *Plum Duff* and *Heart's Desire* to attract the visitors.

My houseboat was moored on Dal Lake, near the capital of Kashmir, Srinagar. Half the city is modern, with roads and traffic and petrol fumes, and the other half is old, with crowded narrow pathways, bridges over gurgling streams and rose-coloured houses that lean as perilously as the Tower of Pisa.

The houseboats, built mostly of sandalwood and rosewood, are large and commodious, with enormous bedrooms, a big formal drawing-room, an open deck where you can sit and take refreshments when sunsets tinge the mountain-tops pink. Big houseboats have cook boats strung on behind, and come with a retinue of servants, including a cook, a shikara boy (with your own personal shikara) and a house boy.

I had a big houseboat all to myself. It was not yet full season and there were few tourists. My house boy was Mr Buktu. Mr Buktu served me China tea. He kept looking at me. In the end he said, 'Excuse me, moddom, but were you here fifteen years ago, moddom – when you were with child?'

I was. Mr Buktu had then been the shikara boy, and my accomplice in a visit to interview Sheikh Abdullah, leader of a breakaway Moslem group, who had just been released from imprisonment. I had asked for an interview, and Mr Buktu had taken me there blindfolded, in the middle of the night. The Sheikh had granted an interview on condition that I had no means of knowing his hiding place.

Mr Buktu and I hugged each other and beamed with delight. Mr Buktu nurtured me at a time I most needed it. Spring had only just arrived and it was still cold. He brought me hot-water bottles at night and lit charcoal stoves during the day. He made green tea spiced with caraway and cloves, which he served in delicate cups, and insisted on cooking meals that would have overwhelmed even the British Raj: Irish stew, mulligatawny soup, spotted dick and stewed apples.

Gulam Mohamad Buktu thought he was about forty-one years old. 'In the villages we do not know our ages, moddom. We say she was born when the aeroplanes came, or the first snows fell, and so we do not know. I choose my birthday when I feel like it. One day my boys say I am in a bad mood. So I say, okay, tomorrow I make my birthday.'

Mr Buktu left school when he was nine. He spoke thirteen Indian languages but could not read or write. He married his first wife in 1961 but she died fourteen months later, giving birth to a son. She was sixteen. Mr Buktu married again, and had four more sons, but one died.

'Till my fourth son die, I was always worrying. I tell my wife, be careful. But all the time this boy play in the water and he is good in the water. But one day he fell in the water and this bloody bugger he die. So since that time I say nobody can help it when somebody has to die. Remember that, moddom, when it is time to die. Nobody can help it.'

In the beginning I mostly stayed on the boat and enjoyed the pale spring sun. But by about the fourth day I was feeling better. Mr Buktu said, 'I am thinking, moddom, maybe you would like to visit Floating Gardens with best bottle of British gin.'

I said I would take the gardens but without the gin. Then I became even more adventurous and I decided I wanted to go pony trekking. Early one morning we drove to Paalgum, a village in the foothills of the alps which used to be a weekend retreat for the British. Here they opened a country club, and played cricket and polo and drank whisky stingers. At Paalgum we would pick up the ponies and our supplies.

Pony men trotted by us on the dusty road, offering their services. Mr Buktu said he had already picked 'our pony mens'. My modest trek was fast becoming an expedition. We set off with a cavalcade of eight or nine pony men, one to carry the bedding, one the food, one the tents, one the pots and pans, and several ponies for riding. The cook's pony was laden with wicker panniers in which were stuffed several squawking chickens. Each day there was one chicken less.

I felt well for the first time in many months. We walked through glades and lush green meadows that rolled down from snow-capped peaks. We walked across springy grass tracks and through forests, higher and higher, while Mr Buktu regaled me with stories about the Abominable Snowman. 'He is definitely definitely seen, mod-dom. Oh most definitely.'

By late afternoon, the sun had gone and it was becoming cold. Mr Buktu led us to a valley where he ordered the pony men to pitch camp. He inspected my tent before he would allow me to enter. My bed was a proper bed, with sheets and blankets. I had soap and clean white towels, and tea in a silver teapot. This was not like the camping I had been used to. We sat crosslegged by the fire and, under the night sky, Mr Buktu continued his story-telling.

'So many things in the heart, moddom. I make a lot of mistakes in my life, not big mistakes but human mistakes, and this way I learn many things. I think if I get children I can make it good for them. Village people is very rough people. I also am very rough people. But I have ordered to my wife that every day my children they have a bath, and I check up their food and I check health. If they have a little bit fever, I cannot sleep.'

Mr Buktu poured tea and whisky from a silver flask and continued, 'I like to play with my sons, and I teach them English every day, moddom. In my sons I have a very good control. Whenever they start bad words, or fighting, or they bring very dirty clothes, I just say, look your hands, look your clothes, don't do that. I get very angry, by the eyes, by the face. But I don't like to beat. Beating is not good for children.

'Want is bad. I say to them if you see people eating ten-star chocolate, I cannot afford it. I will bring you two-star chocolate. I have opened four bank accounts for them. Slowly slowly I give them what I can afford. The biggest most important thing for me is to see my children go nicely in their lives. That is like a holy day for me.'

I lay in bed in my tent and listened to the quiet snuffling sound of the ponies grazing and the water from the river. I fell asleep exhausted and for the first time in weeks I did not think of Jonathan.

Next day I was so stiff that I was unable to walk. I rode a pony. On the third day I was too stiff for the ponies. I hobbled.

When we returned to Srinagar and the houseboat, Mr Buktu told me he might be able to help my son. 'I know holy man, he cure one boy, good family, who is very very very sick, moddom. Sick in the head. Holy man, he tell this boy to smoke hash. All you want is hash, moddom.'

*Jonathan, where are you? If you heard that, you'd be up here in seconds.* When I left, Mr Buktu took me to the airport, and carried a cricket bat I had asked him to buy me for Joshua. Kashmir is famous for its cricket bats, made of willow that grows in the vale. The cricket bat was wrapped in a cloth bag, marked 'Best Test Cricket Bat'. It was so heavy I could hardly lift it. Mr Buktu called it 'a curkie bar' and handed it over with care at the airport. He also gave me a bunch of cornflowers and poppies.

'Yes, moddom, I am thinking, moddom, I am liking you very much.'

'Thank you, Mr Buktu, I am liking you very much.'

I returned to Australia and gave Joshua his 'curkie bar' which he liked very much – and then found the following entry in my diary, which he must have written while I was away.

*26 May   Remember whose birthday it is. Your magnificent son. The one who you have to get a brilliant present for. Cricket whites, cricket shirt, cricket bat, cricket shoes, cricket box, cricket ball, cricket game, cricket hat, cricket book, cricket pads, cricket stumps, cricket jumper, cricket magazine. You can't forget your favourite child.*

*Hey*, he is saying – this twelve-year-old with a wonderful sense of humour which then I hardly recognised – *hey, I'm here. Remember me?*

At the beginning of June I got my first feedback about Jonathan, in a letter from Susan, who was due to return to Adelaide:

*Jonathan is still on Living Room and appears to find it a safe structure. He's settling down well, contributing where he can, and*

*is talking about his feelings at times. He seems to have started
identifying problem areas, and I think is also beginning to trust the
community. Most people like him, although he gets his share of
confrontation. I feel good about him, and think he'll use the program
to get well.*

This is followed by a letter from Jacqui, sent two weeks later:

*Jonathan seems to be getting along all right. We got the report back
from our consultant in the United States, who indicates several things
of interest, but has not made a diagnostic statement. There are
certainly issues of problems in relation to reality, indications of
neurological problems, some possibility of dyslexia, and many
personal areas of conflict.*

*I think Jonathan is not terribly unhappy at being here, and is
experiencing some relief at finding himself controlled. He is still on
Living Room, in partial restraints, and whenever he talks about
getting out of restraints, he has not actually initiated that. To me
that means he is not ready for that much independence. He is
relating reasonably well, and seems to be fairly well liked.*

*I do appreciate your confidence in us.*

*Lovingly,*

*Jacqui.*

Now that someone else was more directly responsible for
Jonathan, I felt as if I'd left the battle zone.

It was too good to last. On 14 August I received a telegram which
read: JONATHAN RAN AWAY POLICE INFORMED JACQUI.

I felt sick. I rang Bangalore several times, but either they could
hear me and I could not hear them, or vice versa. I suggested I
should fly to India. The people at Athma Shakti said, 'Don't. We are
doing all we can.'

I was out of my mind. Georgia, Joshua and the architect remained
calm. They were convinced Jonathan would show up.

Georgia said, 'He's a survivor.'

On 24 August I received an express-mail letter from Jacqui which
explained what had happened:

*Jonathan had gotten off Living Room and was no longer in
restraints. He seemed to be cooperating well and making a good
adjustment. However, after inquiring, I heard of several incidents
the previous day where he had had negative encounters with his peers*

*around such things as turning off the record player, etc. He had
not settled a confrontation about being irresponsible about one of
his jobs and a confrontation was pending about that. At the time
he ran away he was at the boys' building with a staff member
(Hank) standing close by him. He was not wearing shoes or warm
clothing nor did he have any money. He ran quite suddenly and
Hank chased him for some distance but was unable to keep up with
him. Apparently no one was aware of what happened and Hank
lost him when he got into a populated area.*

*We have done all the things we know to locate him and believe
it is unlikely that he has continued to be in the Bangalore area. Since
we cannot imagine where he will have obtained money, we believe
he must have hitched a ride elsewhere (while Hank was chasing him
he jumped onto the back of a vehicle but got off again because it
was moving too slowly.) Anyway, this may mean you will hear from
him or about him before we do.*

*Please be assured of our continuing concern. If Jonathan turns
up in India and you want us to go and get him we will be available
to do so. We are disappointed that this happened as it appeared that
Jonathan was making an adjustment to the community which
would have precluded his acting in this way.*

*Sincerely yours,*

*Jacqui*

On that same day, an official from the Australian Consulate in
Bombay rang to say Jonathan had turned up, emaciated and ill. He
had told them that he was sent to India by his family because they
wished to get rid of him, and that he had been tortured by the clinic
in Bangalore and beaten with iron bars. I said this was not true and
that I wished him to return to the clinic. The Consulate voice
sounded chill, even angry – *What mother is this who has consigned
her son to a strange country where he has been grossly abused, yet
who will send him back?*

The Consulate wished me to fly to India to collect Jonathan. One
hour later there was another phone-call. Jonathan was not seriously
ill. He had dysentery and would be discharged from hospital to the
Consulate within a couple of days. I rang Jacqui, and she sent two
of the medical staff to Bombay to try to persuade Jonathan to return.

Jonathan refused to return to Bangalore. When I spoke with him on the telephone he was adamant. I felt bitterly disappointed. India had seemed like the last chance and yet again he had run away from getting well. Laing wrote much about incarceration of the mentally ill being society's way of ridding itself of people who are too difficult and too painful to live with. There is some truth in this. Part of me did not want Jonathan to return because he had been so difficult to live with. But more than this I did not want him to return, because I was fearful that back in Australia he would continue on a slide downhill and would never get well.

I did not feel capable of flying to Bombay myself to fetch Jonathan home. The plane ride to India had been difficult enough; the one back could be worse. In the end I arranged with the hospital to send a psychiatrist to India to collect him. I had to arrange payment for airfares for the psychiatrist and for Jonathan, and to the Consulate for Jonathan's board and medical expenses.

Jonathan arrived back on 31 August. I asked Brenda to meet him at the airport. 'Under the conditions of his bond,' I said meanly – Brenda was still his supervising probation officer.

'Thanks,' she said sarcastically. She also had memories of Jonathan's previous behaviour.

My disappointment with Jonathan had given way to anger. I had decided I should not see him immediately. Brenda met him and arranged hostel accommodation. She said that he seemed reasonably well. He told her that he had found his way from Bangalore to Bombay partly by hitching, and partly by teaming up with street people and begging for money so he could travel some of the way by train.

Jonathan's period of well-being was brief. He did not keep any of his doctor's appointments. He created problems at the hostel because he sat up at night talking to himself and keeping other people awake. He left the hostel and moved back into squats. He did not keep Brenda informed of his whereabouts. A week after his return he went on community radio and talked about the cruelty of the Indian community, and how his mother had sent him there because she did not love her happy hippy boy.

*Stuff you, Jonathan,* I thought, and pounded along the beach shouting 'Stuff you, stuff you, stuff you.'

'People will think you are mad,' said one of the children.

**23 September**   Jacqui wrote from India:
*It seems that when Jonathan ran away he must have had something like that in mind, since the manner of his running and his behaviour while he was in India does seem to have been remarkably well planned and well organized. I am sorry that that is the situation in that Jonathan did seem to be doing well here, although he did not form significant relationships and was not working very actively on problems. However, that isn't unusual for the first several months so we were not particularly concerned about that. Anyway, I hope that eventually his situation will become miserable enough so that he will be frightened and seek help on his own.*

There wasn't much point in being angry with Jacqui about Jonathan running away. Ultimately he had to accept responsibility for himself – which brought me back again to one of the dilemmas of mental illness. At what point can we expect responsibility? If we do not expect it, will we ever see it? Now, looking back, I think we are right to expect it, but to recognise that when someone is living with the chaos and fear of schizophrenia, responsibility can take a long time to learn. And yes, it is a little like taking a person back to childhood and 'growing them up' again. It requires love and skill and patience.

Two or three years later, I met Jacqui in Australia. We talked about Jonathan and she said to tell him she was very sorry that he had run away. She sent her love and said he would always be welcome to return. Then she produced a Scrabble set and some chocolates and said in her squeaky voice, 'My daughters and I have decided that you are not a schizophrenogenic mother.' One of her daughters, a young woman from America who had been with Jacqui for some years, snarled at me, 'I haven't decided that.' Jacqui popped another chocolate in her mouth and continued her game.

I think of India with mixed feelings. Even though I did not agree with Jacqui's views about the cause of schizophrenia and found some of her methods harsh, I believe she was a highly skilled therapist, and cared deeply for the young people she worked with. It is hard to get formal results of the success of Athma Shakti. Because people stay there for a comparatively long time, the number of those who have completed treatment has not been statistically large, nor is it clear what diagnoses they had at the beginning. But Hank writes that some people do get better, and Susan substantiates this.

Since Jacqui left, the regime is far less severe, and anti-psychotic drugs are now used in low doses, but only when necessary.

I believe Hank would continue to argue that the basis of the illness lies primarily in early childhood trauma, rather than there being any basic biological disturbance – and I still disagree. But, given an ecological view of life, where biology and environment are seen to be in a constant process of flux, what I have no doubt about is the healing power of therapeutic communities like Athma Shakti. Even if all the people who go there for help are not 'cured', they learn to love themselves and each other, and to live fully with whatever strengths and vulnerabilities they may have. Schizophrenia is more than just a biochemical aberration, to be fixed by the right pill. The keys to its management are lodged not just in medicine but in the whole person, and in the world that surrounds that person.

I saw Jonathan only occasionally during these next few weeks after my meeting with Jacqui. My diary seems to be full of ordinary entries, like taking Joshua to the dentist and Georgia to a concert. Then, in about the middle of October, Jonathan turned up, ill and confused. Brenda counselled against 'fixing him up'.

Yet it is impossible not to want to fix someone up if, unfixed, they create havoc in your life. Jonathan had begun harrassing Georgia again. In a few days' time she was to sit for her final school exams – the ones that would determine her entrance to university. We discussed the idea of her staying with friends, but she decided that it would be too disruptive.

*23 October*   Jonathan came, very late, and very convinced that the Russians had surrounded his house and ours. He was dirty, hungry and demanding radios. I gave him a meal. I also rang the hospital but they said I would have to bring him in. The same old story.

*26 October*   Brenda wrote:
*Went to North Adelaide and found a derelict house in Boulton Street. Jonathan was asleep on a mattress inside. It looks as if a couple of other people are squatting there as well. I tried to wake Jonathan but could not. He is in an extremely dirty condition, no shoes, and*

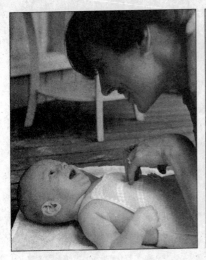

1. Jonathan and me on the verandah of our first house overlooking the water.

2 and 3. When Jonathan was about sixteen months old we went to Europe by boat to visit my parents in London. *Above*, cooling off, and *below*, with me.

4 and 5. Jonathan, aged about five, and Georgia, aged two, drawing happily in the garden.

6. Jonathan, aged about seven, with Georgia
– on holiday by the sea.

7. Jonathan and my mother.

8. Jonathan, aged about nine.

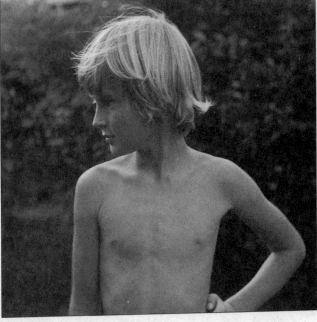

9. Family and much-loved dog Kassim: we were about to leave for Italy where we spent nearly a year living in a village in Piedmont. We both took a long break from work.

10. Italy, 1972: Josh, Georgia and Jonathan.

11. Having a picnic in a French village – we were big on picnics!

12. Jonathan and Ellis: we returned from Italy by sea. Jonathan would be about
eleven by now.

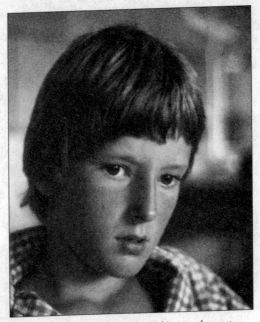

13. Jonathan, aged thirteen. In his second year at high school.

14. Jonathan, aged about fourteen.

15. Jonathan with a friend, Paul, just after we had moved to Adelaide and just before he became ill.

16. Jonathan, aged nineteen: the night before we left for India.

*his feet have cuts and sores on them. Will go back there at a later date and perhaps take someone else with me as it is not particularly pleasant creeping round a derelict house where squatters are.*

**27 October** Jonathan came again. I braved asking him to go to a doctor but he swore and ran off. That night I went to my study and sat up till late, mostly staring out at the sea. In my diary I wrote: *Brenda has discussed whether I should let Jonathan know our new address when we move. Again, I find I can't do this. It seems so wrong, so cruel. There must be other ways of managing – like getting him proper medical help, for God's sake. But I am certainly frightened of Jonathan by now, and so are Georgia and Joshua.*

**30 October** The hospital phoned. Jonathan had been picked up by the police because he was standing on one foot in the middle of the road at peak hour. The police took him to hospital, and he was committed for three days. When I went to see him, he seemed calm. The medication had quickly helped to bring him down; he said he had been frightened by what was happening inside his head. I asked the doctor on duty whether we could have a planning meeting. The hospital appeared to have no plans. I had a feeling they had written him off.

**2 November** Jonathan was released and came straight to the house. He told me he had thrown his medication away. I phoned the hospital and asked why the hell they had discharged him without letting me know and what they thought we should do next. A new, very young-sounding doctor told me that it was my problem, not Jonathan's. Jonathan wanted an alternative lifestyle he said, and I wouldn't let him. Meantime Jonathan was picking up things in the kitchen and banging them down, thud, thud, thud. He pushed past me, then turned and punched me on my arm and then in my stomach so that he winded me. He left by the front door. It looked as if we were in for some heavy weather. I was angry with the hospital for leaving us so vulnerable.

**3 November** Brenda phoned, and I told her what had happened. She went in search of Jonathan:

*I drove down Stepney Street, and met Jonathan walking down the centre of the road and quite spaced out. We talked for a while and he admitted to hurting Anne. I suggested that it would be a good idea for him not to see Anne for a while and any necessary contact could be made through me. Jonathan agreed, but he has a tendency to agree just to get people off his back. While I was talking to him a man called Neil came along and introduced himself as the person Joe was staying with. Neil confronted Joe about needing money for food. He said he was welcome to stay with them but there would be some rules – i.e. he must eat three meals a day with them, he must pay for his keep. Neil also suggested that Joe not buy any more Codral as he looked as if he had been taking too many. Note: Check Jonathan's ear. He has pierced it with a dirty safety pin and it looks doubtful.*

Brenda told me Neil lived with his partner Icia in a semi-derelict house, which had no door and only some of its windows. Neil and Icia were born-again Christians in their early thirties, and practised what they believed by looking after people who were mentally ill or drug- or alcohol-addicted. Icia had been a psychiatric nurse but believed people needed more than medication to get well. Neil and Icia thought they could cope with Jonathan. They said they understood mental illness and Jonathan's need to regress and felt they could provide Jonathan with a loving home environment. I was relieved to think that someone would help.

**6 November** Jonathan came in through the windows in the downstairs front room. He was crazy. It was about midday, Georgia and Joshua were at school, and I was frightened. When Jonathan became psychotic, the level of discordant energy was so immense that I could feel him approaching minutes before he actually arrived. Several times I would wake in the middle of the night with the hair on my arms standing on edge and know that Jonathan was somewhere near. Here was Jonathan on this blue and white November morning, telling me that he had decided to kill me. I made an excuse to visit the corner store and phoned Brenda from a phone-box. She said she would come immediately. We talked about ringing the police, but from past experience they did not always come and Jonathan's hostility was so fierce that I did not feel safe doing this without Brenda's support.

When Brenda arrived Jonathan was lying on the big couch that faced the sea. He was nodding to himself as if he were listening to voices, but he did not speak aloud. We asked if he were hearing voices. Jonathan looked suspiciously at both of us, then said 'No voices.' He said something else but his voice trailed away. Brenda leaned forward and said she could not hear him.

'I said only Anne's voice,' he shouted.

'Where's Anne's voice?'

'Plotting against me. Inside my head.'

'Jonathan, I'm not plotting against you. And I'm not inside your head. I'm here.'

He looked at me, his eyes darting everywhere, and still that racing energy which seemed to fill the whole room, bouncing off the ceiling and the walls, jangling my own energy, so that I felt I was receiving an electric shock.

'God has said that I should kill you Anne, and Brenda too if she doesn't shut up.'

He stalked out of the room, waving his arms. A few seconds later he returned, looked at us both, muttered something and left again. This time he didn't return. Brenda rang the police to see if they could pick him up and take him to the hospital to be certified. They said not unless the hospital agreed to take him in. The hospital said they could make no such promises until they saw him. I huddled up in one of the big armchairs. I felt shaky and frightened. Georgia and Joshua came home and I did not tell them about Jonathan's visit. I went round that night checking all the locks on the doors and windows, but realised that it was simple to break in through the basement, and that I should have had both those windows and doors fitted with iron grilles. I wrote in my diary: *God, what is happening to us all?*

The architect rang to see how I was and I burst into tears. He offered to come over for dinner and to bring a bottle of wine.

Two days later, Jonathan turned up at tea time. He walked in through the front door as if nothing untoward had ever happened. He made himself some tea, and asked if he could stay on and help while Josh and I made a cake. He stayed long enough to eat a couple of slices, and then left.

***11 November***   I was wakened from a deep sleep by the telephone ringing. The voice said his name was Neil, and asked 'Are you all right?'

'Yes,' I mumbled.

'Thank God.'

'Why?'

'Jonathan has just come home saying he's "put out the light in the eyes of the woman he loves".'

'God! Well it's not me. Is he all right?'

'No, he was sobbing. He said he'd killed you.'

'He needs to be in hospital,' I cried.

'He went there yesterday, but they wouldn't take him in.'

'Bastards.'

Neil said Jonathan was no longer staying with them on any full-time basis. He had found someone called Canadian Bob and was staying there. Neil, Icia and Canadian Bob were extremely worried. They felt Jonathan had the potential to harm himself or me. We agreed to meet, and I said that I would have another concerted attempt with Brenda's help to get Jonathan hospitalised. I staggered back to bed feeling I was in the middle of some monstrous nightmare. *How much suffering must we endure before we can get any help? Who is mad, I wonder? Who is mad?*

***10 November***   Georgia was to have her first exam, English, the following day. English was her best subject and she was expected to do extremely well; she had studied hard against big odds. Poor child, I thought as I looked at her taut face.

We went to bed early. At about ten thirty I heard a banging sound downstairs. Jonathan had forced himself in through the cellar door and was climbing the stairs. I sat bolt upright. At all costs he must not wake Georgia. I put on a dressing-gown and ran downstairs. *Keep calm. Make some tea.* 'No thank you,' he said, he didn't want any tea. His eyes followed me as I moved around the kitchen, and even now as I write this I feel you might be thinking I am being melodramatic. But madness is sometimes the stuff of melodrama, and if you don't take it seriously it can become tragedy. Jonathan had one of the kitchen knives in his hand and he waved it at me and ordered me to sit down. I sat down, on one of those hellish high-backed stools, in that clinically white and sterile kitchen.

'Don't move,' he said. He kept spinning the knife and talking to himself. He wore a black T-shirt which was so shrunken his midriff was bare, and his jeans were dirty, tattered and at half-mast. His feet were bare. He had three safety pins dangling from one ear and he had drawn tattoo marks all over his hands and arms with a black felt pen. I again offered him some tea. Oh blessed tea, with all the family rituals it invokes.

He nodded, then he mumbled something a little louder and it sounded like 'I'm going to get you before you get me.'

I asked him to repeat what he had just said.

'I'm going to get you before you get me.' He said it very loudly.

'Let's have some cake first – okay?' As I said this, I thought, *How incongruous, how bloody incongruous. Cut the cake, don't eat with your mouth full, and never kill your mother until you have finished afternoon tea.* He stuffed a slice of cake in his mouth. I told him to have another piece, and said I was going to let the dog out for a run.

We had a general practitioner living just up the road and I ran and banged on his door. He was still up. I asked him to help get Jonathan into hospital, urgently.

He looked embarrassed, as if he wished I would go away. He said he didn't know Jonathan and he did not really know me. But he fetched his bag and came out, out into the night air, along the strip of road that linked our houses, with the sea shining dark in the moonlight. I introduced him to Jonathan and told Jonathan I thought he needed to go into hospital.

'No sir, no sir, I am not sick,' Jonathan said in a whining voice. He continued to spin the knife. 'My mother only thinks I am sick and she's got the army trained against me.'

Dr W said he couldn't see any army and he suggested that Jonathan might feel safer in hospital.

Jonathan disagreed. 'I've got the PLO on my side.'

Dr W then beckoned me into the hallway, and whispered in a confidential voice, as if he were imparting new and important information, 'You've got a very dangerous young man there.'

'So you'll get him into hospital?'

'He doesn't want to go.'

'Certify him.'

'I can't certify him. I don't know him.'

'But he's mad.'

'Maybe.'

'So are you going to leave us here alone with him?' I was shouting, and there were tears of desperation in my eyes. I grabbed the phone and thrust it at him. '*Do something!*'

He hesitated. 'I'll call the police and tell them to keep an eye on you.'

'They may not come for hours. At least help me get him out of the house. Let's call a taxi to take him home.'

Dr W looked relieved and rang the police. He said that I seemed to be an educated sort of woman, even though he didn't know me. What was the implication from this? Ignore all women if they don't have an education? The taxi arrived. Jonathan said 'I'll be back'; and then he was outside, on the doorstep, and I was able to close the front door.

It was then about midnight. I rang Brenda and we discussed whether I should wake Georgia and Joshua, and all go to a motel for the night. In the end I decided to sit it out. I checked the doors and windows, put barricades against the cellar door, and then I went into the kitchen and ate all the cake.

I jumped at the slightest noise. I was shivering. I felt as if I were damned. As if I were some mythological character, that was being punished and would never escape. I thought of Jonathan killing me, and then tried not to think of that, in case I brought it upon myself. Already that year three women in Australia had been killed by their schizophrenic sons. I knew the majority of people with schizophrenia are not generally violent and that tragedies occurred only if people became psychotic and were left without help. It was survival time. I telephoned a couple whom I barely knew but who lived relatively close. Bruce was once a policeman. I begged them to come. They arrived, and we checked the doors and windows again and then dossed down in the living-room. The police came banging on the door at about four in the morning and woke up the entire house. But they came and I was grateful.

The following morning, Georgia and Joshua were white-faced and looked wretched. I wanted to weep for Georgia, weep for Joshua and weep for Jonathan. It was not the time for weeping.

After Joshua had left for school, and Georgia for her exams, I went to Brenda's office. We spent the morning trying to find a way to get Jonathan certified. She took one telephone, I took another. We phoned a number of doctors, including Frank, and although they were sympathetic, none of them could do anything as they had not seen Jonathan within the past week, and this is what the legislation for certification required.

We tried the hospital, and spoke to the registrar on duty, who also said he could not do anything without seeing Jonathan, and that anyway Jonathan had a history of being difficult to treat. Brenda said, 'Oh I see, so you'll only take the nice ones, will you?' I said something stronger.

We rang the police and they refused to take Jonathan to hospital unless the hospital had agreed to admit him. The police sergeant said he was tired of taking people to hospital and having them turned away.

I called the hospital again and demanded to speak to the superintendent. He was away. I got back to the first doctor and told him that if they did not admit Jonathan and any one of us were harmed, I would make sure in advance that every newspaper in Australia would know what had happened. I said that I would make him personally responsible if I won the dead mother of the year award. He capitulated. He said they would accept Jonathan if we could bring him in ourselves or persuade the police to pick him up.

We drove to the North Adelaide police station, which was a small colonial cottage with a flower garden and an air of cosy domesticity. The police sergeant said he would help out only if we found Jonathan ourselves, and if we had a guarantee that he would be certified by the hospital. Back to square one. Brenda spoke to the police commissioner, who said he would see what he could do, which could have meant this year, next year, sometime, never, so we determined that at least we would find Jonathan.

We did the rounds of all the squats. About mid-afternoon, we spotted him heading into a fish-and-chip shop. We raced back to the police station and they called out a van and locked up Jonathan in the back. The paddy wagon looked like an animal box. Inside, in the darkness, Jonathan was sitting with his half-eaten fish and chips. Brenda said, 'I feel terrible. Terrible. There must be better ways.'

I wanted to look through the wire of the van and talk to Jonathan but I could not bring myself to do so. Brenda went and told him what was happening and why. He did not answer.

The police still would not take Jonathan to the hospital without the permission of a sergeant from police headquarters who had to sign the necessary forms in person. They also would not take him until I agreed to pay a conveyancing fee. The hospital still refused to guarantee that they would admit Jonathan. Eventually, the police van drove off with Jonathan to the hospital. Brenda and I stood in the middle of the road and watched it go.

I thought it must be easier to get someone to the moon than into psychiatric hospital. A survey in Australia found that when urgent help was sought for mentally ill relatives, nearly all the families had to go to more than one place before any action was taken. Of those who sent out an SOS to doctors or hospitals, less than half were listened to. The professionals either implied that the relatives were causing the problem, or saw the disturbance as behavioural rather than due to mental illness, or said it was not urgent. One-quarter were simply reluctant to intervene, like my seaside doctor with his black bag who scuttled off into the night. Yet when help was not given, in eight out of ten cases the sick person became worse, and sometimes violent.

A few years later, while I was director of the Australian Film, Television and Radio School, a student came to me in distress about his elder brother who had schizophrenia. A crisis was brewing and he was frightened. His brother's case sounded not unlike Jonathan's. The student's family had tried everything to get the older brother into hospital as we had with Jonathan. A few weeks later, the boy killed his father, by pouring petrol over him and lighting a match. His mother was terribly burned.

Most people with mental illness are not violent, they are usually timid and withdrawn and, with adequate treatment, the risk of violence associated with schizophrenia melts away. Time and again, case studies show that violence occurred only after repeated warnings and repeated calls for help were ignored. The real violence is ours: it is the violence of neglect.

Jonathan was admitted to hospital for a three-day period, subject to review. It was imperative that he be properly assessed, and this time kept there long enough to establish a proper program to help him get well.

**11 November**   I woke feeling a sense of immense relief. I spoke first to the psychiatrist in charge of Jonathan's case and he promised that we would have a proper case conference. Then I met Neil and Icia and liked both of them. Neil was calm and straight, with a friendly humour. Icia was earth-mother gypsy; seemed wise, yet had a fey childlike quality about her. They spoke as if they loved the kernel of Jonathan and saw the madness as a husk they could strip away.

**12 November**   I went to the hospital and for the first time felt that Jonathan's case was being taken seriously. Jonathan was to have a full assessment made of his condition. He was still highly disturbed and was in the locked ward. I was advised that I should have two nurses with me when I visited him. I went to see him most days, and he alternated between begging me to take him home and being angry.

**24 November**   Brenda records:
*Visited Anderson Ward but Jonathan was absent having a brain scan. According to the charge nurse there has been no change at all in Jonathan's condition during the past week. He still maintains that he does not need treatment. Jonathan has tried to escape several times and they realise that if he is transferred to an open ward there is a strong possibility that he will abscond. He is only allowed to wear pyjamas and dressing gown as he will then be conspicuous if he absconds.*

**1 December**   I spoke with Dr P who said there was little change in Jonathan's condition except that he was no longer psychotic. Jonathan had registered a legal appeal against his detention order and the appeal was being heard in two days' time. If his appeal failed, they could extend his detention order for another twenty-one days.

*2 December*   The lawyer who was assigned to Jonathan's case under the mental health legislation, rang me to ask if I would support Jonathan's appeal and pay for his legal fees. I refused.

*3 December*   Even though Jonathan lost his appeal, I was told that he had conducted his case extremely well, better than the lawyer. The hospital would extend his detention order and it would be reviewed in mid-January. They planned a behaviour modification program for Jonathan where he would be rewarded for good behaviour.

*5 December*   Letter from a woman in Queensland, to whom I had sent details of the Indian program:
*I hope your boy is safe. It is a nightmare when you don't know where they are or whether they are all right. You know how people are, if you are working. They tend always to blame the mother. We are sitting ducks.*

*15 December*   Little change.

*17 December*   Another meeting with Neil and Icia. They planned to go to the Riverland for fruit-picking. They had been visiting Jonathan regularly and still hoped that when he was discharged he would join them.

*18 December*   We moved house. We had sold the Marines; now that the architect was only there at weekends, I had found it too lonely and melancholic. I had rented a shabby but pleasant house in the city.

*24 December*   We christened our new home with a Christmas party. The previous evening I had been to a Christmas party at the hospital. Jonathan had been allowed leave from the security ward to attend. Although we both tried to enjoy ourselves, it was a brave but hollow attempt.

*25 December*   Georgia, Joshua and I went to the hospital. We gave Jonathan some books and paints and chocolates and, I think, a new shirt. Joshua brought along his cricket bat and we played French cricket on the grass outside the ward. Jonathan seemed pleased we had come. That evening we had Christmas dinner with the architect. Packing up the seaside house had been like packing up our dreams. I felt bleak and exhausted. In the middle of dinner I developed a sudden fever. I had a high temperature and my teeth began chattering. I sat through the rest of the evening in an armchair with a hot-water bottle on my lap. When the time came to go home, I found that I had been sitting on the Christmas chocolates, and they had all melted.

I do not remember what we did for New Year's Eve that year. Probably I crept quietly away to bed, for I had given up looking for clouds with silver linings. By then I had realised that Jonathan would not get better for a long time.

Just before the end of the year I visited Jonathan on my own and we sat under a shady tree for a while, listening to the cicadas drumming and the faint sound of a lawn-mower.

He broke the silence by tugging at my arm. 'If I had a baby, I'd cry.'

'Why darling?'

'Because a baby is such a beautiful thing. I wouldn't want to hurt it.'

Five
# *Jail Is Heavy*

*I know not whether Laws be right,*
*Or whether Laws be wrong;*
*All that we know who lie in jail*
*Is that the wall is strong;*
                                        OSCAR WILDE

*January 1982*   This is the year when Jonathan shot through to
Sydney and ended up in jail. But we were innocent of all
this in January, when Georgia, Joshua and I were still settling into
our new house.

The house at South Terrace was an Edwardian red-brick villa near
the centre of Adelaide, with a wide front verandah and fretted
woodwork, painted white. It had been a shared house for some years
and it was shabby but welcoming. It reminded me of all
those rented houses I had lived in while I was growing up –
mottled linoleum on the floors, power-points in ridiculous positions, creaking doors and floorboards, and electrical fittings that
sprouted octopus arms of tangled black flex. The bathroom had a
shower that gushed forth a niagara of scalding water one moment
and needle-points of icy water the next. But the house had beautiful
rosy-pink and blue stained glass over the door and in some of the
windows. And it overlooked the parklands with their groves of dusky
olive trees, and handsome avenues of red river-gums. The trunks
of the river-gums were striped grey, orange and cream, and were
home for myriad noisy birds – black and white currawongs, scarlet
and blue parrots, pink and grey galahs. The house had a small strip
of garden in the front, and a concreted yard in the back which was
crowded out by two large iron sheds, an enormous gum tree that
seemed to shed its leaves all year round, and a battered clothes hoist.

Georgia was just seventeen, and had won a scholarship to a
residential college at Adelaide University, so she would only be

home during vacations. Joshua was thirteen, and I had decided to send him back to school as a boarder to get some respite from the traumas of Jonathan. For both of them, life at home must have been like a dangerous ride on a never-ending roller coaster, and I felt relieved that they might now have a calmer existence. But I would miss them, and I looked for someone to share the house with me. This wasn't easy. I needed a particular kind of person to deal with Jonathan. And then I met Mary.

Mary was a sociologist who wrote community drama. She was a slight person, in her late twenties, with a worried look. Mary smoked rollies which I hated. Mary had a big poster of a woman in a garden full of hollyhocks, which I also hated. But I loved Mary. Not just because she did not seem to be particularly perturbed about Jonathan, but because she had an ability to find joyous eccentricity in familiar things. Life with Mary was full of discoveries.

Mary liked baths. I like baths. When times get nasty, instead of reaching for the gin bottle, I have a bath. I sing hymns in baths. I think thoughts in baths. I luxuriate in baths. Maybe I will have to cut back on baths in these times of ecological frugality, but we didn't know about such things then, and baths were my salvation. South Terrace didn't have a bath, but there was room to put one in; even though it was a rented house, and the lease was uncertain, Mary and I determined that we would get ourselves a bath. Cheap.

On the day after she moved in, we discovered that there was an exhibition of old baths at the Adelaide Festival Centre. The baths were displayed on the forecourt, adjoining some contemporary sculpture. There were big baths, small baths, smooth white porcelain baths, baths with claw legs, baths made of zinc and iron, baths with lion legs. We found the most battered of all these baths, which was painted in lime green and much chipped, and we bargained fifteen dollars for it, provided we waited till after the exhibition to collect it. A friend collected it for us in his utility, and helped us plumb it in. We wallowed in baths the entire weekend. We planted a jasmine and a Christmas bush, and the Christmas tree from the party. It was a Norfolk Island pine and would grow twenty metres, so I didn't like its chances of living to old age. Planting in a garden as soon as you move houses must be the equivalent of a dog cocking its leg on a tree: it means, this is home.

I went with Georgia, Joshua and the architect to Kangaroo Island for two weeks' camping holiday. The architect had some beachfront land which was wild and beautiful. We pegged out the area where he would build himself a shack. When we returned from the island a letter was waiting from Neil and Icia, sent from the fruit-picking area of Mildura:

*We have a terrific camping spot right on the Murray, close to town and nicely shaded by big river-gums. It is very hot here so the river is a welcome relief. There is plenty of work and we still look forward to welcoming Joe whenever he is ready . . .*

Jonathan was improved; he had been in hospital for over two months, and so had had time to settle his medication. In order to maintain this stability, Jonathan's doctor and social worker suggested that I apply for him to be placed under the jurisdiction of a body called the Guardianship Board. The Guardianship Board is a legal body that can assist people suffering from mental illness or mental handicap who are manifestly incapable of managing their own affairs. The scope and duration of the guardianship must be specified, and is subject to strict review. In Jonathan's case, the Board would oversee his health care and could order that he continue taking medication – something I had been unable to do.

**27 January**   Jonathan and I appeared before the Guardianship Board of the Mental Health Review Tribunal. The Board consisted of one legal person, one psychiatrist and one community member. I was impressed by their courtesy. Jonathan was shabbily dressed in baggy jeans and a blue cardigan which was too small for him, especially the sleeves. His hands were trembling, and when he sat, his knees jiggled up and down. The medication might have taken away his psychosis but it had left him with the shakes. But he argued his case well and, as he argued, there were those tantalising glimpses of the person he might have been. He said that he didn't have a mental illness, and should be released. I felt I no longer knew him, and I wrote in my diary: *Who is this young man in the shabby blue cardigan who calls the board members 'Sir' and shakes? Who is he?* The boy of seventeen was now a stranger of twenty who had lost his youth. I wanted to reach across and take his hand, but there was a gulf between us.

I told Jonathan that I knew he wanted to leave hospital, but his doctors felt he was not yet ready, and I agreed. He looked down at the table.

The Board decided to place Jonathan under a custody-and-treatment order and his financial affairs were put in the hands of the public trustee.

Jonathan thanked the Board for their consideration. He said that he felt 'very sad' about the decision as it meant he would be kept in hospital for a further three months. 'I do not consider I have a mental illness, sir,' he repeated, nodding his head up and down.

Jonathan saying that he felt 'sad' was potent. 'Sad' is one of those soft small words that sometimes carry more impact than larger declarations. I felt sad too; I would have rebelled at being in captivity at his age or any age, but I also felt immensely relieved. Having his freedom the previous year had not worked; perhaps this would. For three years it had felt as if Jonathan were falling down a bottomless pit. At last it seemed as if someone had put a safety net under him and we could begin the long haul to the surface again. India had seemed like a safety net but he had dived through that one. This time, it might not be so easy.

I went home and told the other children and they looked relieved. Then Georgia said softly, 'He can't be locked away for ever.'

**5 February**   Jonathan absconded from the hospital. The hospital had promised that he would be moved to a halfway house but twice their plans had fallen through. Jonathan had been frustrated and angry. There was (and still is) an acute shortage of any kind accommodation for people with schizophrenia.

I was in the kitchen, absent-mindedly doing the washing up, when there was a knock on the door. A young woman, wearing a well-cut skirt and a neat pin-striped shirt was standing there with an embarrassed look on her face.

'I'm sorry to disturb you,' she said, 'but I wonder if you could do something about the person in the street?'

'What person?' I asked. But I knew already.

'He's lying in the road,' she said in a high-pitched voice. She was trying to sound matter-of-fact, but she didn't fool me. *Should I bluff it out, and pretend that I don't know what she means?*

'He's lying down in front of my car and he won't budge. He says you've turned him out of home.'

Outside, there was a build-up of traffic. Horns were hooting and people gathering. It was rush hour. Jonathan's timing was always impeccable. He was lying in the road, his lanky young body blocking all oncoming cars, in an army greatcoat, bare feet, and with a pink cloth bag clutched to his chest. He was talking, clearly and vigorously. 'My mother has thrown me out of home, honk honk. She's thrown me out of home, honk honk.'

The cars chorused honk honk. Jonathan sat up, crossed his legs, and smiled. It was a wide and beautiful smile. 'Hello Anne,' he said. He rose to his feet with dignity, swung his bag over his shoulder and followed me inside. He had tea and cake, and returned to hospital without a murmur.

*Jonathan, oh Jonathan, I want to weep but sometimes I want to laugh. Sometimes my feelings are so huge, so confused, that I do not know what to do with them.*

**8 February**   Joshua returned to school, his first experience as a boarder. He hadn't wanted to board, but he was good at sport – an open sesame in Australian schools to popularity – and he was also a sociable boy who had plenty of friends. His first letter home said:
*Dear Anne,*

*Guess Who!!!! It's Joshua. Hello, how are you? I haven't done much since I last saw you. Played cricket on the weekend. Got them 4/17 and then they made a recovery and won making 102. I took 3/28 in 16 overs, and I was appointed captain of the House Cricket team ahead of all the year 10s. We lost!!*

**14 February**   On my return to Adelaide from Sydney, another letter from Neil and Icia was waiting for me. They said they intended to travel, doing seasonal work for a year or two, and would still love Jonathan to join them in a few months' time. I thought this was a good idea.

*We could share our lives with him, he could even be working with us. Having his own money for which he has worked could do wonders for him. I can see a big laughing fully conscious Joe being such a precious friend. I hope it can become a reality. I am sure he would be happier here with us on the river than he would be in the hospital. God bless.*

**16 February**  The hospital phoned. Jonathan had again disappeared.

**18 February**  Jonathan turned up in Sydney at the home of an old school·friend, Eric. Eric's mother rang me and said that Jonathan was not in good shape. She asked if I would come.

**19 February**  I flew to Sydney, and found Jonathan lying on the floor of the apartment. Eric had gone out. His mother told Jonathan she thought he was still quite ill, and that he should go back to Adelaide. He refused. I thought, *Poor old Joe, you're so determined not to be ill, so determined not to give in, so stubborn, so . . .* 'Bloody impossible!', I was shouting at him, but he went on lying there, his head buried in his hands, the carpet ruckled. Eric's mother and I drank endless cups of tea, and I was struck with the realisation of how exhausting and frustrating it must be, always trying to escape what is happening inside your head when there can be no escape. Eric's mother said Jonathan could continue to stay on the floor if he wished. He said, 'Yes please,' and I said I would return the following day.

**20 February**  Jonathan suddenly agreed that he would come home to Adelaide. He said that he wanted to get better, and that he needed to stay longer in hospital. The effects of medication from his period in hospital had not yet worn off, and he was still thinking clearly.

**25 February**  Georgia returned from holidays in Tonga, and Joshua sent me a letter from school:
*I've got three terrible teachers. For drama we go to operas etc. I played cricket yesterday. It was a one-day match. We batted first. I came in when we were 4 for 19. I departed at 5 for 71. I top scored with 31 with my new bat. I was hit on the arm. It hurt.*

**10 March**  Jonathan ran away again. He had been making good progress at hospital, so everyone was disappointed. Two days later another Sydney mother telephoned. Jonathan was an expert at hitching truck rides. I braced myself to receive a spate of distressed long-distance calls. This mother put Jonathan on the phone. He sounded spaced out: 'Say hallo to your mother sometime, Anne. Joshua's a little man. Georgia's this terribly beautiful young lady, who isn't sophisticated, she's really magic. Anyway, things will be okay, Anne, right right right, take care, right.'

I decided not to play the rescue game a second time, and this mother agreed. She helped him to find a hostel in Sydney. Perhaps it is amazing that so many people were still willing to help, but we had kept in touch with our Sydney friends and Jonathan still had an extraordinary ability to draw people around him, even when he was at his most quarrelsome.

**18 March**　I went to Sydney to start filming a new ABC documentary series about the changing role of women. With my money from the sale of the seaside house, I had bought an apartment in Sydney, so that I would have a base whenever I was working there, although my home remained the rented house in Adelaide. Jonathan came to see me at the Sydney apartment and I had another go at suggesting he return to Adelaide with me. He thought, and then replied slowly, 'No, Anne, that would not be a good idea.'

He was lying on the floor, and I was in the adjoining kitchen, getting dinner for us both. The apartment was on the harbour, and boats of all kinds sailed past my window, so I spent more time staring outwards than looking in. While Jonathan was speaking, a long black submarine had slipped through the water, and then submerged. One minute it was there, then it was gone. Jonathan was like the submarine.

Jonathan wandered into the kitchen. He was chuckling when he announced that he had changed his mind; he would return to Adelaide to marry his girl-friend. 'She's called Trendy Wendy, and she's my psych nurse. She wants to marry me because she knows I'm cool. I've given her a solid gold ring and we're going to live in Brazil. Being in love is a really good experience.' And then he said, 'In two years I've only eaten three packets of biscuits. I'm getting into good food, apples and radishes. I'm getting better, Anne.'

He scrabbled in my bag and pulled out a pen. 'Write this down,' he said. 'Just sit in the lotus position till your body experiences physical pain and you'll reach a higher state of consciousness. Write it down.'

I wrote it down. I wished he could marry his nurse and live happily ever after in Brazil. His fantasies were sometimes funny, but often made me sad. In Gogol's brilliant *Diary of a Madman* Poprishchin, an insignificant downtrodden clerk whose hair sticks out like hay, and who spends his time sharpening quill pens, goes slowly mad. As he goes mad, he believes that there are logical reasons for everything that is happening to him. Even when he is in an asylum, and is knocked around and cruelly beaten, he still thinks this is some sort of initiatory test for the future King of Spain. Jonathan was teaching me that as illusion and reality merge, comedy becomes tragedy.

Jonathan stayed with me the few days I was in Sydney, and then moved into an inner-city room which he shared with a friend. He was still on sickness benefit, and theoretically this covered food and rent, but in the past he had shown no ability to plan his money and I wondered how long he would survive. I felt mean not lending him the Sydney flat, but I could not trust him there alone. For a start, he'd never close the front door.

My Sydney apartment was one of eight units in a weather-beaten white building, of four storeys, erected on the harbour front in about 1912. It had a Union Jack flying from its forecourt, and a green swathe of grass running down to the water. The building was run by an elected body of tenants' representatives, known as 'the body corporate'. One day, the body corporate wrote me a stiff letter about Jonathan and his noisy music. He looked so strange that residents, who were mainly elderly and conventional, did not like to see him around.

Early in April Neil and Icia returned from fruit-picking and we decided to see if Jonathan could live with them in my Sydney apartment for a few weeks, before they headed for the country again and hopefully took Jonathan with them. Neil and Icia were confident that they could pull Jonathan out of his illness. I thought they were being over-optimistic, but did not tell them this.

We embarked on a program to get Jonathan looking after his health. When the children were growing up I had been obsessive about their teeth and Jonathan's teeth had once been good. Now they were beginning to look black and decayed. I asked Icia if she could help.

Icia pondered. 'How can I give him the incentive to clean and care for his teeth? Aah!' she took out her own false teeth and said, 'Jonathan, this is what happens if you neglect to care for your teeth.' He laughed, and later he asked her for a toothbrush and started cleaning his teeth. I'd like to say it became a regular habit, but no such luck.

Icia wrote in her journal:

*A perfect day at home in this restful beautiful place with Jonathan talking and listening to music. He told me about the dream he had last night of being a little baby and feeling the pain in his head. Anne rang from Adelaide. How happy she sounds.*

Two days later, Icia wrote:

*I can't leave Jonathan here until he's learnt to be more present in his surroundings. Sex Pistols, loud, would disturb any neighbour and these neighbours are in their seventies and eighties. When he has consciously turned the volume down and understands why, I can go. Or maybe he would like to come with me into the city on the ferry. He is sitting tight and angular listening to the music.*

And in another two days:

*Jonathan is snapping and snarling a lot. I say: 'Jonathan, I even have to teach Jamaica not to growl and bark every time at all the people he doesn't like. Because it's not a true way to walk in the world, snapping and snarling.'*

Jonathan had already begun drifting away from Neil and Icia. Living with him was harder than they had imagined. They couldn't leave him on his own, and he was often extremely irritable. His sleeping habits were just as topsy-turvy as ever, and he had begun taking long night walks over Sydney Harbour Bridge and back again. People would report seeing him, walking as if he had a mission with little time to encompass it – his head thrust forward, his bag over his shoulder, his feet bare, and talking, talking, talking. Neil and Icia decided to skip seasonal work for a while and to stay on in Sydney. They found themselves a flat by the beach and told

Jonathan that he was always welcome, but he only visited them a few times. Bondi was off his beat.

There was one visit that it is important to tell you about, because it illustrates the importance of listening to the experiences of people with schizophrenia, however bizarre they sound. Neil and Icia invited Jonathan to meet one of their friends, Peter, who also had schizophrenia. Peter had been an acting student at the National Institute of Dramatic Art when he first developed the illness; now he was in his early thirties and managing well. Peter was a dark intense man with steady eyes.

At first Jonathan paced round and round Peter, talking to himself. Talking was an effective barrier. 'I've got forty black belts. I'm the Kung Fu champion of Kings Cross. I'm the grand master black-belt champion, yeah, yeah,' and he giggled.

Peter held him by the arm to stop him pacing, and looked deep into his eyes. 'Jonathan,' he said, 'are you afraid?'

Jonathan stopped and gazed at Peter. 'Yeah,' he said. 'Shit scared.'

Then he took off on his dance around the room again, this time talking about prostitutes. Jonathan often talked about prostitutes. He imagined that he looked after all the prostitutes in Kings Cross, and saved them from pimps and the police.

Peter said, 'Jonathan, are you lonely?'

'Yes,' said Jonathan. 'I am lonely.'

Peter had understood Jonathan's use of language, and had been able to interpret how he was feeling. People with schizophrenia will often use metaphor and symbols to describe their inner states, but because they have lost their sense of boundary, they are unable to distinguish their inner from their outer worlds, and metaphor becomes reality.

One of the most interesting conversations I have had about schizophrenia was with Russell Meares, Professor of Psychiatry at Sydney University. He talked about interviewing a young woman about her schizophrenia, and asking her, 'How are things?' She said, 'Everything is disguise. It's all green underneath.' Meares said his instinctive response was to dismiss her reply as nonsense, but because he sensed there was meaning behind her strange choice of words, he looked about him. The room was shabby, with peeling cream paint. On the far wall, a speck of green paint was showing through. Meares said, 'Her schizophrenia had made her extremely sensitive to very small details of the sensory environment of which other people would not be aware. While she was in the grip of this kind of experience, where everything was flooding into her consciousness, and nothing could be blocked out, it made life very strange and frightening.'

Jonathan was dropping in and out of the Sydney flat. He seemed to have an uncanny knack of knowing whenever I was there. Equally, whenever I tried to find him, I nearly always succeeded. He'd be padding along some laneway in Kings Cross, dilly bag over his shoulder, bare feet, and noticeable because of his height. He was now 194 centimetres (six foot four inches) tall. He stayed mostly at the Matthew Talbot Hostel for homeless men in Woolloomooloo. The Talbot gave him shelter and friendship which even now makes me feel gratitude for their care. Sometimes he would drift to other shelters, and most of them came to know him.

By then it was clear that Jonathan would not be returning to Adelaide. Adelaide was equated with curtailment of his freedom and this was something he was not prepared to accept. Towards the end of April I received a letter from the South Australian Guardianship Board which said that, as Jonathan was now living in New South Wales, they had decided to cancel all guardianship orders: each state in Australia has its own mental health legislation and there was no reciprocity.

Joshua's fourteenth birthday was in May and as it was holiday time, he came to Sydney. I gave him a surprise birthday party, and Jonathan turned up with a shaven head, and dressed in black: black jeans, black shirt, black boots, and 'tattoo' marks on his hands and arms, drawn with black pen. He wore a string of paper clips dangling from his ears.

The party was good, and Jonathan made immense efforts to belong. I don't think I had realised till then how difficult such occasions were for him. You could see him straining to find the right phrase and, when he found it, he would blurt it out as if he were an actor who was not yet familiar with his lines. People with schizophrenia have to make herculean efforts to stay our side of the line.

By the end of the party, Jonathan was running a high temperature.

I persuaded him to stay, rather than go back to the Matthew Talbot or wherever his wanderings took him. He was ill for several days with some kind of 'flu, and Joshua and I nursed him. The curious thing was that all the time that he had a fever he seemed quite lucid, yet, as his fever subsided, his disordered thinking and behaviour reappeared.

One evening, while Joshua was still with me, and Jonathan was in bed but beginning to recover, a colleague called to take me out to dinner. This was a man who had no idea of my personal life. When Dean arrived, Joshua was sitting in front of the television, watching football.

'Where are you going?' said Josh, his back expressing a hump of disapproval. 'Why don't you have tea here? What time will you be back?'

Dean laughed. Joshua scowled. I tried to look urbane. And then Jonathan appeared. I had hoped he was asleep. No such luck. He had wrapped a towel around his middle but it was trailing on the floor, and you could see that he had been drawing snakes on his stomach and on his chest. He must have raided my sewing basket because instead of paper clips he now wore two long chains of safety pins dangling from his ears. I introduced him to Dean, and Jonathan shook hands, bowing politely as the towel dropped still further. Then he joined Joshua in front of the television.

I poured two stiff whiskies and gave one to Dean. Suddenly, and unexpectedly, the door-bell rang. I opened it to a third young male, who stood there in saffron robes, carrying a copy of the *Bhagavad Gita*. Like Jonathan, his head was shaven, and he was almost as tall. This was Simon, Ellis's younger son by his first marriage, who had just become a member of the Hari Krishnas.

'I have brought you some vegetarian rice,' said Simon.

'Yuk,' said Joshua.

'We're going out,' I said firmly.

'Have dinner in. It's cheaper,' said Simon. He had given some Krishna tracts to Dean, who was leaning forward in his chair looking fascinated at us all.

Jonathan stood up, still clutching the towel, and peered down at us from his great height. 'You should eat rice, Anne, it's good for you.'

'We are going out,' I said. I looked around me, at Jonathan, at Simon, at Joshua, and knew that at any minute I might burst into tears.

Dean said, 'We are going out'. Dean wore red shoes and was not easily thrown. He was also almost as tall as Simon and Jonathan.

We were almost out the door when Joshua delivered his parting shot. He didn't even bother to turn his head; he knew it would make its mark. 'I'll be waiting up for you.'

On another day Simon returned to show us photographs he had taken of an international Krishna gathering in India. Krishna temples are sumptuously ornate; they glitter with gold and jewels. Jonathan rocked back and forth, looking and listening. For a brief moment I wondered if he might become interested in joining. Perhaps this would be his salvation. The movement is highly structured, and structure was good for Jonathan. But Jonathan wasn't interested. He looked at the photographs and said, 'Some power-trip, man.'

A couple of days later, Josh and I were due to return to Adelaide We were catching an early plane which meant leaving the apartment by 5.45 in the morning. I did not like the idea of turfing Jonathan out at this hour, as he still wasn't completely recovered, so I suggested that he might leave later in the day, or even stay another night if he felt he needed it.

The following morning, back in Adelaide, I had a phone-call from Jenny in Sydney, who had always made Jonathan welcome if ever he turned up on her door, and who lived near my Sydney flat. Jonathan had gone beserk in my apartment in the middle of the night. He had thrown wine and china out of the window, followed by books and records. He had turned the music up full blast. He had locked himself in. The neighbours had called the police but Jonathan had refused to let anyone in. I cannot remember how or why the police were able to contact Jenny, but they had, and she had gone round and persuaded Jonathan to open the door. I flew to Sydney to deal with the damage and to calm down the neighbours. By the time I arrived Jonathan had disappeared.

I rang Andy, the psychiatrist friend who had persuaded Jonathan to go into hospital that first time in Sydney over two years ago. He came and gave me a hug. He also gave me a lecture. He said I should stop trying to fix Jonathan up and stop trying to pretend that everything was normal, because it was not. Jonathan would not get better, he said. He might improve, but there was not going to be any miracle cure, and I had to let go of thinking I would find one. I remember we were standing in one corner of the living-room, and it was about midday. The harbour looked grey and chilly. Andy took me by the shoulders and made me look at him when he said, 'Let go.'

Andy also told me to stop pretending I could cope on those occasions when I could not. When Jonathan was most angry, it meant he was also most frightened. 'If you're acting like Mary Poppins, how do you think he feels? His rage is to protect himself and there you are, apparently totally unmoved. Tell him how you feel.'

By June Jonathan had become very speedy and I felt that he was heading for another crisis. The medication from Adelaide had almost worn off, and his world was becoming dark again. He glittered with an extraordinary energy. He said he was into amphetamines and I tried to talk him out of them. He became angry and swore at me. He said that I was a she-devil and he'd throw me out the window. I remembered Andrew's advice, and I burst into tears.

Jonathan looked at me for a couple of seconds, and then put his arms around me. 'I reckon we're both in a bit of a mess,' he said. 'I'll make you some tea.'

But it was only a moment of sanity. Jonathan refused to go into hospital, refused to go back on medication, refused to see Andy again. 'No, no, no,' he said.

My helplessness showed in my dreams, like the one I recorded just before my birthday in June:

*I am with a group of people in a park, having a picnic. I notice my knee is suppurating. I am not very worried at first, then the wound spreads and I see that there is a crack around my knee cap. I touch it, and to my horror, the whole of my knee cap comes off in my hand. I look down into a vast black hole. I am really alarmed but no one takes any notice.*

*Now, I am looking to the centre of the universe. It is dark, and getting darker, but then I see a dim shape, the husk of a flower or a fruit. I am scared to touch it because I think it might be dead. But it is alive, and tough. I cannot pull it out and I am relieved. But the hole is still growing, deeper and deeper. I put my knee cap*

*back and I tell everyone what is happening, but no one seems to
care. I spray disinfectant around the wound and it appears to heal,
but I know it hasn't. I know there is a huge hollow there that will
not go away.*

A month later I dreamt that my body fell apart and that I had to
stick it together with sticky tape.

July in South Australia meant winter. We lit fires and went for long
walks and at weekends went into the hills and drank mulled wine.
I don't particularly like mulled wine, but it seemed a sociable ritual
and I joined in gratefully. One day I went out for a walk and came
back to find the house was on fire. A red-hot coal had fallen onto
the rug because I had forgotten to put up the fire-guard. The hearth
rug blazed immediately. The kelim underneath, which was a tribal
rug made of natural fibres, took longer to burn. The floorboards
were smouldering, and some of the furniture was singed. We were
lucky it had not spread further. I saw it as a sign that I needed to
take more care.

Early in July I received a Sydney telephone call from a Salvation
Army officer who asked if I knew that Jonathan had been in jail for
five days. He had noticed him sitting in the back of the cells. He
said the charges were serious.

At 8.20 on the morning of 8 July, at the back of St Vincent's
Hospital in Sydney, Jonathan and another young man had hailed
a taxi. The other man had asked to be driven to the Commonwealth
Bank in George Street. Both were behaving in a strange manner,
and the taxi driver was suspicious. He adjusted his rear mirror
so that he could observe them. The shorter man was talking with
Jonathan in a tone that could not be overheard. At the town hall,
the man had got out, saying he was going to the bank. He ran
across the street but Jonathan was still sitting in the back and
the driver asked him where he wanted to go. Jonathan refused
to speak to him. The driver said that he would drive once round
the block while Jonathan made up his mind. Jonathan still did
not answer. The driver then pulled up at the nearest police station,
where Jonathan obligingly accompanied him to the detectives' office
on the third floor. Here he was interviewed and said that he and
the other man had intended to frighten the taxi driver with a knife
into handing over his money.

Jonathan gave his occupation as male prostitute and said that he needed the money because he was a heroin addict. He signed a written transcript of the interview and was charged with three counts: conspiracy to assault and rob; armed with intent to commit indictable offence; carrying a cutting weapon.

I have no way of knowing whether Jonathan intended holding up the taxi driver, but I think it unlikely. Jonathan had a propensity for confessing to all misdemeanours, real or imagined – perhaps because he found it difficult to separate the two. Just before he was arrested, he had left this note in my Sydney flat:

*Remember the rules. Always say you have something to hide. Yes sir. Turn into a babbling scared baby, yes sir yes sir yes sir, and then write out a confession. This is what counts in court. After they have told you what you look like, they will ask you for your honesty. You must tell the truth and nothing but the truth or else they will bust your darling mother, bless her scared heart. I hope she will save you from their honest cruelty. Now what they can do to hurt you is say that the lizard used sex against his will. This is their done magic.*

Nor have I any way of knowing whether Jonathan was in fact a male prostitute or, by now, a heroin addict. His similar claims in the past had been delusional. But I did know that, in view of the seriousness of the charges, I would need to get him a lawyer, as in the past he had failed to organise legal aid. I rang Andrew, our Adelaide lawyer, to get the name of a good solicitor in Sydney, and Brenda to contact the New South Wales prison psychiatric service to make sure that his medical history was known. I wrote to Jonathan telling him what I had done and saying that he could make up his own mind as to whether he used the solicitor, but recommending that he did.

The solicitor went to see Jonathan in jail, and Jonathan told him what had occurred (the following is a transcript):

*Police are hassling me continually. I pretend to be mad and they leave me alone. Everyone wants you to be a conformist robot. I have taken heroin, I was into it, I don't know if I had a habit. Maybe I did. I took a bottle of codein cough syrup a year ago. I would prefer jail or half-way house to nuttery. I will always tell the truth because I have metal in my brain.*

The immediate issue was whether Jonathan should plead Guilty or Not guilty. We had no way of knowing what evidence the taxi driver would give, and whether Jonathan had in fact threatened him. Jonathan said he had not. Jonathan decided he would plead Not guilty. He agreed to accept a magistrate's order to have treatment if this were proposed.

The case came up at the end of July, and I flew to Sydney to attend. Jonathan had instructed the solicitor to seek bail. I said that unless I could be sure Jonathan were receiving ongoing medication, I would not be willing to stand bail.

The District Court was a big grimy Victorian building on the corner of a busy highway. It was already crowded. Groups of people were waiting outside on the steps and inside, in the entrance hall. They were the anxious, the lonely, the frightened. A few, the better-dressed brigade, seemed relatively collected. I sat in the back of the court, and wondered what Jonathan would look like when they brought him up from the cells. Jonathan appeared in jeans and some sort of orange sleeveless jumper. I couldn't see his feet. Like most court proceedings I have ever attended, it was hard to keep track of what was going on. People seemed to bob up and sit down, and make statements in voices that were impossible to hear. Suddenly I became aware that the solicitor, the nice kind avuncular solicitor, was on his feet, asking for bail. He said that the mother would take the prisoner to hospital, and that the hospital would admit him.

I had no guarantee that, once released, Jonathan would accompany me to any hospital, and I knew that no hospital would take him simply to provide an alternative to jail. They would keep him as an involuntary patient only as long as he was legally a danger to himself or others. I stood up in court, and in a voice that I did not recognise as my own because it was so taut and harsh said, 'Unless my son is on a long-term treatment program, I will not stand bail.' I looked at Jonathan but his head was hanging down.

The magistrate said, 'This is a very sorry situation.' I sat down feeling sick. I feel sick as I write this, so many years later. Why did I not bend heaven and earth to keep Jonathan out of jail? Why did not I take him to hospital – at least try? Because I feared he would either run away before he reached hospital, or that they would not admit him, or that he would run away later. And I did not want to be responsible for him any more. So Jonathan stayed in jail, and I felt cold despair. Hell, oh hell, this is a very hard part to write. So many bear-pits to fall into, so many tears. But sometimes you just lose the energy to try yet again.

I was not allowed to see Jonathan after the case, and I could not stay the following day, so I wrote him a letter:

*I am not willing to bail you out because I am no longer willing to be responsible for you, and this is what standing bail means. I do not want to act as your 'policeman' – to see that you don't take any more drugs, nor to see that you front up in Court when required. I love you. I have not abandoned you. I will never abandon you, but I feel it is time you started taking responsibility for your own actions.*

I finished writing the letter just before I caught the plane back to Sydney. Pale winter sun made the harbour shimmer with light, some sparrows were fluffing themselves under the lemon tree, and it was a beautiful morning. But I felt heavy, and then I heard a snatch of information on the radio which absurdly cheered me: 'If your bird is poorly, inspect his droppings. Count them each morning. Now that might sound a strange thing to do, but you'd be surprised how many bird fanciers count the droppings of their birds.'

**6 August**  I wrote to the solicitor saying I no longer felt happy about continuing to use him.

*I fully understand and accept your efforts to get Jonathan bail; what I don't understand and accept was your persistence in exploring avenues which you knew quite clearly were not viable. Namely, you pressed for cash surety knowing full well that I wouldn't give it and why, and you assured the Court that the doctor would admit Jonathan to hospital equally knowing that no such undertaking had been given, and why.*

*If at any time I find a place to which Jonathan can go, and which he also finds acceptable then, and only then, will I agree to standing bail.*

*I am sorry this has happened, because I really did appreciate your concern.*

Brenda's efforts were under way. She had been in touch with the Probation and Parole Department in Sydney, and both she and our

Sydney psychiatrist friend Andy had contacted the prison psychiatric service. The prison report to Brenda was that Jonathan was out of touch with reality but aware of his surroundings. He had been having fits.

**16 August**   I was still haunted by my decision not to bail out Jonathan. Jonathan's former psychiatrist at the Adelaide Hospital suggested that I see him every fortnight to give me support.

Jonathan's new solicitor told me we would need to engage a forensic psychiatrist to give a medical report on Jonathan. I would have to fly to Sydney to see him. Dr T was a short, dapper, grey-haired man, with more bounce than sensitivity. He wore a dark suit, a pale silk tie and he talked in a clipped voice. He prodded me and said sharply, 'Which one had the gene, eh mother, eh?' I could only shuffle disconcertedly and say I really didn't know.

And neither does anybody else. The genetic picture about schizophrenia is still cloudy. There is a tendency for the condition to run in some families, although many people who develop schizophrenia come from families that have no known history of the illness. Even in identical twins, who have exactly the same genetic make-up, there is only about a fifty-fifty chance that if one twin develops schizophrenia, so will the other, regardless of whether the twins are brought up together or apart. The brothers, sisters, and children of a person with schizophrenia have a ten per cent chance of getting the illness compared with one per cent for the general population. Where both parents have schizophrenia, the figure rises to forty per cent. It is now generally believed that what people inherit is an increased predisposition towards the illness, rather than the illness itself.

Dr T visited Jonathan in jail, and reported:

*He first experienced abnormal mental phenomena – hearing voices giving him commands, such as 'kill yourself' or 'you're hopeless, cut yourself', at about the age of seventeen years; they would sometimes appear to come from inside his head, sometimes from outside his head – the latter when his mental state was wildly abnormal in other ways. Other abnormal mental phenomena included feeling that he was 'under the control of some outside force', that 'his own thoughts were being broadcast to others' and that 'some of his thoughts had been inserted into his mind from elsewhere.'*

When spoken to by the undersigned and closely questioned, the client was adamant that he had not had LSD, and that he had not had heroin. Marijuana, he said, helped calm his abnormal fear and anxieties. He had told people he had had LSD trips in order to explain some of his strange hallucinatory experiences.

Although at the present time he is stabilised on the prescribed psychotropic drug trifluoperazine (stelazine) the undersigned has no doubts that the client suffers from Schizophrenia – Hebephrenic type (International Classification of Diseases (ICD) World Health Organization, Geneva 1978) No. 2951, defined thus in the Glossary to the ICD: 'A form of schizophrenia in which affective changes are prominent, delusions and hallucinations fleeting and fragmentary, behaviour irresponsible and unpredictable and mannerisms common. The mood is shallow and inappropriate, accompanied by giggling or self-satisfied, self-absorbed smiling, or by a lofty manner, grimaces, mannerisms, pranks, hypochondriacal complaints and reiterated phrases. Thought is disorganised. There is a tendency to remain solitary, and behaviour seems empty of purpose and feeling. This form of schizophrenia usually starts between the ages of fifteen and twenty-five years.'

Because Jonathan had decided to plead Not guilty and there was a backlog in the courts, it was likely he would have to wait a long time before his case was heard. He was being held in the Special Observation Unit of the jail, a section reserved for prisoners needing protection or with psychiatric illnesses. I was making trips to Sydney for production work for the ABC, so was able to visit him every two or three weeks. In the first three months he became thinner and thinner, till he looked like a stick-insect, so fragile I feared he might break. His eyes would be downcast, he would speak only a few words. I used to stand there not knowing what to say: 'Georgia sends her love . . . It's quite cool outside . . . Joshua sends his love . . . What's the food like? . . . How are you feeling?'

The prison system is brutal: the dingy waiting-room where you sit, listening for your name to be called; the cage into which the prisoner comes to talk to you through the wire and the distance between you; the warders that hover near because these are their orders, the lack of privacy, the fact that you are not allowed to touch;

the chill that settles on your soul and the harshness of love in hiding, so that even a smile becomes a blessed event. I went home after one visit and re-read *The Ballad of Reading Gaol.*

One afternoon the warder gave me a message that I should talk to the nurse on duty in the Special Unit. She seemed like a warm person who was trying to appear cold. She said that Jonathan had become so withdrawn that they were worried about him: I was allowed to see him and to go and have body contact. We deprive people of their liberty as a punishment but we also deprive them of human touch. Jonathan was sitting on a trestle bed with his head in his hands. He was wearing boots that were too large, and clothes that were too small. His legs were crossed and one foot kept jiggling up and down. His hands shook. When I touched him it was like touching a bundle of fragile bones, a marionette in khaki. I thought, *I don't know how much more of this I can stand.* That was the only contact visit I was allowed to make.

The next time I saw Jonathan he was back in one of the wire visiting cages, standing on one leg. It was the same stork posture that he had taken up when he first became ill, that night in Adelaide under the plum tree. It seemed like a hundred years ago.

I remembered something I had read, about modelling behaviour and language to promote empathy. It was an idea of Milton Erickson, the great humanist psychologist, and the father of modern medical hypnosis. Erickson did not solely use formal hypnosis, but pioneered naturalistic methods to get his clients to relate to him and to work with him. This might sometimes involve the therapist matching the client's movements and language to develop empathy and acceptance. And so, that early morning in Long Bay jail, I stood on one leg like a stork looking calmly at my son who stood on one leg like a stork, both of us ignoring the wire that kept us apart. I swayed and wobbled a bit, but I stood there for three or four or five minutes, and then Jonathan put down his tucked-up foot and burst out laughing. 'You look silly,' he said. We still did not talk much, but there was no need.

One day I went with Icia who had slung a shawl around her shoulders and swung her hips as she walked into the jail, looking more like Nell Gwyn than someone suitably subdued for a visit to a prisoner. Icia greeted Jonathan with a wide smile, said that she longed to give him a big hug, and then stood smiling at him in contented silence. Every now and then all three of us would laugh. It was another meeting that needed no words such luminous moments happened rarely.

*5 November*  Jonathan was still in the Special Observation Unit and the solicitor was still trying to move him to an outside hospital. Still, still, still. How much longer would he be held before his case was heard? A senior probation officer talked with Jonathan to see if he had any better idea of the responsibilities of bail.

'Joe, do you know what will be required of you if we manage to get you bail?'

No answer.

'Joe, you will have to keep in touch with us, and not break the law. Do you understand?'

No answer.

'Do you want bail, Joe?'

'Yeah, when I get bail I'm going to get me a motorbike and be one of the beautiful people again. Yeah.'

*8 November*  The solicitor had been trying to get the charge against Jonathan dropped. The Attorney-General refused.

*18 November*  I took a book into Jonathan and received a docket: *Receipt for Prisoner's Property: Received the undermentioned articles on behalf of prisoner No. 2460 1 paperback. New.*

*29 November*  Jonathan's court appearance was brought forward to 6 December. He was still going to plead Not guilty. Gradually, Jonathan was beginning to look better. His half-brother Simon was visiting him with the Hari Krishnas who had a program of teaching yoga and meditation in jails. An occupational therapist was teaching painting once a week. He played chess. Various people were keeping an eye on him, like Neil and Icia, and Clare, our loving Irish friend who had spent Christmas with us that year when Jonathan first became ill. During the holidays brave Georgia and Joshua visited him.

*3 December*   Jonathan's case was now postponed till the following year. He was looking better than I could remember. He stood with his head upright. He looked into my eyes. He had energy in his voice. He said jail was heavy, but hospital was humiliating. He said he was cold.

I made one more visit to Sydney just before Christmas, and I took him a new navy-blue pullover, lanolin-treated for arctic conditions and some more paperbacks. As I left he called out, 'I hope you're behaving yourself, Anne.'

Six
# *Tough Love*

*'Mid pleasures and palaces though we may roam,*
*Be it ever so humble, there's no place like home.*
                                        J. H. PAYNE

***January 1983***   I sit here in a shower of memories tonight. It is strange writing about things past: I know what is to come and I can change nothing. Sometimes I can look back calmly, other times I am engulfed with memories. This year begins with good memories. I was in Hong Kong, waiting to fly into Beijing with a South Australian friend, Pat Kelly. We were about to set up a tour by the Sydney theatre company, Nimrod, of Chinese universities. I hoped to arrange an accompanying film.

***2 January***   We flew into Beijing, where the temperature was minus eighteen degrees. We wore parkas, track suits, thermal underwear, two pairs of gloves, scarves and woollen hats. Most of the Hong Kong Chinese who were visiting Beijing seemed to be wearing mink. Beijing offered a khaki-coloured sky and a khaki landscape.

The Beijing Hotel was built on a grand scale. My room was vast, with a massive wooden bed, an impressive desk and armchairs, and heavy plum-coloured curtains. In the foyer, men and women paraded in enormous fur hats while pale winter children darted in and out of people's legs. Young Chinese men in dark glasses who had been on visits to Hong Kong swaggered by, festooned with electronic gear. People sat on elegant gilt chairs drinking tea and cocoa, and eating small cakes.

This was China some four years after the end of the cultural revolution. A whole generation had been starved of creative and intellectual development and there was a thirst for contact with the

West. Our interpreter, Huaren, was clever, quick and charming. When we met her in Beijing she wore a dark-blue Mao suit; her clothing became increasingly colourful as we moved further south. We visited five universities to discuss what theatre they would like to see and all of them asked for Shakespeare, Eugene O'Neill, Arthur Miller, John Steinbeck and, in the University of Xian, for some reason, Lady Gregory was also in demand. We proposed some Australian drama and they politely said yes.

We had arrived in China at the beginning of Birth Control Month and everywhere we went, from one end of that vast country to the other, we were regaled with messages reminding us that birth control is a glorious task. Banners carrying birth control slogans festooned the buildings; street stalls did a brisk trade in condoms; television 'soaps' were about the perils of unwanted pregnancies; operas and 'pop' music were about the horrors of large families and the joys of small. What campaigns had there been for mental illness, I wondered? None, I was told.

For part of the way we travelled by train, and stayed awake most of the night talking, talking, talking – two Australian women and one Chinese. We talked about our husbands, our lovers, our work, our children, our politics. We snuggled down under padded red-and-white check quilts and the train attendant brought tea in big metal pots. I wrote in my diary fragments of my thoughts, fragments of our conversation:

*. . . Where is Jonathan, Jonathan of the wild eyes and the fluttering hands? . . . Put the memory away, pack it up in paper, tie it with string, seal it with sealing wax . . .*

We drank more tea and peered out at a siding. It looked like a film scene, set in a landscape so vast that everything human-sized was dwarfed and bleak with cold.

*My husband was sent to one of the universities in the far north of China. I only see him once a year. My sister brings up my son. He is ten years old. It is better for him in the country than in Beijing. When he is older he can come to live with me. It is perhaps difficult for you to understand . . . Many many Chinese women feel very sad that their husbands are not good to them when they have their children. They are not sympathetic, and their women can never forget this . . .*

The train lurched and rattled over the tracks. We lurched too, spilling boiling tea on our quilts, eating barley sugar, talking as if we had known each other all our lives.

*... Jonathan pierced his ears with three holes for three seashells. Georgia pierced only one of hers. So did Josh. ... Acupuncture is used for hysterectomies in China ... Three doctors told me I needed a hysterectomy. One said you wouldn't hang on to a rotten decayed old tooth, would you? Well that's what you're doing with your womb ... no back ache? ... no, well you soon will have. ... Have a Jaffa – they're what all Australians eat at the movies ... My uterus is still here, thank you very much, and doing very nicely ... Still there are very few women in high positions in China ... I think we need to educate the men ... my hot-water bottle is cold. ... Fill it up with the teapot.*

We said goodbye to Huaren at Guangzhou. One year later the Nimrod Theatre Company with John Bell was able to visit China and played to thousands of students and academics across the countryside. Alas, we were not able to raise enough money to make the film.

As soon as I returned from China, I plunged back into the worry of Jonathan's court case which was due very soon. He was still in jail. Whenever he was moved to the ordinary section he would stand on one foot making strange noises until he was moved back to the Special Unit. He said that he was frightened in the ordinary part of jail and had been raped. It was probable.

The solicitors made representations to the Under-Secretary of Justice and to the Attorney-General's Department to have the case against Jonathan dropped. They sent me a letter saying that in the interim could I please send the sum of two thousand dollars by way of a retainer and on account of costs already incurred. There would also be the QC's bill.

In February I received a jubilant phone-call from one of the solicitors. I thought she was going to tell me that Jonathan was about to be released. Instead, she said, 'We think your son may not have schizophrenia.'

'Oh yes?' I said.

'He's really a very interesting young man, who wants to live in the countryside and grow carrots.' I see from my notes that I also wrote 'keep rabbits', but that could have been sarcasm.

'Oh yes,' I said again. And left it at that. Never throw away all your hope cards. The QC, who was a good man (as were the solicitors good women and men) was chairperson of a psychiatric halfway house, and Jonathan had agreed to go to one of these once he was released.

*1 March*   The day before the trial and the young solicitor rang sounding distressed. She and the QC had gone to see Jonathan to reconstruct the story of his arrest. He had been at first withdrawn, and then rambling. The strain of the coming trial had set him back again. Finally, he beckoned imperiously for a piece of paper and a pen, turned his back on them and wrote: *I dismiss you. I dismiss you. I dismiss you. Get fucked. J. B. Esquire.*

'What do we do?' said the solicitor.

'Go on acting for him', I said wearily.

At seven o'clock that night the QC rang me in Sydney. The Attorney-General had withdrawn the main charges. There had been no evidence against Jonathan of any substance. He had not once threatened the taxi driver, neither verbally nor in any other way. He would still be charged with being in possession of a cutting instrument.

So in spite of a long history of mental illness, Jonathan had been kept in jail for nine months, without trial, and for what ultimately turned out to be possession of a penknife, eight centimetres long.

Dr John Grigor, then head of forensic psychiatric services in Victoria, has said that, arguably, jails are the biggest mental hospitals in our country. In the United States many studies have consistently demonstrated that about twenty per cent of jail inmates are seriously mentally ill and in need of psychiatric care. Up to five per cent are acutely psychotic. Commentators have speculated that rates of mental disorder have increased in the last thirty years in prisons and remand centres, and that this could be the unintended consequence of de-institutionalisation, and of a worldwide trend towards more stringent procedures for involuntary commitment to mental hospitals. Even when beds are available, many psychiatrists are reluctant to admit people who are chronically mentally ill. Many of this group are being arrested for minor criminal acts that are really manifes-

tations of their illness – either acute psychosis, or the poor judgement and impulsive behaviour that is part of chronic mental illness.
Their crimes are usually petty ones – failing to pay a bus fare, petty
theft, vagrancy – the kind of crimes Jonathan kept committing. A
young man picks up a brick and smashes the plate-glass window
of a retail store because he sees a dinosaur jumping out at him. A
young woman is repeatedly arrested for walking out of restaurants
without paying because she believes she does not need to pay. She
says she is the reincarnation of Jesus Christ. In a research study in
Portland, Oregon, almost all the families of mentally ill people
reported that when their ill relative had committed a crime, it was
after a psychiatric crisis. Over half the respondent families had tried
and failed to have their relative committed to a hospital just before
the crime was committed. Some said they were even relieved when
the arrest was made, since 'At last he got some help.'

I read this study, couched in the necessary formal language of
acadame, and a sentence like the last resonates. What was it I had
said when I heard of Jonathan's arrest? – 'At last he'll get some help.'
But what a terrible indictment of our health services it is that we
have to wait until a mentally ill person has committed a criminal
act before we can get this help.

Brenda had advised me that I could take some decent clothes
for Jonathan if I arrived early at the court-room. I handed them over
to two of the Sydney probation and parole officers, and then learned
that the detectives who had arrested Jonathan were there. They were
displeased that the main part of the charge had been disallowed
and told me that Jonathan was a heroin addict.

The hearing of the charge concerning the cutting instrument was
brief. Jonathan was given a one-year bond. He walked out of the
court-room looking good and sounding good. I wasn't sure what
we should do with this first day of freedom and, as returning to the
flat seemed like an anti-climax, I asked if he would like to go to
Bondi. He said yes.

We had a surreal day on Bondi Beach. It was still warm. We walked
along the beach, not saying much. We bought pizza and icecream
and milkshakes. We swam. I did not ask any questions about the
past, nor did I ask questions about the future. Jonathan seemed so
happy that for the moment, questions would have been out of place.

He was like the old Jonathan, before he became ill.

We went back to Kirribilli and Neil and Icia had arrived. We had dinner together and he held our hands round the table and said, 'God, it's wonderful to be with the people I love so much.' It was a good moment.

Jonathan had agreed to check in with the halfway house the following day. He did nothing about it. Icia asked him if he were going to stay in Sydney or return to Adelaide. He decided to think about it before making up his mind. That night he began to be edgy and the next morning his irritability was worse. Given the trauma of having spent nine months in jail, this did not seem surprising. I returned to Adelaide where Joshua had an exeat from boarding school for the weekend, and Georgia had also just arrived. She had decided to move back home. She was just eighteen and Josh was fourteen. Jonathan was twenty-one.

Jonathan rang and said he had also decided to return home. I met him at the airport and we drove through the parklands that surround the city of Adelaide. On the way, as if by some quirk of fate, he spotted Simon the Street Poet and Clayton Pring. He hopped out of the car while it was still moving.

'I'll be back soon,' he called out.

He came back an hour later and paced up and down the kitchen while I cooked dinner. He was excited but quite rational. I can remember being overjoyed at how normal he seemed. We ate in the courtyard, under the big tree and the clothesline. During dinner he became argumentative with Georgia.

The following day Joshua returned to school, and Jonathan slept in. We had an early dinner, and Jonathan was even more irritable and again began to pick a quarrel with Georgia, calling her some vile names. He snarled at me, and jerked some mineral water across the table and into my lap. I told him to go for a walk and cool off. He stomped off, talking to himself, and sat cross-legged on the footpath, rocking backwards and forwards.

I had to go up the road to borrow something from a friend – I forget what – so I left the house for about an hour. I guess I misjudged the degree of his disturbance – this was a serious error of judgement.

When I came back two police cars were parked outside the house and the scene looked as if a bomb had hit it. The road was strewn for several metres with debris. Georgia was white-faced and in tears. She said that after I left Jonathan burst into the house, grabbed armfuls of china and glass, and threw them on the road. He scattered books and tore up papers. He pulled pictures off walls and jumped on them. He flattened radios with his hands. He stomped on clocks and hurled them across the road. His rage was formidable. Georgia screamed at him to stop, but he pushed her away as if nothing would halt him. Georgia ran to the nearest neighbours to phone the police. The police took him to hospital.

Georgia was distraught and in shock. I called a good friend, who was now also our family doctor, and he came round and rang the hospital, to be told that Jonathan was calm again. It took two hours to sweep up the wreckage in the street and we did not finish till past two in the morning.

The following day Georgia had left for university when I rang the hospital and spoke to the superintendent. This was not the hospital where Jonathan had spent so much time the year before because we were now living in a different catchment area. The doctor said that Jonathan was much better, and was on his way home. I stopped and took a deep breath. On his way home ... Jesus ... I couldn't believe it ... *on his way home*. I looked out the window and sure enough there was Jonathan loping down the road.

Jonathan kicked open the gate with his foot, came up the drive, into the house, pushed me to the ground and put his foot on my head so that my face was pressed into the carpet. He called me 'cunt' and 'whore' and 'she-devil'. He demanded, 'Give me that chain, and that bracelet, lady,' and then tried to tear the chain off my neck. He took my arm and jerked it behind my back and marched me round the room. I yelled in fury and pain. I told him I would call the police. He slammed me against the wall. Then he wandered around the house, picking up one or two remaining articles, like my watch which was by my bed, a radio that he had missed, some papers which he tore into pieces, some jewellery. Eventually he left, with loot in his pockets and in his arms. I call it loot because this had been a plunder. At the front door, he said, 'Watch it bitch, I'll be back.'

I rang the hospital, and spoke to the doctor who had been giving me advice and support. I snivelled on the phone in a voice that

I no longer recognised because it sounded like a whine. I said, 'I'm frightened.' The doctor said that I had to stop rescuing Jonathan. Perhaps he was wondering why I had let Jonathan come back to Adelaide. Georgia had also said I should not have let him come home. I did not want a lecture; I wanted help. The doctor said I was right to be scared. I should take out a restraining order and maybe get a security guard on the house. If Jonathan appeared again I should call the police.

I rang Brenda. She also said to take out a restraining order, and that I should think about getting a watch-dog or moving interstate. People have to do this sometimes, said Brenda. I could just swallow the notion of a restraining order, but not the idea of three members of the family moving interstate for protection against one sick one, and the watch-dog idea seemed the worst of all. Everyone said that for my own safety and the safety of Georgia and Joshua I must break all association with Jonathan.

I did not want to stay in the house that night, and neither did anyone else. Georgia had just got back from a lecture. She decided it was better if she left home and lived with friends. Mary had been away for the weekend and had just returned. She decided she would also move out for a while. Joshua was at boarding school. That left me. I felt on my own. I was on my own.

That night I stayed with friends. The following day I returned to the empty house which still looked as if a bomb had hit it. I needed to talk with someone who had been through similar traumas, and so I rang Betty, a woman I had met a few months earlier who also had a son with schizophrenia. When you are wounded, you need someone who knows your hurt and your shame. Because I felt shame. I thought, *What kind of a person am I, that my son could do this to me? What will they think of me, the grey ghosts of self-judgement?*

Betty said, 'Fuck 'em.'

Betty took in the piles of broken glass and china and said 'Oh my Gawd.'

Betty was large, generous and funny. She believed in horoscopes, Bach flower remedies, witches, tarot cards, the labour movement, the power of women and the power of love. She had taught herself about literature, history and politics while she was feeding her three children, and learned Ovid and Virgil to train her mind. Betty was married to Dave who was tall and wiry, and called people 'Love'. They lived in a house with a big back-yard with fruit trees and vegetables and, inside, every room seemed full of books, papers and people. Their house attracted people.

Their youngest son had developed schizophrenia when he was nineteen. 'He went to Cactus Beach to surf, and one of his mates got through to us to say he'd gone off the air. We had to get the flying doctor service to get him back. They put him on the phone to us. "It's Mum," I said. "Mum? Oh Mum!" he said, as if I were a fish from the sea.'

When I recounted my current saga of woes, Betty peered at me and said, 'Listen, my love, if you gaze for long into the abyss, the abyss gazes into you.' She chuckled. 'That's Nietzsche in *Beyond Good and Evil*.' She seemed to radiate an inexhaustible inner strength. We moved into the kitchen and drank tea. Betty was wedged into the space behind the green laminex kitchen table.

'Lie to them,' she said. 'Fall apart. Say you're going to have a nervous breakdown. That's the only way the buggers will listen to you. You go in there all calm and collected and they think, "Oh she's all right. She's not front-line casualty. She's coping."' She chuckled and then patted my hand. 'I'll send round Dave,' she said.

Years later we talked and she remarked, 'It's funny you know, because I thought you were so calm and coping because you were organised. Even the piles of glass were organised. Impressive.'

The moral of that particular story, reinforced by Betty's earlier admonitions, is that there are times in life when it is foolish to pretend you are coping. Betty helped me learn to show how helpless I felt – and to ask for support.

Betty's Dave turned up that afternoon. Dave was just retired, and he quietly went round the house, fixing up catches on windows, and noticing small jobs that needed repair. He brought spanners to mend dripping taps, axes to chop up wood, and on two or three occasions he stayed the night because I was frightened to be on my own. But most of the time I stayed with various friends and only came back during the day in order to work. The hospital said that this was wise. I also had security guards to check the house. Finally, I went to the police station to fill out a form requesting a restraining order – a legal order forbidding Jonathan access to the house. In a few days' time, after processing, this would have to come before a magistrate.

It was hard to take out the order. It went against all my instincts as a parent and against all my values about home. Home was the place where you could always go. And yet here I was turning Jonathan away when it was the terror of his illness that had made him behave this way.

Two days later at about midday I returned to the house to fetch some books and found Jonathan sitting on the verandah. I made myself walk up to him: 'If you ever again behave like you did on Sunday, I will charge you. I am scared of you when you carry on like that, and so are the others. For the time being I do not want you near the house. I have taken out a restraining order with the police, which says you must stay away.'

Jonathan said 'Yeah, right, orright, *orright*,' and then wandered off into the parklands and sat under a big tree, cross-legged, staring at me. I went inside and shut the door.

Jonathan had been jailed for nine months awaiting trial on a charge that was dropped and for which there had never been any evidence. During that time he may or may not have been raped. He had been released with no counselling. He then had a homecoming fraught with emotion. Given that schizophrenia is almost certainly triggered by stress, it was small wonder that he blew when suddenly he was thrust into the expectations of an outside world.

Jonathan began haunting the neighbourhood. Sometimes he appeared in the back-yard, but ran away when I came out. Once he climbed in through the window and stalked around the house picking things up and putting them down again. He had returned to the squats to live, and was drawing sickness benefits, but as the Guardianship Order on his financial affairs had not been lifted he had to go to Brenda for access to his savings so he could buy a mattress, blankets and some clothes.

**15 March**   Brenda wrote:
*I had a talk with Joe as to how he is going to survive, and where he can get free meals and a shower.*

*I also made it very clear to Joe that I will help him in any way possible, that he can live his life as he wants to and I will not take any steps to put him in hospital. However, if he harms anyone and if he continues to harrass those living in his mother's house, I will take action. He agreed with me, but the message will probably get scrambled in his mind. He is not keen to go on the invalid pension because he is still talking about trying to get work. The trouble is that he is too mixed up to manage any kind of job.*

That same day I went to the Magistrate's Court to make application in person for the restraining order. I had to explain my reason for needing one. The magistrate looked at me over his glasses and said, 'But can't the boy get help? Why isn't he in hospital?' I said tartly that I wished that he would ask the hospital that same question. As I left the court, the police told me that because Jonathan did not have any fixed address, they might be unable to serve the order, which would mean it could not be enforced.

I returned to South Terrace alone, and felt the most terrible desolation. Georgia and Joshua had both been forced to leave home. Security guards were watching the house. Jonathan was still crazy. And I was helpless and frightened.

Sometimes I slept at the house out of bravura: I would not be turned out of my own home. But I would wake at the slightest rustle outside. The security guards' torches would flicker through my bedroom window and startle me so I would sit upright, pretending that I wasn't alarmed. Once when the moon was flying high and I had been woken by a possum – or was it a cat? or was it my errant son? – I marched through the house in my bare feet shouting, 'Go away, Jonathan, go away! Leave me alone, Jonathan, Leave me alone.' As I clambered back into bed, I thought ironically of all those statements about mothers who clung to their children and would not cut the umbilical cord. God, I'd cut it, burn it, blow it up – anything to get rid of this burden that would never give me peace, and which left me so exhausted I did not know how I could face each day.

Easter fell at the beginning of April, and I suggested Georgia, Joshua and I all meet at the house on Easter Sunday – in an attempt at re-creating some kind of normal family life. We were joined by Mary who was still lodging with friends. Everyone squabbled, and I lost my temper. 'Tough,' I said. 'Yes, it would have been better if Ellis hadn't died; it would have been better if Jonathan hadn't gone mad; it would have been better if he hadn't wrecked the house. It would have been better if none of these things had happened. But I can't change them and neither can you. So we can go on being miserable and beating each other up, or we can accept what's happened and give each other the best time we possibly can.'

I stormed out and walked round the parklands. When I returned the tea was made, the hot-cross buns were in the oven. It wasn't a brilliant Easter, but it wasn't bad.

About a week went by and there was a knock on the door. It was Jonathan, looking healthy and happy, and as if nothing untoward had ever occurred. He wanted to show me the clothes he had just bought from the opportunity shop: an air-force jacket, khaki dungarees and a pair of fur-lined boots. He was beaming with pleasure, like a child who had just bought himself some new toys. I knew I was being inconsistent, but I found it impossible to turn him away.

'Hello Anne,' he said, and put his arms out and hugged me. 'Do you like my new clothes?'

'Yes.' I said. 'But I still feel upset about what happened, and I don't want you around.'

A few days later Jonathan appeared again at the front door. 'Got a light?' he asked. He had a weedie hanging from his lips. He was still wearing his dungarees and boots but not the air-force jacket. He said he had lost it in the hills. Instead, he had draped a Fair-Isle cardigan around his shoulders. He sat in a cane chair on the verandah, and crossed his legs.

'Do you like my boots?' He looked admiringly down at them.

'Yes,' I said.

'I'm a vegetarian. Think I look better?'

There was silence. I pulled up some weeds. Again, I knew that if I were going to stick with that restraining order – the one that still hadn't been served – I should by now have called the police. In the clear light of day, it seemed ridiculous.

He went on: 'I've been having a good time. Been seeing some guys who are into feminism. I decided I was wrong to deny you your rights. I was being chauvinistic. In fifty years or five hundred years when the feminists get really strong, you might turn round and deny us our rights. So I'm sorry.'

'Okay,' I said. There were no more weeds left to pull.

'This guy, he was with some feminists and he tried to turn them round, really beautiful girls, but they gave him a hard time. So I reckon you've got to respect each other's rights.'

'Yes,' I said. 'So please bring me back my watch.'

'I didn't take any watches, didn't take any watches, didn't take any watches.' He scratched the dog Liza, who turned upside down and waved her legs in the air.

'She got cancer?'

'Nope.'

'That's good, because if she had I was going to take her away to some mates in the country who can cure cancer.'

'She hasn't got cancer, and I do *not* want you to take her away.'

'You'd miss her if I took her away, wouldn't you?'

'I would.'

The night games continued. I would hear trees whispering and think it was Jonathan. I would jump at every sound. He would break in, sometimes in the middle of the night, sometimes very early in the morning. He would climb in through the bathroom or the study window. Sometimes he broke windows, sometimes he forced locks. Sometimes he hid in the back shed and slipped in through the kitchen door when no one was looking and locked himself in the bathroom. Sometimes he rang the door-bell. I would hear his breathing outside my window, or imagine that I heard his breathing. There would be a clinking sound from the back door, and I would see that he had pushed the key out of the lock and a piece of paper would appear under the door trying to pull the key close to the door so that he could grab it from the outside. The more we locked him out, the angrier and more lost he became. We would know he had come because of the trail of cigarette butts and the smell of dirty socks.

Once he broke in at about two o'clock in the morning through the bathroom window, but then could not get into the main part of the house because we had locked the door from the outside. I called the police. The police came, but said that the restraining

order had not yet been served. I said, 'Well, now's your chance.'
They said they had left it behind. I unlocked the bathroom door
and Jonathan was sitting on the lavatory, shivering. He wore a torn
plastic raincoat.

'Excuse me, excuse me,' he said. 'I had nowhere to go and Anne
said it would be all right.'

'No, it is not all right.'

'Why not go to the Sallys?' said the older policeman.

'Closed.'

'Why didn't you go earlier?' I said.

He thought for a moment, as if he were hanging onto every
sentence very hard, so as not to let the words fly away. 'I thought
I could stay. And I am sick.' He coughed and hung his head.

*Bastard, Jonathan! Get up off the lavatory. Stop playing pathetic,*
*bastard!*

I can't go on writing as I feel so distraught. How could I have
done that to my own son, when he was sick? How could I have
turned him out in the middle of a winter's night, when outside it
was raining and freezing cold? I can still see the two policemen,
shuffling their feet, not liking what was happening, and one of them
saying, 'Please yourself, ma'am, but they say blood is thicker than
water.'

Come off it, Anne, the reality is that in Jonathan's last two years,
he twice threatened to kill you; he bit you, had his hands round
your throat and semi-throttled you, hit you, terrorised Joshua, threw
Georgia around; he smashed up your possessions in Sydney and
in Adelaide. He ran away from every possible kind of help. He did
not have to sleep in the park; he did not have to break into your
house in the middle of the night.

The policeman asked Jonathan: 'Do you know there is a warrant?'

'Yes.'

'Then why do you come here?'

'Because it is not very just, is it?'

The older policeman who had a pink face and a sandy moustache
said he did not intend to carry on with this kind of talk any longer.
'What do you want to do?' he asked me. 'Charge him?'

'No, just move him on.'

'Well, come on son.'

Jonathan got up off the lavatory, his jeans at their familiar half mast, his feet bare, his raincoat flapping. 'All right, all right, all right. I'm very sorry. Excuse me. Excuse me.' He leered at me as he pushed past, towards the front door.

The rain was sheeting down. 'Please try and get him into Hillcrest Hospital for the night,' I said. The policemen nodded. A breakdown truck was parked outside our paling fence – for broken cars but not for broken minds I thought. Jonathan talked to the police on the street corner for a few minutes. He kept shaking his head. Then he padded off down the road.

*Home is where the heart is,* I thought. *Home is the place where they never turn you away. Jonathan has no home. What sentimental bilge. He has a home, but he abuses it.*

*I hate you Jonathan, I hate you, I hate you. I hate you for your manipulation, your whingeing and whining, your refusal to look after yourself, your bullying. I hate you.*

The next day Georgia said sadly, 'It's best to go away and forget him. He'll never get better.'

Brenda said, 'It's best to go away and forget him. He'll never get better.'

She also said that he would probably be round in her office, any tick of the clock, asking for more money. She was right.

I do not want to write this book. I find it painful. I find it depressing. It scratches old wounds so they have no chance to heal. I am sick of the word 'schizophrenia'. I am sick of madness.

I remember other times when Jonathan used to waken me in the middle of the night, and I am sick of those memories too. The phone that rang in Sydney, and when I picked up the receiver I heard his voice and he was crying. It was about two in the morning. The harbour was black and glittering and I made myself listen to my son's crying and his voice saying, 'The cops are going to arrest me because they say I have a drug-running ring. And the prostitutes can't save me. And the police say they'll bash me. And there are two guys waiting outside the phone-box. Anne, save me. They are going to kill me. Save me.'

So in my mind, I can see him in the phone-box, and smell him, and feel the fear, but I do not know if there are two men outside, waiting to kill him, or if the police are waiting to bash him, or if there are prostitutes waiting to save him. Or where the phone-box is. Or what I can do. So I say, ' Get into a taxi and come round here if you are frightened and I'll pay the taxi this end.'

And he goes on crying and then puts down the phone.

And there is silence.

The doctor said I must tough it out: otherwise Jonathan would not learn respect, he would do it again. Brenda said the same.

Looking back, the scenario with Jonathan had become like guerilla warfare.

*10 April*   I went to the country where a friend had lent me his house near the sea. I took our dog Liza, and walked for hours, in rain and storms. Sometimes I shouted 'Whoop whoop whoop' and the winds howled back, 'Whoop whoop whoop.' At night I lit fires and listened to the radio and read. I dreamed I was on a hill in a barren ochre land, looking down at a compound in which were lions and tigers. Outside the compound there were other animals – elephants, giraffes, zebras and horses. Some were grazing. Some were frightened. I knew I had to open the wire gates of the compound, and I was frightened because I thought the lions and tigers would eat me, and eat the other animals. I wanted to warn them but I did not know their language. I had to open the gates. I had been commanded. So I opened them. The lions and tigers walked out, and joined the other animals. They ate no one. Not even me.

When I returned, I thought *I am not going to play this game any longer with Jonathan. I will open the gates of the compound.* When I saw him in the parklands I went across to him. I put my hands on his shoulders and said that he might come into the house during the day, but only when I was there. And that he must not come during the night once the lights were out and we had gone to bed. Jonathan said, 'Orright,' and came in and had a mug of tea.

Jonathan was now living at Whitmore Square in the William Booth Memorial Hostel, run by the Salvation Army. The William Booth is a substantial red-brick building which has lace curtains at the windows and emits the unmistakable smell of food. The verandahs have handsome blue cast-iron lace-work, and the eaves are pie-crusted. It has rainbow-painted seats facing a concrete-paved square.

When I went back to see it fairly recently the privet hedge had had its top lopped off, and there were two new Red Cross clothing bins. Next door was the Salvation Army shop where Jonathan and I had shopped for pots and pans and clothes – because it was no use buying new ones, they would be lost within days. In the window was a display of shirts and dresses, on wire hangers that had been twisted upwards, so the garments looked as if they had wings and were about to fly away.

The Square with its many trees was a place people from the Hostel could just sit. Once I had seen Jonathan sitting there, and on impulse had picked him up and driven to the sea. We drove past the white oleanders and palm trees that lined the main highway, past the green railings of the cemetery, the privet hedges, the urns and obelisks, the grave-stones. We walked on the beach and Jonathan said, 'When I die I shall come back as a fish, but don't tell the police.'

By now Mary had found somewhere else to live, and so Dean moved in. Dean was my friend and colleague who had first met Jonathan in Sydney with Simon, my Hari Krishna stepson. Dean felt he could cope with Jonathan, and I was glad of his support. Sometimes Jonathan kept to the limits I had set him on visiting the house, and came for showers and food and a change of clothes. Sometimes he still broke in, even when he could have knocked on the door. Joshua suggested we should leave out notices saying: *Please do not break in. Food and sleeping bag in the shed.* We did, and sometimes it worked and sometimes it didn't. Sometimes he would wake us all up and stand on the doorstep, bowing politely as if he had stepped out of a Victorian novel: 'Excuse me, excuse me, I am sick and malnourished and I have nowhere to sleep.'

'Go to St Vincents.'

'They won't have me.'

'Go to the Sallys.'

'They won't have me.'

'Go to hospital.'

'I haven't got the fare.'

'Here is the fare.'

Once he said haughtily, 'My doorman will be round at the weekend,' and strode out into the night.

Everyone told me that I must be much tougher. 'You have to be tough...You aren't tough enough...it's called tough-love...tough it out so that he will be forced to face his illness and seek help...he doesn't have to be homeless...he doesn't have to be on the streets...if you aren't tough, we cannot be responsible for your safety any more.'

Listen you guys (it was mostly guys), if you'd been prepared to take him into hospital and keep him there until his mind was clear enough to face his illness, all this wouldn't be happening. How about *your* being tough? Okay, I know he kept running away, but that's par for the course. If you couldn't deal with the difficult ones, then how the hell did you expect me to?

In May Jonathan was in court on a charge of possession of Indian hemp. The magistrate asked Jonathan why he carried a Swiss Army knife. Jonathan said, 'So that I can frighten rapists away from young women. My mother gave it to me.'

'I find that a difficult one to substantiate,' said the magistrate. He remanded Jonathan in custody and ordered a Probation Services report.

Brenda wrote the report and then went to Adelaide jail where she read it to Jonathan. She said that he was saner than she could remember. He talked for quite some time about the pain in his head, and how people did not see him as he wanted to be seen. He said that people were frightened of him, and this hurt him deeply. He said that he loved me very much and did not want to cause me harm. He talked about Georgia and Joshua and felt sad that he no longer knew them.

Jonathan called in immediately after his release. He sat at the kitchen table, with his head in his hands, and wept. He wept most bitterly, and as I held him and tried to comfort him, I felt my own tears running silently down my cheeks.

'My head is blowing apart. I can't stand it much longer.'

'Please, darling Jonathan, go and see Frank or someone for help.'

He jerked away. 'Rhubarb, rhubarb, rhubarb, excuse me, when I come to see you that's all you talk about, fucking help, fucking psychiatrists.'

'I feel so helpless. What should I do?'

He shook his head.

I suggested that he started coming round again more regularly, a huge sigh of relief because I was scared. He was big for a start. And I had no sense of limits on what would happen if he did go off.'

The winter months passed with periodic crises and some quite long periods of calm. Georgia came back for weekends and so did Josh, and I remember one Sunday giving them a death notice I had cut out from the weekend newspaper.

> *Mothers are special and wonderfully wise,*
> *As she grows older, we look back with love,*
> *Knowing that mothers are gifts from above.*
> *And when she goes home to receive her reward,*
> *She will dwell in God's Kingdom and keep house for the Lord,*
> *Where she'll light up the stars that shine through the night,*
> *And keep all the moonbeams sparkling and bright.*
> *And then with the dawn she'll put the darkness away,*
> *As she scours the sun to new brilliance each day.*
> *So dry tears of sorrow, for mothers don't die,*
> *They just move in with God and keep house in the sky.*

days later, a woman member of an education committee I asked me, 'How do you combine your busy life with house I was tempted to give her the poem.

ber was spring, and blossom in the parklands, and the ng with green. Jonathan began striding to North Adelaide ain, over one bridge, back by another. September was 's birthday. He had remembered it, and so had I. I had book and a cassette, even though I knew it would I asked him what else he wanted. He said that he r the ballet. He was adamant about this. So I bought e ballet. As I had not been certain if he would show ared any special food, but when he said that he ay tea, we went and bought a cake and iced it It was a limp and depressing ceremony. I had tions. I do not know if he ever used the ballet r to find out. The birthday cake and asking eminded me painfully of those earlier times, to fly. Now his wings would not even lift

that he came for meals and to listen to music.

'Can I stay the night?' he said sharply.

'No, because I don't think it's good for either of us. Come during the day, but not at night.'

He got up and walked around. 'Humpty Dumpty sat on a wall . . . Humpty Dump . . . Dump, dump . . . And all the King's horse and all the King's men, couldn't put Humpty . . .' his voice trailed away. 'I suppose I'm luckier than most. I have nice clothes, and a nice home, and I look pretty good.'

I think I was about to say something about still needing help, but stopped myself just in time. If we keep telling people they need help, they will stay helpless. It must also have been profoundly demoralising for him to have conversation always focused on fixing up his illness.

Jonathan was looking at himself in the mirror and laughing. 'Jeez, I look rough.' He pulled at his hair which was long and straggling. 'Too long, and smelly.'

'Would you like me to trim it?'

'Yeah. And I'll wash it and have a shower, and I'd like some clean clothes.'

He came out of the bathroom with his hair shining, wearing one of the spare pair of jeans and T-shirts I kept in a plastic bag hanging in the back hall. He looked great. He took my arm and said, 'Take me for coffee.'

So we went for a walk, arm in arm, and sat in a coffee bar having cappuccinos. It was a brief respite. In the coffee bar he began to look anxiously around him. He frowned. He lowered his eyes. He closed his mouth tightly. He retreated. In front of my eyes he retreated. Poor Jonathan, trying valiantly once again to have a life like everyone else. But the horrors seemed always to be lurking.

On the way home he grabbed my arm. His eyes narrowed.

'Don't-go-down-there-you-fucking-stupid-bitch-don't-go-down-there-it's-a-fucking-uranium-mine.' There were tears in his eyes. 'It's a fucking terrible world.'

He started walking, faster and faster. I had to run to keep up with him. 'Fuck off,' he screamed. ' They're after me. Fuck off.' And he disappeared round the corner, running as if the Devil were at his heels.

Many people with schizophrenia talk about the feeling that their senses and sensitivities are exposed, vulnerable and raw; that it feels as if they bear all the evils of our world, coursing through their bodies and through their minds. Howard, a young doctor who has schizophrenia, writes to me his view of our 'normal' society:

*In a schizophrenic state:*

1. *Shooting animals for sport is mental illness*
2. *Driving a motor vehicle worth more than $60,000 is mental illness*
3. *Hoarding as though one can drink out of more than one glass at a time is mental illness and*
4. *Playing cricket, football and golf instead of doing something useful is clearly mental illness.*

On my birthday I went to Louey Mascara. Louey was a clairvoyant. She read gypsy cards, tarot cards, teacup leaves, the I Ching, runes and people. The best treat was when she read tiny scrolls of Chinese parchment, exquisitely lettered and stored upright in a beautifully made sandalwood box. Louey lived in a neat house with a neat path, flanked by upright roses and tidy shrubs. In the garden there were stone Buddhas and stone frogs and plastic dwarfs.

The inside of her house was festooned with religious statues of all kinds, from Buddha to Jesus. She had a singing canary, two budgerigars, and fed a tame magpie. Her house was always full of flowers and her china was decorated with orange roses and orange poppies.

Louey was a beautiful woman, somewhere in her late fifties, and like Betty, generously built and generous in her disposition. Her clothes were colourful, and she wore lots of Indian jewellery.

She told me that this year was the year of the dark night of the soul. Four years from now I would not be living in the same house. One key became two. Jonathan would journey into the outer reaches of space, and he might come back, but he might not. I neither believed Louey nor disbelieved her. What she had to say was not nearly as important as the way she said it, for Louey was a wise woman, who spoke in metaphor and gave sound counsel.

At the end of July I had work to do in Queensland, researching a film script. The architect came too, and we had a holiday afterwards, but it was not a relaxed time. I realise the architect has all but disappeared from my story, yet we were still clinging to the ritual

of our relationship and neither of us was yet ready to let go.

On our way home, we were in Sydney when Georgia rang, in tears. 'Jonathan is here and he's mad again. Um, I guess I'll be all right. Dean will be back soon.' A few minutes later she rang again: 'Oh no,' she said, 'He's singing to himself with the record player and I just can't stand it.'

Jonathan had been so much better lately that this flare-up was unexpected. I felt impotent because of the distance.

When I got home, Georgia talked more about what had happened. 'Jonathan sat in the kitchen and raved. He said, "Georgia, if you cross your legs and wear an earring it means you're a member of the PLO Crack Squad." And I said, "I cross my legs because it's more comfortable that way." So he looked at me and said, "You wouldn't be having me on, would you?"

'He kept going round saying, "Mustn't drop crumbs, mustn't make a mess, mustn't be a naughty boy, mustn't in the bath, naughty boy Jonathan."

'And I put his washing in the machine and said going now?" and he said, "Oh excuse I, I could in my underpants, now could I, George?"

'And he talked about you. He said, "A does look a bit battered. You might th battered, but she might have looked

Dean had then returned, and here.'

'Sorry mate, not at night.'

'I've got rights, haven'

Later, he broke a w of the beds. In the brought him tea "No staying th into the lau

Jonath these two Years later to meet. I was never be sure how when I remember get

him off the ground. I find that I have tears in my eyes.

In the beginning, writing this book was excruciatingly painful: like living the whole seven years through all its peaks and troughs, with no time out for the light and ordinary things of life. I thought I would have to abandon the book. I kept asking myself why I had not taken stronger action to get Jonathan hospitalised, or why I had not protected Georgia and Joshua better. Once I had the outline of the story down I found that I could be more removed. But every now and then I lose that distance and I am back – in this funny shabby house, with this tall loping young man, his face grey and ill-looking, his mind racing and exploding with a monstrous discordancy, and now like a plaintive child's, wanting his birthday cake and his birthday treat.

I had come to understand that Jonathan's terror was often huge. I learned to make plenty of space around him. If, when he came, I was frantic or fearful, it was better not to spend time with him, because my tension would exacerbate his. His acute sensitivity would detect the slightest hint of dissembling on my part; honesty was essential. This same sensitivity meant that he found it almost impossible to cope with too many questions, too many statements, too much of anything. He would explode or retreat. If my presence were calm, he would find calm. I had to recognise, though, that if he were psychotic, there was a limit to the extent I could contain him just by my presence.

One afternoon Jonathan came to the door, wearing his Tibetan jacket again. Don't ask me how he still had it, but there it was, and there was Jonathan, this time looking joyously colourful. As well as the jacket and jeans, he wore a pink Fair-Isle jumper, a black waistcoat, a yellow shirt, and a blue windcheater.

'Can I do some washing, please?'

'Sure.'

'Can I have something to eat?'

'Sure. Spaghetti okay? And there's some fruit. What have you been doing?'

'Nothing much.'

'How are you?'

'All right.' His hands were stained with nicotine. He held them under the table.

He ate his lunch in silence, and drank his tea in silence, and sat in silence for over two hours. Eventually I said, 'Talk to me.' He raised his head with a start, as if I had pulled him back into another world, and then he jerked to his feet and began walking round the kitchen and through the house as if he were participating in a race. He was talking so quickly it was hard to understand him, particularly as he did not once draw breath. In ten minutes he covered dictatorships in South America, Thatcher's Britain, Marxism and Communism, and corruption in the United States of America. The theme was exploitation and oppression. It was an impressive performance which he halted as suddenly as he had begun. He jackknifed from his considerable height and lay stretched out on the kitchen floor where he fell fast asleep. When Brenda called in for tea she nearly stumbled over him. She said, 'When you're an old lady and senile, he'll have recovered his sanity and be looking after you.'

*2 October*  Brenda and I went to a public meeting which had been called in order to form the first Schizophrenia Fellowship of South Australia. The hall was packed out, mainly with families seeking support and practical advice. At this meeting the young woman who said that she had cured herself with an orthomolecular approach stood up and urged everyone not to give up hope. She had learned to manage her illness, she said. She deserved an ovation for her courage. Instead I had a feeling people viewed her with sceptism; one of the problems of having a mental illness is that even in a sane period people will not take you seriously.

A few days later I went to meet people at the Victorian Schizophrenia Fellowship, which was the first Australian group to get under way, and already had a network of support groups. I wanted to find out the best way that I, as a journalist, could help. The tales that relatives told sounded familiar. I felt relieved that at least our abnormal experiences were normal. A woman was asking about how to deal with her nineteen-year-old son.

'If he plays up, put on your coat and leave him,' said someone.

'What if I find the window broken when I get back?'

'Better than you being broken.'

'They gave me tablets for him to take but never any kind of back-up. I thought we could manage. Three months and he was off the planet and so was I.'

A thin woman with sad eyes said, 'My son wanted me to say I was the Virgin Mary, but I couldn't. And now he's run away, and he's only eighteen.'

Next door a group of young people with schizophrenia were discussing their problems. They sat around the room in a cloud of cigarette smoke, some were withdrawn and gazed down at the floor, others were animated and kept the conversation moving. Many had involuntary movements of their arms and legs – side-effects from their medication.

'I want to come off my medication,' said a pale young man in a low voice.

The others were sympathetic but advised him against it. When he insisted, they tried to get him to discuss it with his psychiatrist and to get support from his friends.

A woman who carried a note-pad and pencil, said eagerly that she wanted everyone to help her hold a Fancy Hat Dance. 'Yeah,' said a young man with keen eyes that darted around the room, 'if you haven't got a head, get a hat.'

Margaret Leggatt, director of the Fellowship said, 'Confront the problem, and the earlier the better, before the illness becomes chronic and the family is torn apart.' She said that this was difficult for our culture. We do not set limits when someone is sick, and we 'do' things for sick people instead of encouraging them also to take responsibility for themselves. Some years back Margaret conducted a major research study, as part of her doctorate thesis in sociology, looking at what happened in families when a son or daughter was diagnosed as suffering from schizophrenia. 'I found that research a shattering experience. I could not believe that there were so many families out there coping with probably the most difficult illness that I can think of. Sons and daughters were developing really bizarre symptoms, so that their behaviour was disorganised and very frightening, but their parents were getting no help or support. Instead, they got terrible blame.' Margaret has since been a major force in helping to establish Schizophrenia Fellow-ships around Australia. She is a woman in her early fifties, charming, tenaciously persuasive, and capable of fierce anger and exasperation at the neglect of schizophrenia.

When I arrived back from Melbourne, I found Jonathan was at home with a friend called George – 'Call me Grizzly Bear, call me Griz.' Griz had long hair in a ponytail at the back, and short hair cut into a stubble at the front. He had very blue eyes. Griz and Jonathan sat in the kitchen and smoked their way through a pack of cigarettes. Griz wore an army greatcoat, and a grey waistcoat with pearl buttons. He was heavily tattooed, mostly with romantic messages and drawings of hearts and roses. Even his fingers and his ears were tattooed.

Griz said, 'Joe will be all right, 'cos I am a healer. No one else will live with him because his pacing drives them nuts.'

'I do it to block out the sounds I don't want to hear,' said Jonathan who was again wearing several jumpers of assorted hue.

'I don't mind him pacing because I can block him out with my pictures. I see things in colour. Pink means stop. Green means stay. And I can look at you and project someone else's picture on your face.'

Griz rolled a cigarette. Joe rocked back and forth. Griz continued, 'I'm gentle. I don't harm anyone. They let me come and go at the hospital because they know me. I first went there seven years ago when I tried to kill myself because my best friend had died in a head-on collision with a lorry. I was only a boy. Now the psychiatrists are really interested in me, because they try to make sense of my visions. I've been touched by God.'

'By God?' I asked, pouring the tea.

'It happened when this rope appeared out of nowhere. I knew it was meant for me. If it burns at both ends, it means you go into infinity, but if it only burns at one, it means you've still got time on this earth.' Jonathan giggled.

Griz continued. 'Sometimes I click. I click all over. I have these callouses on my fingers and thumbs and its because of the clicking. Sometimes my back clicks.'

'I am in bands sometimes, punk bands. The last one was called Murder Weapons. A film crew came once and they were interested in me, but that was when I was good-looking. Now I have no teeth and tattoos. So I make my own films. I close my eyes and I can see it all. I can look at people and know what they're thinking about.

'My father and mother died when I was thirteen. My mother ran off with a Jugoslav. She kept saying she'd go and we didn't believe her. My dad married again. I was the eldest, and I looked after my eight brothers and sisters. I was always teased at school and beaten up because I was different. Then my dad committed me and he didn't want to know about me any more.' Griz sighed. Liza was lying on his greatcoat and, when he and Jonathan left, he insisted on leaving his coat for the dog.

Jonathan came back several times with Griz. They were sharing a room together, and Griz had become protective. 'I'm going to make it really nice. We've got a bit of carpet from the welfare, and candles and some flowers we took from the trees in the square.

'Joe will be all right, but it will take time. When I heal someone I take on their illness after a while. I'm on downers to calm me, otherwise I'm pretty psychotic. Joe wears too many clothes. It's not healthy. Look after him. He's okay. He thinks differently. Like me. That's all. Don't worry.'

Griz stopped coming and Jonathan said he had gone interstate to escape his visions. They had been giving him a rough time, he said. Griz wasn't the only one; Jonathan's visions also seemed to be causing trouble.

On 8 November the neighbours called the police because Jonathan was standing on the footpath making so much noise that they could not sleep. The police came but as usual did not take him to hospital. We did not know where he went.

I had come to a decision a few weeks earlier that it was time to leave Adelaide. The architect and I saw very little of each other now. We had exhausted the goodbyes and the reconciliations. My work had run downhill and I felt if I went to Sydney I would have more chance of earning a reasonable living again. Joshua only had two more years of schooling so it was not a bad time for him to move, and Georgia was about to enter her final year at university and could share the Adelaide house with friends, and then join us in Sydney if she wished. I did not know what Jonathan would want to do.

I planned to fly to Europe with Georgia and Joshua, see my brothers, one of whom lived in Sweden and the other in Italy, and return in January in time to pack up our belongings and leave for

Sydney. I had even made an offer on a Sydney house. I had thought carefully about leaving Jonathan, but the truth seemed to be that whether we were around or not made little apparent difference to the state of his mind, but it made a huge difference to mine. I discussed it with Brenda and with Jonathan, and tried to persuade him to move out of the squats and into one of the Salvation Army Hostels during the period we were away in Europe. I was still not supposed to interfere in his life, but I did not like to think of him with no place to go, so I arranged to pay for his board for the next couple of months, even if he did not use it. I knew it would be difficult to explain to Jonathan why I was taking his brother and sister, and leaving him behind. He would feel it was one more example of the bitterness of his situation. But I could not go on living my life around his, and I told him that I was not taking him because I did not feel he was well enough to come. He appeared not to listen. He turned up on the morning that we left, and I felt mean and wretched. I remember him that day wandering off into the parklands, a solitary figure in faded blue jeans, his jacket hitched over his shoulders, his head bowed, his feet dragging on the ground.

Seven
# *The Ideological Din*

*Where is the life we have lost in the living,*
*Where is the wisdom we have lost in knowledge,*
*Where is the knowledge we have lost in information?*
T. S. ELIOT

*January 1984*  When Georgia, Joshua and I arrived back from overseas, Jonathan was on the front verandah of our house, pacing up and down. Brenda had collected him from one of the squats.

Jonathan looked well and pleased to see us. He wore jeans, hitched up with a tie round his middle and his usual odd assortment of T-shirts and jumpers, and said vaguely that he had been living with friends. Because I hadn't seen him for some time, it was like meeting him anew. I was struck by his unpredictability. One minute he would be drinking tea with us in the kitchen, the next racing round the house, picking things up and putting them down, and twice disappearing in the middle of a sentence to take a shower.

Joshua and I were due to leave for Sydney in two weeks' time, but during those first few days back in Adelaide, I felt as if I were not yet ready to go. I walked up and down the beach, trying to make up my mind.

I tried visualising life in Sydney, but I saw nothing. I came home and announced that we would stay in Adelaide. I realised this was a complete about-face and that everyone would be angry with me. They were. But coming back had felt like coming home. I knew also that while I was away I had created a fantasy that the architect and I would be able to find true love again.

The architect said, 'Stop writing me into your scripts.'

'But they're loving scripts,' I said hopefully.

'Yes, but they're yours, not mine,' he said. He had already met someone else.

193

For a while I made myself feel better by plotting childish revenge, like spraying his car with graffiti or infiltrating millipedes into his house, despite the fact that when I went overseas, I had already said goodbye. I was glad, anyway, that I had made the decision to stay on in Adelaide.

A few days later, a Buddhist nun called Janey turned up at our house and sat cross-legged on the floor, talking about madness and drinking herbal tea. Once she had been an actress I knew in Sydney and I had met her again by chance the previous day at the Adelaide markets. Her head was shaven, her eyes were deep blue. She said she had recently been committed to a psychiatric hospital and that this had caused deep trauma. I felt defensive and told her that I had several times committed Jonathan and would do so again if I thought it were necessary. She listened and replied gravely that she was sure I would do whatever was right.

While she was talking, Jonathan wandered in and squatted on the floor. Janey was talking about the ashram in the Adelaide hills where she lived. Jonathan was interested. He peered at her through his tangled hair. 'You seem like a nice lady, are you mad?'

'There is no such thing as mad. There are altered states of consciousness.'

Jonathan said, 'What's your politics?'

'I'm a Buddhist nun.'

'A spy?'

'No, a Buddhist nun. You should come to our ashram.'

'Why?'

'It is a place of peace. You could work in the gardens.'

'How much do they give you?'

'You give them.'

'How much?'

'Sixty dollars a week.'

'Sixty bucks! If you're doing the work, how come they don't pay you?'

Jonathan closed his eyes. He began talking to himself. 'Now see here, Joe, you need a place to get your head together – good food, good living, safe place, nice lady. . . . Yeah, but sixty bucks? Yeah, but you do have problems, Joe, your head's all wired . . . but sixty fucking bucks . . . hey, that's a rip-off.'

Janey looked calmly at him. 'It's your choice,' she said. Jonathan walked out of the room.

Janey had self-published a large paperback book called *HELP!* The book invited people to share Responses, Ideas, Questions, Herbal Tea, Fruit Juice, Ecco, Laughter, Love, Tears, Peace, Janey. *HELP!* was printed backwards. It would have been easy to smile at its naivety, but *HELP!* was the story of one person's experience with asylum, and I remember again Jonathan's remark the year before, 'Jail is heavy. Hospital is humiliating.'

In *HELP!* Janey wrote:

*I was threatened, talked down to, treated as if I had no intelligence, allowed no privacy, and a lifestyle that had taken me 33 years to carve out for myself was scornfully dismissed.. During my first few days I was whisked off without warning by several strange doctors and quizzed as if I was in a concentration camp for idiots. They kept firing ridiculous questions at me, like 'Who is the Prime Minister of Australia?' 'What does it mean "People in glass houses should not throw stones?"' I am still having trouble with that one. I was told to wear a nightie and a dressing gown for the first twenty-four hours. Fortunately I did not possess one. As an insane person, one has no rights, is afforded no dignity. In spite of requests not to, the majority of staff insisted on calling me Janet.*

*The drugs made me feel like a rotting vegetable. I was terribly tired, but I wasn't allowed to rest. Never. Patients always have to be seen to be doing something, yet there is never anything appropriate to do. We were always being urged to 'go bowling' or to be made up by a beautician. I would never want to do these things. Why should I be forced to when I am in hospital? Why should I be told I am not co-operative when I refuse?*

*I went into the laundry and got the squeezy washing container and squirted the liquid soap out all over the sink, symbolically trying to get rid of the blackness I felt surrounding me. Blackness was literally closing me in.*

*When doctors learn how to love, and to stop being so scared about becoming involved with the patients, they could then truly learn how to heal. At the present time, the kitchen staff and the cleaners are the ones where warmth flickers the most.*

Janey's writing exemplifies the rejection by so many people of psychiatric hospitals. It is not that the hospitals are bad. It is not that the staff are cruel. Mostly they are dedicated people who do a difficult job for not much money and little acknowledgement. But few hospitals succeed in providing the best kind of environment for sick and frightened people to get better.

One morning, not long after Janey's visits, Jonathan called by in a dirty and dishevelled state. He had a gold stud in his nose, and wore one earring from which dangled the cat's bell. He was talking rapidly to himself, 'This is Jonathan talking to Jonathan. Roger, over and out. Jonathan, can you hear me, Jonathan? I am lonely, Jonathan. Roger. Over and out.' I spoke to Brenda, who said she felt he was becoming psychotic again.

January he was well. February he deteriorated. March brought my appointment as chairperson of the South Australian Film Corporation and chairperson of the government's Children's Interest Bureau. The Minister of Community Welfare, Greg Crafter, had called round one Friday evening to ask if I would help get the Bureau going. I thought he should know of Jonathan's police record and the fact that it might happen again. The Minister said that my experiences with Jonathan were one of the reasons he had asked me. The two appointments brought several media interviews. In one, I was sitting in the front room of our house, answering questions about juvenile delinquency. Out of the corner of my eye I saw a foot appearing over the window sill. A foot in a black and rotting gym boot. A foot, a leg, an arm, a face at the window. A grimy face, almost hidden by hair. Through the window the spectre crawled and slipped silently across the room, behind the camera. No one noticed. I breathed a sigh of relief.

Two minutes later there was a knock on the door, Jonathan entered. 'Excuse me, excuse me, I am a triple certificated psychiatric black belt and I am on a diet of water and black magic.' He bowed elaborately, shook hands with the interviewer, the camera person and the sound recordist, and left.

Joshua was coming home from boarding school most weekends, and sometimes brought friends to the house. He often looked anxious, and I thought he might be worried that Jonathan might suddenly appear. One Sunday I was in the kitchen, clattering my way through a pile of dishes, and Josh and three friends had just made themselves orange drinks. Jonathan wandered in, talking very earnestly to himself. He had tied numbers of strings and ribbons around his wrists to ward off the evil eye, and he had a beanie pulled low over his brows, even though it was a warm day. When Jonathan wore a beanie like this it was to insulate himself, from both the forces of the outside world and the voices of his inner world. After he had left, Joshua's friends said, 'Who's he?' and giggled.

I felt my neck muscles become tense. I wondered what Joshua would reply. Josh said casually, 'Oh, he's my brother Jonathan.'

'What's up with him?'

'He's got schizophrenia. It's a mental illness,' said Josh, sounding as if he'd said 'It's a sprained ankle.'

Oh wondrous moment, well done Joshua! And I smiled around the house for the rest of the day. I have not written much about Georgia and Joshua, largely out of respect for their privacy. For a long while, I did not know what they thought or felt because when I asked them they did not tell me. Their feelings were locked away. Perhaps the only place they felt safe was inside themselves. Perhaps that is true for all of us – except for those who have an illness like schizophrenia which takes even that inner sanctuary away. But Joshua's directness was one of several indications that gradually, we were all beginning to be more open about our lives. Even Jonathan could talk sit on the kitchen floor, blanket around his shoulders, and talk with a stranger – Janey, the Buddhist nun – about his wired-up head.

In between coming home at weekends, Joshua was writing cheerfully grumbling letters from school which made me feel good whenever I received them.

*Dear Anne,*

*Every weekend I have to write a stupid letter. It's quite pointless because I waste 27c every time I write. I usually see or speak to you and they make me write this dumb letter too. I've spent all this time talking about this absurd letter. I honestly think it's all so pointless. All this ink has been wasted. I'll probably have to buy a new pen!*

Summer shimmered into autumn, with little change in Jonathan's condition. A woman rang from the Adelaide Unemployed Youth Centre and said did I know that my son Jonathan was living in Adelaide. Yes, I said, I did. Oh, she said, sounding surprised and disbelieving. Then did I also know that Jonathan was attending the Centre, and was anxious to improve his lifestyle.

'Fantastic,' I said.

'We think his problems are just a matter of poor self-esteem,' she said coldly.

'Yes,' I said, because I could not raise the energy to say anything else. She then rang Brenda who advised her to take things at Jonathan's pace or he would back off and disappear. Jonathan called round and was exuberant about the Centre. He said he could do pottery and leather-work there. He suggested we went for a walk. The late afternoon sun was still hot on our shoulders and bees were busy in the rose gardens. Jonathan smelt a large pink cabbage rose, of the kind that must surely have been called Dame Josephine or Lady Clara, then he spat on the pavement, first to the left then to the right.

'What do you do that for, Jonathan?'

'I am killing my enemies.'

Two weeks later Jonathan was asked to leave the Centre. The social worker rang to say he did not fit in. 'His behaviour, manner and appearance are inappropriate, and we are losing quite a few of our other participants. If he wants to join the world he will have to change.'

*3 April*   Brenda wrote:
*Jonathan in office, looking very dirty but making sense. Wanted money for mattress, blankets and some clothes as he says he only has the clothes he is wearing. Phoned Public Trustee office, who were most reluctant to authorise expenditure. They gave me the impression that Jonathan was not entitled to the money, even though it is his!*

In April we were given three months' notice to quit South Terrace because the house was wanted for offices. Jonathan had been coming round two or three times a week but, without explanation, the visits stopped. I made enquiries through the police, at the hostels and the squats but no one had seen him.

At the end of April I received a phone-call very late at night. The voice was high-pitched and dramatic, 'Good evening, darling. I'm

Louis the hypnotist and I am ringing from Sydney. I thought you'd like to know that I have someone here who you're very fond of. You mustn't be angry with him. It's your son Jonathan.

'I make films darling, and Jonathan is a very beautiful young man with lots of talent. We are all very excited about him. We're living in the biggest house in Bellevue Hill, and he can stay here as long as he likes. He has just had chicken and champagne. I know he's a bit mixed up especially after being kicked out of home, but I promise I won't blackmail you, darling. Not even a teensy bit. What you have to say to me?'

'Leave Jonathan alone.'

'You aren't cross with me, darling?'

'Leave Jonathan alone,' I said in cold fury.

Jonathan came on the phone. His voice was dim and furry, as if he were speaking from the end of a long tunnel: 'Hello Anne.' I heard a click and the phone went dead. The silence lasted a long time. I went to the kitchen and made tea, banging the spoon in the teapot and scalding myself as I drank.

A few days after I'd heard from Louis the hypnotist, I had to go to Sydney, and I went straight to Matthew Talbot, the hostel for homeless men where Jonathan most often stayed. I need to tell you about the Talbot because it became important to Jonathan and important to me. It was built in depression times and is a brick building that has grown in all directions, upwards and downwards, in a part of Sydney known as Woolloomooloo. This area was once subject to the seediness of all industrial waterside areas. Today large parts have become gentrified; but the Talbot remains and I hope it is never exiled to the suburbs in the pious hope that its residents will follow. They won't go. They enjoy the anonymity of city living, and the excitement of nearby Kings Cross with its strident mixture of nightclubs, cafés and refuges of all kinds.

At any hour of the day or night, there will be bodies stretched outside the Talbot, on the pavements, leaning against the walls, or in the patch of green that passes for a park. White bodies, black bodies, drunken bodies, lame bodies, old men who still cling tenaciously to life, and young men for whom life may still hold promise.

On this particular late afternoon, a cluster of men were catching the last rays of sunshine before going inside. Drink bottles and cans littered the footpath. A stocky little man with bandy legs rolled his way purposefully down the laneway on his way to book a bed for the night. And there, right outside the entrance to the Talbot, sat a familiar figure, a tall lanky young man with a dilly bag by his side and a multi-coloured striped beanie on the top of his head. He was examining a bare and grubby foot. He looked up at me and grinned. 'Hallo Anne.'

I went up and hugged him. 'How are you?'

'Spinning out.'

'Have you left Louis the hypnotist?'

'Yeah,' he said. And looked even more closely at his foot. 'He was a rip-off.'

I asked Jonathan if he wanted to come back to Adelaide with me. He said No, he liked Kings Cross. I felt apprehensive about leaving him in Sydney and went inside to find Ray Bourke, one of the managers of the Talbot, and someone I had known ever since I had made a documentary about homeless men some years previously.

The first notice you see as you enter the Talbot is written on a blackboard in white chalk, *Everyone MUST shower and use some soap.* The main office checks new arrivals, and if they are 'under the influence' (drunk) or drugged, they have to go to an area known as the Annexe for seven hours to cool off. Everyone else is admitted, although another notice near the canteen says, *You are asked not to seek a bed here if you have got a job and received your first pay.*

The Talbot offers:

*Accommodation and pyjamas; All meals;*
*Clothing; Showers and towels; Soap and razor;*
*Laundry facilities; Medical clinic; Luggage storage;*
*AA meetings; Money security; Half-way houses;*
*plus other services.*

If I were adding to that list, I would include friendship and care. On this particular day, when I went to find Ray he was on the telephone, saying, 'I think he's also saying he's prepared to go on medication again – because he's feeling so bad with his illness. It's important we handle it right.' Ray is a lay-brother of the order of St Vincent de Paul. Like so many of the helpers around the place, he is a voluntary worker. He is a big cheerful man with a bald head and a reassuring sense of solidity. Ray promised to keep an eye on Jonathan and said that he could be sure of a bed whenever he wanted. He said they sent people out looking for the regulars if they didn't turn up after a couple of nights. They were vulnerable, and were often robbed or bashed. *Oh God, don't let Jonathan sleep on the streets. Don't let him end up in a drain-pipe or floating upside down in the harbour. Find him, Ray Bourke, find him wherever he is and bring him back safe.*

When I returned to Adelaide, it was June and mid-winter. I began research for three one-hour radio programs about schizophrenia for the ABC's Science Show program to be called, 'One in a Hundred'. The new television series about women, which I had made the previous year, went to air. And the removalists came. While we were packing up, I looked at the lists by the telephone and on the fridge door, which had accumulated over the years, and wondered now that Jonathan was in Sydney whether I would need them again. The lists had grown and now included therapeutic communities with names like Laughing Waters and Rainbow's End, the Hari Krishnas, welfare officers from the jails, a plant nursery that might give work, caravan parks all over Australia, and the owner of a pizza shop in North Adelaide who had offered to let Jonathan live on his farm and help pick tomatoes.

The move to a new house was bearable mainly because we found ourselves living in the most welcoming of all our Adelaide homes, in a street lined with acacia trees, where old men and women walked slowly and carefully and children wobbled on their bicycles. The corner store sold sweets in bottles and locally grown fruit. The storekeeper wore a black wig, fashioned in early Beatles' style. The house was a generously built stone villa, with deep pink and apricot stained glass, and a garden full of fruit trees and roses. It was a house of peace and plenty. Josh moved home, and Georgia lived close by.

One morning I received a phone call from a close friend in Sydney. She had just been told that her seventeen-year-old-son had schizophrenia. He was very tall, this young man, with a sensitive face, and dark in his beauty as Jonathan had been fair.

'When I went away to work it happened: he had an attack. Took off his clothes, went to the house of these friends and appeared in their bedroom late at night, naked. They called the police. He went to hospital. He jumped the wall, and we all ran after him, down the road. When he came home, later, he said he was going to walk to Melbourne. He kept saying, "A man's got to do it".'

My friend walked by her son's side, late at night and in the pouring rain. Her son said, 'You won't be able to make it. I'll carry you.' They were wet and cold. They walked some more. My friend suggested it might be better to drive than walk. He agreed, and so they turned back to get the car. When they reached home, he said, 'The human being has tremendous potential because it is harnessed to energy. That energy can make you fly. Boil a cup of milk,' he said, 'to help my energy.'

'Yes dear,' she said, 'yes dear.' She boiled the milk, and he went to bed.

A few years earlier, the same friend and I had been driving through Adelaide together when we had passed Jonathan stalking along the road, regardless of the traffic. We had stopped and given him a lift. He had asked after my friend's son, who was then only about twelve or thirteen and apparently quite normal. 'He's like me, you know,' said Jonathan. 'The same as me.' I had thought, 'I hope not,' and my friend must fervently have thought the same but she was too polite to say anything. Most people with schizophrenia, however well they are managing, are able to recognise the illness in each other. Jonathan it seemed had recognised the illness before it had even manifested.

July was busy. Apart from the radio documentaries, I was now developing a proposal for a book on schizophrenia. Some time during this month, I went up to Sydney for a couple of days, and headed first for the Talbot where I was told that a psychiatrist was now running regular clinics. Ray thought it would be a good idea if I talked with the psychiatrist. Neil Buhrich was a youngish man, dark, with a mobile face and a quietly ironic sense of humour. I liked him. Jonathan was also at the clinic, pacing up and down an exceedingly small room, while two nurses and Buhrich and I watched and listened. For five minutes he held forth about the wickedness of his fucking mother. She was the black toad at the end of the tunnel, the scream at the top of a cliff, the arsehole of the world, the witch to end all witches. Suddenly the tirade stopped.

Jonathan looked around him with some sense of triumph. Buhrich said, 'I take it you're not very pleased with your mother.' Everyone burst out laughing.

Jonathan also giggled. 'Yair, I reckon,' he said, and then suggested we went outside for a Coke. We sat in the canteen underneath plaster statues of Jesus and Mary. A burly man in singlet and stubbies and wearing a green baize apron was setting the tables for tea. In an adjoining space, rows of men, young and old, were watching television.

Jonathan had found a straw to drink his Coke, and blew into it making bubbles. He grinned with delight. 'I think I should tell you that in a manner of speaking, I have taken up spitting again. Yesterday, I spat on the ground and it was a good spit, a volatile spit and it smelt of Dobermann.'

His voice was speeding up. Thoughts were clearly racing through his brain and his speech was trying to keep up with them. 'In the Darlinghurst Police Station, I killed fifteen coppers, so if you don't believe me, you'll have to go and find out. I am a member of the IRA, the Red Brigade, the PLO and the KGB. I am in good nick. Good solid jail nick. A girl gave me this bracelet. She's my au pair and she is a prostitute in a nice way. I am going to attack the juvenile black bar for not being helpful to me. It will take a lot of gentleness and love. I have three brains. Maybe four.'

In some ways, Jonathan had made progress in the four months since he had been living at the Talbot. It was the first time he had remained in stable accommodation of his own free will, and the first time that he had asked for medication. This was an immense step forward. In other ways he was worse. His physical health had deteriorated, he had bad sores on his legs and arms and, in a big city, he was much more vulnerable to harrassment than he had been in Adelaide. Once or twice he was beaten up. But he seemed far more settled than I could remember. Matthew Talbot suited Jonathan because it imposed no demands upon him. So many psychiatric programs have unreal expectations. They require people to conform to standards which perhaps they cannot meet, or to fit neatly into one diagnostic category. A more integrated philosophy and approach would mean that mentally ill people who have physical problems, and physically ill people with mental problems, and all the rest of us who can't be tidied up to suit bureaucratic needs, would get cared for in holistic ways. At the Talbot, Jonathan and people like Jonathan, the frail, the vulnerable, the poor, the unwanted, the non-conformist, can find acceptance.

I felt I was beginning to breathe again. Georgia and Joshua were both going well in Adelaide. Josh was still at school, Georgia at university. The house was a lovely place to live. And I was enjoying my work. I decided that in October I would go overseas to research both the book and the radio series. I would begin by attending an International Symposium on the Psychotherapy of Schizophrenia to be held at the Yale University School of Medicine in October. After Yale, I would go to New York and then zigzag my way across the States, taking in Toronto, and then to London. It wasn't a particularly structured visit in a research sense, but it would give me a flavour of current medical views, and I wanted to see how people were coping with the illness in North America and in England.

I found myself in New England at one of the best times of the year, with maple leaves turning scarlet, crisp mornings and clear blue skies. The symposium was held in a large wood-panelled hall, with red seats and a duck-egg blue carpet in the auditorium. I turned up for the keynote address by Theodore Lidz. Lidz was then in his seventies, and was still a powerful man. He lumbered up to the podium, emanating confidence. He said the conference came at a critical time in the history of schizophrenia. One hundred years of biological research had led us up blind alleys; schizophrenia was not a dysfunction in the brain; the fault was more likely in the programming than the hardware.

Lidz claimed he had traced the illness to the suffocating attention of mothers who, by living through their children, prevented them from developing a separate identity. He had developed the concept of 'marital skew': believing that when this type of mother was partnered by a submissive, indifferent, or negligent father, lack of what he called 'a firm parental coalition' led the parents to compete for the child's loyalty and affection, and caused the child to have a confused or inadequate ego base. Towards the end of his keynote address Lidz also had a blast at schizophrenogenic mothers, and described them as domineering, over-protective, over-involved and hostile. He was right about hostile.

One of the next sesssions was a family session, where a panel of experts were discussing case histories. I arrived to hear a male voice pronounce, 'It is my concern that schizophrenics have feelings just the same as anyone else.' The panel was discussing a young man called Joseph. The psychiatrist, presenting Joseph's story in a dry well-mannered voice, informed us that Joseph had been a conformist, socially regressed and under-developed child, who had shared the parental bed. Now, as a young man, Joseph was intelligent, verbal, sensitive and depressed. He was attractive to psychotherapists because of his intelligence. Joseph had fellatio fantasies, masturbation fantasies, passive anal intercourse fantasies, persecution complexes, delusional masochism, and his mission was to be the familial victim.

Joseph's problems were seen to stem from maternal dependency. We were told he had an aggressive, domineering, hard-to-please father, and a mother who had the kind of murderous maternal behaviour that made you shiver.

A therapist who wore gold-rimmed glasses, a dark-blue suit and a pink-striped shirt, and who spoke in a heavy Viennese accent, said solemnly, 'I would tell Joseph, it is absolutely forbidden to mingle your bodies.' The panel nodded approvingly.

The presenting psychiatrist was beginning to sound anxious. 'I came in touch with the unnameable. I was pushed to the limit which is the limit beyond which one cannot go at the risk of death. I began to feel disgust. I saw death, or chronic illness, lingering in the back-wards.'

Theodore Lidz lumbered up to the front. He proclaimed, 'The boy wanted impregnation by the therapist to incorporate his father. This is not unknown amongst New Guinea tribes. This must be addressed.'

I leave the hall for black coffee with two sugars. Normally, I never take sugar.

Later, I attended a seminar on misconceptions about psychotherapy and schizophrenia. The psychiatrist who gave this session was a big man with a powerful personality, thick black curly hair and a loud voice. He said that people with schizophrenia live in chronic terror. 'The first thing I tell my patients is that I will not let anyone kill you. Catatonic stupor is a special state of overwhelming terror. It is a successful evolutionary device. Reptiles become catatonic when terrified.'

I wrote *CHRONIC TERROR* in my notebook. *Oh Jonathan, oh yes, sometimes I could touch your terror.*

This psychiatrist was also pungent about parents: 'If you spend time with schizophrenic families, you see they are mixed up and ill. None of these families provides the essentials. All communicate defectively. They are intrusive and impervious of the child as a separate individual.'

A young man with red hair and a bushy ginger beard said that the notion of chemical imbalance was a myth. 'Chemically imbalanced people cannot dialogue.'

I wrote, *But perhaps they can talk?*

Red Beard continued: 'People invest in psychoses as a life choice. Therapy has low visiblity. So what have we been reduced to? Dispensing drugs?'

A white-haired woman raises her hand. 'How many of you were in hospital before 1955? By the grace of the new medication, thousands were given a chance of living for the first time since their illness began.'

A very young and earnest woman in the audience said, 'We need to dialogue with the biochemical therapists. Psychiatry has turned the clock back one hundred years, to a time when we believed little could be done. But many schizophrenics become both productive and sociable.' She gave upmarket examples of people who had beaten the illness and were now professors, symphony orchestra players, college students. 'They no longer play their mothers' poisonous games.'

Anger and guilt flooded my being. I tried to hold onto the anger but I was still too cowed to make any kind of statement from the floor. Instead I sneaked around, hoping no one would discover my true identity as a noxious parent, and then I met a fellow culprit, one who apparently had much more confidence than I. His name was Adam, and his son Daniel had schizophrenia. Adam was a businessman in playful mood. He wore Gucci jeans, high-heeled boots and lots of silver jewellery.

I also met Martin, a young psychologist from Pittsburgh, Pennsylvania. His neatness and precision was carefully wrapped around a zany sense of humour. Martin prefaced his sentences with 'I don't know if you notice . . . It seems to me . . .' He had been well trained in communication skills. He belonged to the newer professional breed who saw the problem of schizophrenia as multi-factorial. He said people were looking for direction. 'When someone is ill, everyone is looking for us to say, "Do this and it will be better." '

*Spot on, Martin. Do this and it will be better.* Instead of that void of helplessness where you feel so alone. I liked Martin. He talked about his patients as people, not as cases. Some two years later, when he was feeling burned out by his work, he wrote to me:

*Those of us who work in the trenches in the US mental health system bear the stigmata along with those who suffer with mental agony and who bear our treatment. I work with the most remarkably gifted, creative and compassionate people who are looked upon with disrespect by the rest of the hospital community.*

I went to a workshop run by a psychiatrist called Loren Mosher who looked to me like Groucho Marx. He was dressed in a crumpled linen jacket, and radiated an infectious warmth and enthusiasm. Mosher was folk-hero and veteran of many mental-health wars. Late golden sun streamed through the windows of a dark-panelled room which was packed out.

Mosher had focused much of his work in establishing effective healing environments. He believed in setting up ordinary houses in ordinary suburbs, with a high staff-to-patient ratio and minimal hierarchy. 'You have positive expectations. You focus on giving your client increasing responsibility. You have clearly defined practical goals that everyone understands – like "Don't piss on the floor", "Don't hit people." You follow people through into the community and you build up an extensive network of support.

'Our staff are trained "to be with", not "to do". Having to do something is usually based on staff anxiety, not on patient needs.'

As Mosher spoke I remember Janey, the Buddhist nun, and all those afternoons with Jonathan when I had found the best way of reaching him was simply by being with him, not by trying to fix him up.

Mosher said, "Treat people as normal, like them, be warm and friendly, and they will have much more chance of getting better than if you treat them as sick and keep as far away from them as possible.'

I went to plenty of other lectures and workshops and, by the end, it seemed to me as if the old guard were on the way out. I have concentrated on writing about the beliefs of the old guard because, as personalities, they still held such sway at the symposium. But new approaches were gaining acceptance.

Back in New York, I met Muriel Shepherd and Ros Rosnan, representatives from the National Alliance for the Mentally Ill, the biggest mental illness advocacy group in the United States. Muriel was a journalist, a wiry woman in her fifties with long greying hair. She sounded vague but wasn't. She had a daughter of twenty-nine with schizophrenia. Ros talked admiringly of how much Muriel had achieved.

Ros was a retired teacher and a widow. Her only son had schizoprenia. She was large, Jewish, asthmatic, with a self-deprecatory sense of humour.

'My son has said, "You shit, I'm going to murder you." And I've said, "Anything else troubling you?" ' Ros had dark circles under her eyes and didn't look well. She invited me to a monthly parents' meeting at St James's Church, Madison Avenue.

Muriel said that only twenty per cent of people in the United States acknowledge that schizophrenia is a biological disorder. She said what NAMI needed was a celebrity whose child had schizophrenia. A film star had done a commentary for a documentary called *Interrupted Lives,* but had not come out in the open about the schizophrenia that was allegedly in his family. 'Families are so dreadfully isolated. It's the feeling it will go on and on forever, without a break. This country is so health-oriented, we find it hard to accept the idea of long-term illness. But we're beginning to know that people do get better as they get older.'

Ros leaned back in her chair. 'By that time I'll be dead.'

I talked about Australia. Ros said, 'My, oh my, it's the same story.' We arranged to meet at an Association gathering at St James's Church in two days' time. St James's is an upmarket church but the people who went there that night were all ages and backgrounds. Many look tired, the kind of tired that had become a way of life. There were raffles at the door, a babble of voices and then the chairperson, who wore glasses that looked as if they would fly off into orbit, demanded quiet. She was obeyed.

The guest speaker was a plump, sandy-haired psychologist who ran a New York psychiatric day centre. He said he had a doctoral degree and spoke from two decades of experience. He was not untouched by mental illness: his younger brother had Down's syndrome and had been able to live all his life with his parents. Relatives of the mentally retarded were way ahead of the mentally ill in learning to cope and in lobbying, and their experience ought to be used.

The audience questioned him vigorously, 'We all know about those people who come into hospital at 11.30 and are out again by 12.30. Like a football. What are your priorities?'

The psychologist said, 'With some trepidation I make my position clear, although it might not be popular. I feel there has been too strong a biochemical bias taken by organisations like yours.'

A woman said, 'My daughter gets given so many drugs, it would put an elephant in a coma. She is my only child. She comes from a happy home.' She was weeping and wringing her hands.

The psychologist said that it took time to adjust medication. He swayed backwards a little, 'Please do not misunderstand me, I am not advocating abolition of hospitals, but we need to be aware that closing off normal social networks makes re-entry into life very difficult. Hospitals tend to be hierarchical and a premium is placed on social control because of over-crowding, whereas it is important to give patients as much opportunity as possible to run their own lives.'

A white-haired elderly woman asked with great intensity, 'How do you get someone to accept help? How do you get someone to go to a day centre?'

'I wish I knew. I'd bottle it and sell it,' said the psychologist sadly. 'Resistance to treatment is a self-protective behaviour. I level with the person and say you are a free agent.'

By the time Ros and I left the church it was dark, and a cold wind was blowing. Ros said, 'They're not free agents. That's bull.'

I caught a commuter plane to Syracuse, and a national conference run by NAMI. At Syracuse airport I bumped into Ros again. She showed me photographs of her son. 'You see, my son's okay, uh? If he weren't ill. You know what I mean?' I saw a picture of a dark-haired sensitive-looking young man. I knew what she meant.

About two thousand people attended the NAMI Conference, which was held in the ballroom of the Holiday Inn, and I was invited to join a table with Bob and Meg, academics from the mid-west. They were white-haired, courteous and gentle. They neither looked nor sounded like the kind of people who would have a son who had been in jail twice, tried to kill himself twice, and who believed that his mother was trying to poison him. They said their son had received most help at an orthomolecular clinic in New York State, not necessarily because of the orthomolecular approach, but because the staff were dedicated and loving.

The session began with the chairperson telling us that one of the speakers was not able to come. 'He has had an emergency of the kind we are all too familiar with. We as parents and relatives are literally fighting for the lives of our adult young.'

She introduced the keynote speaker who had been with the President's Commission on Mental Health and now worked with a government mental health department. She had black hair pulled back in a knot, heavy black eye make-up, and wore a black dress with a demure neckline, black stockings and high-heeled black pumps. When she spoke, she clasped her hands in front of her, as if she were singing tragic opera. I called her the Black Queen.

'Many of you have faced one of life's most devastating tragedies, risen above it, drawn on spiritual help that can only come through walking down the same pathway. We welcome our partnership. Together we will move beyond the pain to find new life and new beginnings.'

The audience was restless. A short, phlegmatic woman stood up and said, 'I am tired of waiting, tired of clichés, tired of being told how good we are. I want my cookie now. Many of us are only just hanging on.'

An elegantly dressed woman called out, 'We are living a day at a time, but a day at a time is getting shorter and shorter for some of us. We are not prepared to spend any more energy studying the problems. We know them. Now we want to move forward.'

Black Queen replied, 'I am empathic with your concerns. We will move forward, through our four-year plan.'

A woman shouted, 'We cannot wait four years. We don't want a plan. What we need is just a little more money for a couple of case managers. We need it now.' People were on their feet, cheering and stamping.

Black Queen looked rattled. She raised a limp hand. 'It is very, very clear that a great many frustrations have occurred over a very very long time. I concur with you absolutely.'

The chairperson said wryly to the audience, 'I am glad that you are all so upset. Until we develop an advocacy role as vocal and unrelenting as Mental Disability we are not going to prosper. We have asked for posters, messages, a community education program. We have not seen those posters. We have not heard those messages. We need messages that say, "I am a schizophrenic and can be a good neighbour." "Schizophrenia" is still a frightening, ominous, misunderstood and misused term. Unless we get public acceptance we will not get our families into the community where they belong.'

'I agree. Absolutely. Absolutely,' said the Black Queen.

A man rose wearily to his feet and asked, 'Are you aware that in Buffalo there are patients on the floor, patients being beaten up, raped and subjected to acts of bestiality, patients dying of neglect?'

Black Queen murmured something about 'a report'.

'I was told that a year ago,' said the man. 'I am still waiting and people are still dying. One of them was my daughter.'

A pretty brown-haired woman said softly, 'I am also painfully aware, since it involves my own son, that there are 15,000 schizophrenic people in New York prisons. I would like to know if your commission has investigated the quality of care in New York prisons? I would like to suggest that persons with brain disease should not be in prisons. We have decriminalised alcoholism but not mental illness.'

Speakers called for reform of state hospitals, and told of those where beds were less than thirty centimetres apart, where a change of underwear came only once a week, toilets had no doors, and where patients shuffled from ward to ward looking for somewhere to sleep. 'How can they find the energy to put back a life shattered by mental illness, when the daily experience of living is so debilitating?'

Towards the end of the conference, there was a session given by a medical research scientist, Dr Courtenay Harding, whom I had met previously at Yale. She opened her session by stating, 'My most important message is that you have got to have hope, and the person with schizophrenia has also got to have hope because that helps the natural healing process.'

Courtenay Harding's work is part of a number of worldwide studies looking at the long-term outcomes of people with schizophrenia. Until recently, most of the literature indicated that people who had the kind of schizophrenia with repeated relapses were set on a downward path of degeneration. There had been almost no records of what happened to people with schizophrenia over a lifetime. The Vermont study in which Dr Harding was involved managed to track down almost all of 269 people who were in the back wards of Vermont State Hospital and were released in the mid-to-late 1950s. The researchers discovered that well over two-thirds of these people were living useful active lives in the community. They were free from symptoms, they were able to care for themselves, and were closely involved with family and friends. When they were asked how they had got better, many of them talked about feeling 'a curtain lifting' – like a biological straightening of the body. Even the one-third who still had some symptoms were nearly all managing to cope in the outside world. Perhaps, in youth, denial of the illness and natural rebelliousness makes schizophrenia hard to bear. Perhaps, as the years go by, people can come to terms with the illness, and learn to live in a way that will not precipitate it. Courtenay said, 'We forget how far people have come. The grass grows slowly, but it does grow.'

A woman in the audience raised her hand: 'I have had schizophrenia for nearly thirty years. I am almost fifty, and I just graduated. I have got there, slowly.' The audience cheered and applauded.

Courtenay showed slides of elderly people with wonderful faces who had struggled with schizophrenia all their lives. 'They have travelled such long and valiant journeys, fighting their illness. They have found safe harbour. Our expectations are too rigid. My 86-year-olds taught me that in one lifetime there is room for just about everything.'

Courtenay's speech was moving, and many people in the audience were in tears. I felt my own tears, and a desire to get home. With this good-news message and renewed determination, perhaps we could steer Jonathan to safe harbour. I realised that throughout these last few years we had been given little hope. Schizophrenia had been projected as a degenerative disease. If you're told you're going to get worse, why struggle to get better?

At the end of the conference I talked with the brown-haired woman who had asked all the questions about jail. Her name was Madeleine and she had two children. She had also had a husband, until her son shot him. She and her husband, a college professor, had been through all the hoops trying to get treatment for their son, but no hospitals would keep him long enough to stabilise his medication. He disappeared for several months, lived as a homeless person, and then returned home, acutely psychotic and malnourished. He believed his father was trying to kill him by getting fatter as he became thinner, so he shot and killed him. His plea of insanity failed, and he was given the maximum jail sentence. None of this would have happened if he had received proper treatment.

That night I wrote in my diary, *Shit, shit, shit,* which was neither elegant nor original, but I was tired and felt helpless at the pity of it all.

I returned to New York and 42nd Street, where I renewed acquaintance with Adam, the parent whom I had met at Yale. He picked me up at the hotel in an open-topped Mercedes which he drove with furious impatience. We went to his apartment overlooking 44th Street. It was a loft-apartment, furnished with Italian designer furniture and lots of glass and chrome.

Adam told me he was Jewish, a businessman, successful, and married to a woman whom he described as an extremely talented artist. Daniel was their only son who had a normal happy childhood until he was about thirteen, when he began missing school, no longer studying, wanting to sleep all day and stay awake all night. He became interested in photography but gave it up when he thought the chemicals were poisoning him. He joined the Boy Scouts and gave that up too when they asked him to cut his hair. He was alarmed by any competitive sport. And, from being a child of great imagination and creativity, particularly in art, his grades began to drop off until by the time he was fifteen or sixteen, the school was threatening to expel him.

Adam continued, 'When Daniel was about seventeen, we became very scared. We'd be in bed at night and all of a sudden we'd wake

up and there was Daniel standing at the door way, looking at us
while we were asleep. Boy, is that frightening. Because, boy, he's
just kinda standing there, staring, and it's about two or three in the
morning, and you think *Oh my God.*'

As I listened, sitting in this strange apartment with this strange
man, listening to the story of his son Daniel, I realised how similar
it was to the story of my son, Jonathan. That was to happen so many
times before I arrived home.

Adam jiggled the ice in his glass of whisky, and said morosely,
'Doctors go out of their way to convince you that you are not to
blame. Okay, so you listen to them, but deep down you have guilts
that nobody knows about. You recall experiences when you yelled
at your son – ah, like once when I said, "When you are going to
draw something worthwhile, instead of cartoons all the time?" God,
do I hate myself when I recall that feeling. Probably lots of parents
yell at their children but for me I have that guilt.

'I have tied my son up on the floor to stop him pulling knives
on me. I have hugged him when he has spat at me. I have put boxes
on the stairs to warn me if he was coming to me while I was asleep.
I have hired a companion to be with him twenty-four hours a day.
But he sees things that none of us see and I don't know how to
reach him.'

I made a quick trip from New York to Washington, as in both
cities I had people to see at the Equal Opportunities Commission,
and I particularly wanted to meet Dr E. Fuller Torrey, the man responsible for the best layperson's book on schizophrenia I have
read – *Surviving Schizophrenia*. Fuller works as a clinical and
research psychiatrist at the St Elizabeth Hospital in Washington, and
he also has a master's degree in anthropology. His views about the
illness are clear and unequivocal:

1. It is a brain disease.
2. The limbic system and its connections are primarily affected.
3. It often runs in families.
4. The brain damage may occur very early in life.

Fuller's sister suffers from schizophrenia, and perhaps this helps
explain his degree of commitment to helping overcome the myths
that surround the illness. 'People with schizophrenia are the lepers
of the twentieth century,' he says. 'The magnitude of schizophrenia

as a national calamity is exceeded only by the magnitude of our ignorance in dealing with it.'

I went to Toronto next, to visit some of the Canadian Friends of Schizophrenia organisations. June Beebie was one of the key people in the Toronto branch. She was a bright woman, warm and efficient. One of her sons had schizophrenia, and killed himself with a knife, three years before my visit. She says she knows how she loved her son, she knows what kind of a mother she was, she knows that she did not cause her son's illness nor his death, and that this is her armour and her strength.

June's son Matthew became ill when he was seventeen. He was embarrassed by his schizophrenia, and did not want to be called 'a crazy man'. June said, 'I think one of the reasons schizophrenia has been in the closet for so long is that parents do not want to embarrass their sick relative. Matthew's gone now, and the rest of the family encourage me to speak up, because unless parents are willing to talk, I don't know how else we're going to have people understand.

'It's always hard on the other kids in a family. I've known kids who say, "something terrible's going on and I'm not going to stay around and be made a schizophrenic". So families have the first sorrow of one of their children developing schizophrenia, then a second sorrow of their other kids leaving home. I appreciate why many kids don't want to talk about it, and I don't know why mine are different. Maybe it's because they watched what we went through trying to get help for Matthew. Even when he was known to be sick, nobody would listen when he said he was going to kill himself. They released him from hospital and he did kill himself. I think his brothers and sisters now see that it has to be discussed. If people understand that schizophrenia is a medical illness and not something that the person brought on himself, I think the sympathy and care will be there, the way it was for polio, the way it is for cancer and multiple sclerosis. But there is still an assumption: you did it to the kid, you take care of it.'

From Toronto I returned to New York for two days' further research on the ABC programs, and then I flew to Madison to meet Mona Wasow, Professor of Clinical Social Work at the University of Wisconsin in Madison. One of her three children, David, had schizophrenia. Mona hailed originally from west-side New York and a Polish-Jewish family. She was redheaded, funny, warm and clever. Her house was full of books, music, pictures, rugs, and many photographs.

We walked to the nearby lakes with a rug, a bottle of sherry and some cheese, and although we hadn't met before it felt as if we were old friends. As we sat by the lake, seven stout ducks swam importantly past. Like Jonathan, Mona's son David began to fly apart at the onset of puberty. He began truanting from school when he was fifteen. He had big mood swings. Mona and her husband took him to one psychiatrist who referred him to another who declared that David was a fine intact youngster. When he was sixteen, his mood swings became even greater. He had active hallucinations and felt people were out to destroy him. He began to wander away from the house, barefoot, for days at a time. He would tell his parents that he was heading for Alaska. In July that year he was pronounced to be paranoid schizophrenic and, because he was psychotic, was involuntarily committed to hospital where he refused treatment and could not be made to take it. In November he ran away from hospital and six weeks later was found starving in a cave in the woods in sub-zero temperatures. The mental health laws would not cover his re-admission to hospital, and the only way of ensuring his shelter was to charge him with truancy and put him into juvenile jail. He ran away again and did not turn up for another several weeks. This time he was emaciated, filthy, in rags, and psychotic.

Mona said, 'This was his hard-won "freedom". He walked through the front door, curled up on the floor in a corner and stared into space. I handed him some food. He stuffed it into his mouth like a small baby and went to sleep.'

More court cases ensued with legal debates about whether David was dangerous to himself and could be compelled to have treatment. Meantime he stayed in the juvenile detention centre. 'If bad genes or bad parenting killed half of him, the state laws were destroying the other half. He deteriorated rapidly.'

In the six years that followed, David, like Jonathan, was on the run. Social services and health services gave up on him. He was put out on the streets as part of 'reality therapy' to get him to conform. He was dragged through courts. Thousands of dollars were spent on state defence lawyers to protect his civil rights. Not one penny was put forth in court to protect his mental health.

Madison, where Mona Wasow lives and works, has now some of the best model community treatment programs for chronic mental illness anywhere in the world, in part due to her own pioneering efforts, including an excellent book, *Coping with Schizophrenia*. Her son David is a participant in these programs; he has rarely been rehospitalised and is quiet and unobtrusive. But he has had to live in dozens of different places and many times has had to be rescued by his mother, who has found him filthy and skinny, with boils on his body, no food, no sheets on the mattress, and chaos in his room congruent with the chaos in his mind. Yet, because David isn't violent, and has been kept out of hospital, he is listed as a statistical 'success' in the de-institutionalisation movement. In an article about the need for asylum for the chronically mentally ill, Mona wrote: *That is not how he looks to me. I think he looks like a giant, broken, plastic throwaway toy. And he breaks my heart.*

From Madison, my journey took me to Denver, Colorado, and to a Holiday Inn where hotel staff were dressed up as pumpkins or witches because it was coming up for Halloween. A pumpkin called me a taxi to my appointment with oil millionaire Jack Hinckley.

In one of the most controversial verdicts in American legal history, Hinckley's son, John, was found Not guilty by reason of insanity on a charge of attempting to assassinate President Ronald Reagan in March 1981. John Hinckley was sent to a maximum-security mental hospital in Washington where he was diagnosed schizophrenic.

After the verdict the Hinckleys received thousands of letters, much of it hate-mail, but one letter hooked Jack in a way none of the others had. 'Your name is mud,' someone wrote, 'You've got nothing to lose. Why don't you speak out for the mentally ill?' Jack Hinckley retired from his oil and gas exploration business, sold his house, and moved to Washington and with his wife established the American Mental Health Fund, to educate the public about mental illness and to raise money for research.

Hinckley was in Colorado for business on the day I saw him. He checked his watch and said he would give me precisely thirty minutes. He was balding, powerfully built, powerfully spoken. His eyes were an intense clear blue and he maintained a direct gaze. He told a familiar story. The Hinckleys have three children. At the time the shooting occured, the elder son, Scott, was working in his father's company. Diane was married. Their younger son, John, was a gentle aimless young man of twenty-seven, who had been unable to complete any college course or hold down a job since leaving school. He had a history of feeling unwell, but doctors were unable to find anything wrong and none picked up on the seriousness of John Hinckley's mental condition. A psychiatrist said that the problem was immaturity and counselled against hospital because he said it would make a mental cripple out of him. He devised a treatment program which involved withholding financial support and not allowing the young man home. His father now says, 'If mental illness is involved, "tough love" is the worst thing you can do.'

Oh yes, Jack Hinckley, I know about tough love too. Tough love was what I practised when I sent Jonathan to Sydney, the first time he was diagnosed schizophrenic. Tough love led me to call the police and put him out in the freezing rain early one morning in Adelaide, a memory that still pierces me. You and I know about it – Mona Wasow, and June Beeby in Canada, and all the other thousands of parents who are told to put their mentally ill children out of home, in the naive belief that they will learn to cope because they have to.

Young John Hinckley, obsessed by the actress Jodi Foster, wrote to her on the same day he shot at Reagan, urging: *please look into your heart and at least give me the chance, with this historical deed, to gain your respect and love.* In May 1982 Jack Hinckley took the witness stand at his son's trial and he broke down and cried as he said, 'I am the cause of John's tragedy. We forced him out at a time when he just couldn't cope. I wish to God that I could trade places with him right now.'

Much heated debate followed the use of insanity as the defence in the Hinckley trial, and the consequent Not guilty verdict. The insanity defence dates back to the thirteenth century, when it was known as the 'wild beast test', meaning that if someone's madness makes him behave like a wild beast he cannot be held accountable. Criticism of the insanity defence resulted in calls for reform or abolition. Some states abolished it altogether; others passed legislation restricting its use. Jack Hinckley attributed the public outrage over the verdict to ignorance of mental illness and to a desire for revenge. He said that he often wonders what would have been the attitude toward his son if he had been driving a car near the Washington Hilton that day in March and had suffered a seizure and ploughed into the presidential party in an out-of-control car, causing the same amount of damage.

'Even some of our friends still don't understand that John is sick. You can sense they're being nice to us, but at the same time they don't believe it. Most people believe that a mentally ill person has to have a certain look about him, and if he's not frothing at the mouth or beating his head against the wall, he can't be sick.'

A study undertaken by Hinckley's American Mental Health Fund in 1988 found that sixty per cent of Americans still thought that people with mental illness were malingerers, and could 'pull themselves together'. In Britain, in 1991, nearly seventy per cent thought that schizophrenia was a 'split personality', conjuring up images of Dr Jekyll and Mr Hyde, the prototype for uncontrollable evil. And in Australia, in 1991, while just about fifty per cent knew schizophrenia was a mental illness or disease, twenty per cent still thought it was caused by parental treatment. Such widespread ignorance of the nature of the illness has led organisations around the world to focus on community education. As an example of the kind of ridicule that still surrounds mental illness, Hinckley has quoted the marketing of a new novelty gift, consisting of a bag of Georgia peanuts wrapped in a tiny straitjacket and labelled 'Certifiably Nuts'. This doll-like item came complete with a patient history and a certificate committing it to an insane asylum. At the pull of a string, it emitted frenzied giggles.

More recently, in 1990, a major study on American attitudes to chronic mental illness showed that although nine out of ten respondents associated mental illness with chemical imbalances in the brain or environmental conditions, nine out of ten also thought it was caused by alcoholism or drug abuse, and nearly six out of ten thought it was due to lack of discipline.

From Denver I flew to Los Angeles and, on a Sunday morning, checked into an airport hotel that smelled of stale air-conditioning and cheap room-fresheners. The curtains and the bedcover of the super king-size bed were made of quilted gold satin, frayed at the edges. Outside the sky was smog-grey. Planes thundered in to land every few seconds, and no birds sang.

I was aching all over, with what my father would have called the Sickness Mongo (he called all unidentified illnesses the Sickness Mongo) so I decided to spend the day in bed, watching television. I felt too feeble to do anything else.

I turned on the remote-control gadget, and learned that, Glory Allelujah, the apocalypse was nigh. The commentator of the program had well-oiled dark hair, a ginger moustache, and wore a shiny blue suit, red tie and red handkerchief. 'Boy, am I glad Jesus is coming, because we need him, oh glory, we need him. AIDS is like a time bomb, there's a hole in the north pole, the Soviet Union is producing tremendous weapons of war, New Age witch-doctors have infiltrated the big corporations. The Bible says the only unpardonable sin is not to believe in Jesus. He is going to come secretly in the twinkling of an eye, leaving the sinners behind. Call now and our beautiful counsellors will send you a new birth certificate as you begin this exciting new journey with Jesus Christ.'

He leapt to his feet and waved an impassioned hand: 'The night will come when you tune into your TV channel and the screen will be black. We will be gone. The Lord will have called us into the heavens but you will be left behind, groaning in your misery and your heart will fail with fear. Call now!'

'Call now,' flashed on the screen, but instead of calling us to God it was flogging the world's smallest coffee maker, the world's only talking wristwatch and the world's only personal environmental sound machine.

I moaned, and turned off the television. *Oh Jonathan, Jonathan, what am I doing in this insane city listening to this insane evangelism which sounds even loopier than you at your most psychotic?* I telephoned Georgia and Joshua and was relieved to hear them sounding so cheerful. The following morning I flew the short flight to Palo Alto, and Carl Rogers, on the last leg of my North American journey.

Carl Rogers was one of the leaders of the human potential therapy movement, a system rooted in the belief of the essential goodness of humankind. Rogers came from a mid-western farm tradition, trained as an evangelical minister, and then discovered that his true bent was psychotherapy. In his long and distinguished career, he developed a system of client-centred, or non-directive, therapy which was widely practised and studied. The therapist made few demands upon the client, offered an atmosphere free of threats, and did not direct the client into any particular channel. The therapist's role was to clarify what the patient was thinking and feeling.

Palo Alto was also the home of the Western Behavioural Sciences Institute and a meeting place of many of the people I had read so avidly in the 'sixties. I arrived early in the morning, full of anticipation.

There weren't many people at the airport and I found a small bus driven by a large girl who was a discus thrower. I asked if she could drop me off at a small unpretentious place by the sea. 'Travelodge?' she said pertly. I said, 'No.' She took me to a place which she said was near the sea, old-fashioned and 'homey'. It was a two-storey building of serviced apartments, probably built in the 'fifties, and I liked it and stayed.

I rang Carl Rogers because it was Halloween Night and I hoped naively that out of the essential goodness of humankind, he would invite me to a Halloween party. He could not remember our letters, including the arrangements we had made, and said tetchily that he was very busy but might have an hour on Thursday. It was then Saturday. I wandered aimlessly around the shops where pumpkins competed with early Father Christmas and were winning. I was depressed and decided I would treat myself, so I bought a really good bottle of wine, oysters, smoked trout, strawberries, a wine glass and a linen napkin – and took it all home and had a feast while I watched the Mondale–Ferrari presidential election debate on television.

The beach outside my window was small and tight and full of fat dirty seagulls and thin clean joggers. I went for modest walks and jogged for a couple of seconds every so often. The eucalyptus trees around the university made me feel homesick. In between these shopping and jogging expeditions I read at the university library, went to the movies and some art exhibitions, and started writing up notes. When Thursday came, I took a cab to Carl Rogers's house. It was a pleasant, low, modern house, set in the hills, with a large garden and magnificent views. He invited me in; it took a while for both of us to relax.

Rogers's view of schizophrenia accorded with the dominant views of his time, namely that schizophrenia was a psychosocial response to an alienating environment and that the most healing tool that the therapist could use was to establish a loving and trusting relationship with the person who had schizophrenia. He also had a strong and shining belief that behind the curtains of silence, the hallucinations, the strange talk, the hostility and the indifference, there was a person who could be reached, a soul in hiding. I also believe this. Throughout Jonathan's illness, either in moments of stillness together, or in moments of alarm, I caught glimpses of Jonathan. But the moments never lasted long. Whatever was causing the distortion of his sensory processes would reassert itself, and all the old terrors and defensive behaviours would reappear. Yet he would always know what was happening, no matter how crazy he appeared. He would register fear and humiliation – his or others' – and love and anger. He remembered it all.

At the end of the interview I was quite tired and Rogers promptly called me a taxi. On the drive back to town, his own car passed the taxi, and I wondered why he had not given me a lift. Then I reflected that perhaps if I were eighty-two, I would conserve my energy by keeping encounters to a minimum.

The next day I returned some books he had lent me. It was hot and I was eating a pear which was smeared from ear to ear. Unexpectedly, Rogers opened the door. He looked at me and began laughing. He invited me in and was much more welcoming than the day before. Perhaps on that day, the words of our interview had created their own obstacle. Rogers once wrote about a schizophrenic client:

*I told him that being with him was like being with an Indian, because we both sat silently not saying anything, and yet I felt a good deal was going on between us. For the first time in a long time, he really laughed at my comment, and I am sure he got the point.*

The last leg of my journey was London. Among the people I was to visit was R. D. Laing – psychiatrist, poet, musician, scholar and existentialist philosopher and perhaps the most influential of the family causation theorists.

Laing's work was embedded in the history of his time, when authority in the western world appeared to be crumbling and social revolution fired the imaginations of the young. It was the time of human-rights activists, anti-Vietnam-war demonstrators, the Beatles and Joan Baez, mescaline and marijuana, flower-power and hippies. Every established institution was under challenge, including the medical profession.

Laing's questioning of traditional psychiatry was born of his experiences as a young psychiatrist in the army, followed by two years as a clinical psychiatrist in a Glasgow hospital where he had come to the painful realisation that he would not like to be treated in the same manner as his own patients. He rejected the use of drugs, insulin and electric shock. He criticised the alienation that occurred between psychiatrists and patients. His views were to polarise the world of psychiatry into a medical establishment, which was held to represent repression and segregation, and an anti-psychiatry faction, which championed the rebellion of madness.

Laing grounded his work in practice by establishing a number of residential communities to provide alternative treatment, including the celebrated Kingsley Hall in London. Kingsley Hall was a place where people could undertake the voyage of madness and were said to emerge cleansed and liberated, and where Laing's exploration of alternative treatments included the therapeutic use of mescaline and LSD.

My interview with Laing was unusual. I had written to him from Australia and had received a prompt reply saying that his fee was one hundred pounds. When I telephoned him in London, his secretary reminded me of the one hundred pounds.

Laing was then living in North London in a white house which was once a vicarage and had a leafy front garden. The large black door bore a polished brass plate, engraved with the word *Laing.* Laing was nowhere in view. His secretary greeted me by asking, 'Have you got cash?'

I said, a little primly, that I hadn't got cash but I could pay by cheque.

'We need cash,' she said tartly.

Laing appeared. His hair stood on end, his clothes were crumpled, he wore one pink sock and one blue and he paced around the room looking agitated.

'D'you want tea or coffee?' he said. And disappeared almost as abruptly as he had arrived.

As soon as he had gone his secretary leant forward and hissed at me. 'We want cash because we haven't enough money to pay the milk-man.' As the house was a fine and well-ordered building, purring with the sounds of domesticity coming from upstairs, there seemed to be some kind of dissonance between the two worlds.

I emptied out my wallet and counted out thirty pounds, all I had on me. 'I'll keep ten for my taxi, you can have twenty, and I'll pay the balance by cheque.'

Laing came back into the room and grinned, showing one missing front tooth. 'That'll be a help,' he said, and then once more disappeared. His secretary explained that a cheque due to be paid into the bank had not yet arrived; there had been a hitch. Suddenly Laing's voice growled behind me. 'I can't do the interview; I'm zonked.' He looked zonked. And I felt it. So, wearily, I picked up my tape recorder, only to have him pilot me into his study saying, 'Don't leave me. I'd like to talk, but I won't be recorded.'

As he talked, his intellectual stature was unquestionable. His ideas soared in all manner of wondrous directions. Every now and then he rolled his eyes backwards; other times he ran his hands through his hair. He spoke so rapidly it was hard to keep pace. At the end of over an hour, he said, 'Come back in three days, and you can have your interview.'

When I returned, the house was closed and shuttered. I rang the bell but nobody came. I rang and rang with mounting anger. The window upstairs was suddenly flung open and Laing's head peered down at me. His hair was wild. He was in his pyjamas. He clutched his forehead. When he let me in it was obvious that he had a monumental hang-over. His room was littered with glasses, bottles, overflowing ashtrays. But he did the interview, slowly and with much heavy breathing.

He was scornfully dismissive of my earlier reference about schizophrenia being 'a sane response to an insane environment'. 'I never said that,' he said, in the kind of voice that had dealt with such a charge many times before. 'I said that the experience and behaviour that tends to be diagnosed as schizophrenia is much more socially intelligible than has come to be supposed by most psychiatrists. That generalisation still holds.'

He similarly denied having said that families played a causal role in the development of schizophrenia. He said that he had never been concerned with the aetiology of schizophrenia. Yet the book that he co-authored with Aaron Esterson in 1964, *Sanity, Madness and the Family*, presented a perspective of schizophrenia that centred around the nature of communication within families in which one of the members had schizophrenia. Particular focus was given to the parent–child relationship. The book was a landmark in its time, and led to a review in *New Society* which claimed:

*This study throws doubt on the traditional view of schizophrenia as an illness with specific symptoms and its own pathology: it suggests rather that some forms of madness may largely be social creations and many of their symptoms no more than the tortured ruses of people struggling to live in unlivable situations.*

It is perhaps a reflection of the turmoil of the times, and the need for a fresh approach, that there appeared to be few challenges to the fact that this slender evidence of only eleven case studies was used to support a whole new psychiatric thesis. So that the next part of my interview with Laing amazed me. Laing said that he had also investigated a group of so-called 'normal' families, and had found the nature of communication within these families in many ways much more depressing than the communication in the families where one member had already been diagnosed as schizophrenic.

'We never did much with that, partly because it was just so depressing,' he said.

I don't think I really took in the full import of what had just been said until much later. If I had I might have shouted at him, 'Why didn't you publicise it? Why didn't you ever talk like that in the days when you were God, and parents were the miserable sinners?'

We went on to explore Laing's view of the current biological approach to schizophrenia. 'There is a biological component to everything,' he said. 'There is a biological component to this conversation. There is a biological component to anxiety, isolation, to every emotion, to every thought and to every feeling. It may well be highly likely that there is some specific biological hormonal biochemical disorder in schizophrenia. Some people when they are psychotic don't look healthy. There's a change in the colour of their skin and their eyes. It looks as though there is something working away in them which is pretty subtle and which hasn't been definitively discovered. But I don't think we can express our total reality by our chemical transactions. You can't see consciousness down a microscope. I don't like talking about such a thing as the soul, and I don't like falling into dualism of two substances, the soul and the body. At the same time, Aristotle said that the soul is to the body as vision is to the eye. Very subtle statement.'

In my final question, I asked him to assess his life's work. He looked irritated. 'If you ask me that question at ten o'clock in the morning I would give you a different answer to the same question at four o'clock in the afternoon. I really don't know. I wish I could have contributed more to dissolving some of the misery there is in this whole field.' He was silent for some little time as he gazed down on the ground. Indeed throughout most of the interview he had looked everywhere except at me or the microphone. This time when he looked up, he did look at me. 'But there's no point in reflecting too much on that,' he said. 'I've still got other things I am trying to understand – lies, deceit, jealousy, paranoia, there's a whole nestful.' He chuckled, and rose. The interview was over.

Then I set out on a journey to find Mary Barnes. Mary Barnes had been a young nurse living and working in London when she was diagnosed as having schizophrenia. After a period in hospital, she had found her way to Laing who, together with his colleague Joseph Berke, had just established Kingsley Hall. Berke later wrote a book about Mary Barnes, and the Royal Court Theatre turned it into a play. Mary Barnes became a symbol of freedom from the oppression of psychiatry. She had been allowed to make her journey through madness, and was said to have emerged, re-born.

I discovered that Mary Barnes was living in one of the therapeutic houses that Joseph Berke was still running. She was by then a woman in her sixties. She was short and generously built, overflowing her bright orange caftan, and with long grey hair hanging almost to her waist. She was immensely welcoming, and had a child-like ingenuousness about her. She said that when she was at Kingsley Hall,

Ronnie and Joseph built a wooden womb for her to lie in, so that she could experience regression. They allowed her to rub shit on walls and in Ronny's hair but when she started rubbing it in other people's hair the community got fed up and made her grow up. She felt she had come through the experience of schizophrenia in a healthier way than if she had been kept locked up in hospital. Sometimes she still became 'distressed', which she said could be 'a little bit like being psychotic', and then took herself off to therapeutic communities in Cornwall or Scotland. These gave her sanctuary. Now she was leading an active life, corresponding with people all over the world, and painting large religious canvases in acrylic paint which she stacked in layers around the walls of her very small room.

I enjoyed my time with Mary. I enjoyed her enthusiasm, her interest in Jonathan and her friendliness. I believe she is different from the kind of person she might have been, had she not developed schizophrenia. Equally, she is probably different from the person she might have been had she endured a lifetime of psychiatric institutions. She has learned to manage her illness, and perhaps she epitomises what people mean when they say, 'Cured, no. Recovered, yes.' The fact that she still has to seek refuge when she is feeling vulnerable is to me yet another indicator that there may be times when people with a severe mental illness will need asylum, but not asylum as we know it today. Rather, an asylum that means sanctuary, and if people are so psychotic that they are in danger of harming themselves or others, then Ronnie Laing's unorthodox and surprising suggestion was, 'What's wrong with a brightly coloured padded cell?'

I was almost at the end of my journey when I visited the British Schizophrenia Fellowship in the London suburb of Ealing. The stories I heard were wearily familiar. They were the same as those I had just encountered in North America, and the same as we were battling in Australia. Even today, there has been little change. Getting sick and psychotic people into hospital either to prevent a crisis or at the time of a crisis is still a major issue. An immense gap exists between the professional view of the illness and the home experience. And families are still saying that de-institutionalisation has dumped people from hospital to family, or out on the streets, without any proper support.

The principle of de-institutionalisation is a grand one; it is the way it has been administered that is wrong. De-institutionalisation was born in the 'fifties out of compassion and optimism, when the new anti-psychotic drugs at last enabled people to have some control over their illness. Hospitals rapidly emptied out their overcrowded wards, so that, in countries such as the United States, the United Kingdom and Australia, hospital beds have been cut by as much as seventy-five per cent in the last fifteen years. But as ill and vulnerable people moved back into the community, the mental health dollar stayed locked up in hospital care. Of our mental health expenditure in Australia, seventy-five per cent still goes into hospitals and only twenty-five per cent into community care where ninety per cent of people with a serious mental illness are treated. As a result most community health services are underfunded, inadequate or non-existent, and sick people and their families are bearing the brunt.

De-institutionalisation has also brought the shameful phenomenon of the homeless mentally ill. In the United States and the United Kingdom this issue has become a national scandal. In Australia the problem is just as severe. Up to half the homeless in Sydney and Melbourne are mentally ill but, perhaps because our climate is kinder, the homeless are less visible. Instead of living in cardboard boxes they doss down on park benches, get a bed in a police cell or crowd the hostels that still have room – even though they were not set up for this purpose. The Sydney City Mission, where Jonathan sometimes stayed, has seen a rise in its mentally ill clients from fifteen per cent to seventy-five per cent over a two-year period.

One of the problems of de-institutionalisation has been a failure to acknowledge that the long-term mentally ill are not all of the same kind, and some do not always cope well on their own in the community. Nor can they necessarily conform to well-meaning professional expectations of rehabilitation. We are reluctant to confront this issue because it might mean a curtailment of their liberties. Involuntary treatment will always present us with a difficult dilemma. But when someone is acutely ill and denying help, I believe we have a responsibility to ensure their safety and, beyond this, to ensure that they have some chance of getting well. It may be that this can come about through involuntary treatment within the community; it may be better handled in hospital. We should not be wasting time on ideological arguments, in which *where* we treat mentally ill people becomes more important than *how* we treat them. What is needed is a comprehensive range of services, including suitable places for them to live.

Right at the end of my trip, something unexpected and distressing occurred. I was visiting friends on a cold London evening towards the end of November. Outside, there was a slight grey drizzle and inside, warm lights and the smell of dinner. Agnes, who was in her nineties, greeted me: 'There is bad news. Your friend who has a son with schizophrenia – her boy has just died.'

I felt a deep sadness. I rang. My friend's voice was flat and grey. 'People are saying it is all for the best. I do not feel like that,' she said, in her quiet measured way. Her son had jumped from a great height. He was nineteen. And now he was dead.

After I had put the phone down I wept. I wept for June Beebie in Toronto. I wept for all those other families who had lost people they loved. I wept for the safety of my own son.

*Dear God, let him stay alive*, I wrote in a turmoil of confusion and despair that night, the aching for all those young deaths, the memories of snatches of conversation about the children who were always a little different, a little more vulnerable, a little less able to fit into the norms that we have made for ourselves; the children whom we tried to protect, yearned to make safe, but who kept slipping from our grasp.

Late in December, when I returned to Sydney I went to see my friend. She was white-faced and there were hollows under her eyes. There were writings and photographs of her son, on the table in front of us, on the floor, on chairs, everywhere I looked in this room which had become a room of mourning and a room of memory.

She said, 'What can I do?'

'You know he wasn't angry with you.'

'Oh I know all that,' she said impatiently. She flipped through a loose-leafed folder of notes, projects for his university entrance exam. 'It's the burden,' she said. 'If only I'd stopped him. "Where are you going?" I'd asked him. And he'd said, "Out". "Do you want me to come with you?" I'd asked. "No," he'd said. So I didn't. Ah, but if only I had,' said my friend.

'When he found out he had schizophrenia, he was frightened. "I don't want to be a bag man," he said.' She looked at me. 'We have got to do something to stop any more taking their lives.'

At the memorial service for her son, there was a reading from the Second Book of Samuel, on the death of Absalom:

> *And the king was deeply moved,*
> *and went up to the chamber over*
> *the gate, and wept; and as he*
> *went, he said 'O my son Absalom,*
> *my son, my son Absalom! Would I*
> *have died instead of you,*
> *O Absalom, my son, my son!'*

# Eight
## *The Throwaways*

*And I will show you something different from either*
*Your shadow at morning striding behind you*
*Or your shadow at evening rising to meet you;*
*I will show you fear in a handful of dust.*

T. S. ELIOT

Okay, Jonathan, so if I am going to finish this book, I have to make peace with you, because when I have been writing it for more than a couple of days, I begin to feel you with me. I think I see you sitting on a bench in the rain. Or walking away from me down the road. Mostly I see you as you were in the last two years of your life. Your hair is long and you are talking to yourself – secret conversations that belong to another world. You laugh, and it seems you are laughing at everything, at the absurdities of life, and the profundities of those absurdities. You are nodding your head while I write this. You are here, but not here.

*Do you mind that I am writing this book?*

*In a manner of speaking, no.*

*So does that mean No?*

*Yes.*

*What would you want me to say?*

*Tell it like it was for me.*

*I can only guess.*

*Tell it like I told you once – when I said, 'The message of everything is love, and I'm doing the best I can.'*

The nearer to the end it gets, the harder it becomes. The file marked JONATHAN – DEATH is on the floor, and I keep kicking it away.

*December 1985* Georgia, Joshua and I went to Sydney after Christmas and arrived just in time for New Year's Eve. Georgia and Josh went out with friends. I found Neil and Icia, and together we

231

tracked down Jonathan. He was wearing a long black coat almost down to his ankles and had a daisy in his buttonhole. The four of us caught the bus to Watsons Bay, on the harbour front, and bought fish and chips and champagne. We clambered up a small rise and found ourselves in the midst of a gathering of old people. I do not know who they were, or where they had come from, but we sang and danced with them, and Jonathan waltzed around and around with Icia and Neil and me, and the moon winked a joyful eye.

Jonathan wanted to come to a musical play about David Bowie. As a boy Jonathan had groomed his hair to look like David Bowie. He had put up David Bowie posters in his room and played David Bowie records. The night before the play, when I rang him at Matthew Talbot to make arrangements, he was angry because his money had been stolen. 'I want to know: do you intend to give it back to me as a poor honest boy who's been ripped off? Because it's just my human rights.'

When I suggested that he should meet us at the theatre, he said, 'If you're too mean to bring your chauffeur-driven capitalist car and pick up a man who just demands his rights, then I'll curse you into damnation.'

The following day, I rang up the Talbot and spoke to Ray. He said, 'Oh dear, he's not right to take out, Anne. He's really dirty, dear, and quite angry.'

'What would you do?'

'I'd let him be.'

'But I've promised him and he doesn't forget.'

'Then bring some clean clothes because there's nothing suitable here.'

We did a whip-round at the house where we were staying and arrived at the Talbot with an assortment of shirts and jeans. Jonathan was hovering outside. He was no longer stroppy. He went off and came back with two of the clean shirts over his two dirty T-shirts.

We went to an Italian café and ordered spaghetti and carafe wine. Jonathan said that the wine was a bad vintage and the carafe was corked. In between his complaints he giggled. The waiter was polite.

The theatre was in the Rocks district of Sydney, down by Circular Quay, a place full of pubs and restaurants and tourists. A small crowd of young people were singing on the pavement outside one of the pubs and some of them were dancing. I felt sad when I looked at Jonathan and saw the contrast between his world and theirs.

Jonathan sat through the first ten minutes of the performance and then spent some time pulling a grubby pink button-up cardigan out of his dilly bag. He put that on over his four shirts. Then he wandered out, and sat hunched up in the doorway to the theatre, where we found him at the interval. He was staring ahead of him, oblivious to the crowds and to the dazzling beauty of the harbour front. Hell, oh hell, sometimes I still needed to pretend he was okay.

When we dropped him off at the Matthew Talbot, three or four men were sprawled drunkenly outside the entrance. Jonathan rang the bell and a tall man with a battered face and black oiled hair let him in. I had seen this man before and he beamed at me; he spoke with a strong Irish accent, 'How d'you think he's doing, Anne?'

'Okay,' I said. I was despondent; the night out did not seem to have brought much joy.

The man with the battered face squeezed my hand. 'We'll pull him through, dear. God will see to it.'

The following week, I went with Jonathan to a jazz concert in the park. It was a beautiful late afternoon at the height of summer, and we wandered through the crowds trying to find somewhere to sit. The park was bursting with people. We had to weave our way through tents and picnickers and children queueing for icecream and hot dogs. We found a giant Moreton Bay fig-tree and made ourselves comfortable, perched on its roots. The sun was hot but Jonathan was still wearing his many shirts and his pink cardigan from the David Bowie concert. I went to buy two icecreams, and when I came back he said, 'You are very kind.' The music had started, and his whole body moved to its beat, arms, legs, feet, head, and the icecream went uneaten and dribbled down his hand. When the music stopped he said, 'Tell Bronwyn [a friend] she shouldn't do art therapy. Art therapy is just an excuse to be slack about art.'

He sucked the melted icecream off his arm and looked at me for quite some time without speaking. Then he said, 'I've got to look after you in your old age because you're my mother. You know I'd do anything for you even if I stop you getting beaten up by the cops. Because someone's going to take advantage of me. If only you had got yourself together I think you should have got a divorce, just animally. If it was me, personally, I would have done so and taken all his cook books. He wasn't wise. I thought I could save him from mortal doom and then he bloody well died. I want to hang on to the past to change my way of life. I can't let go of it. I don't want to hurt anyone. I'm just this young man who wants to have a good time. I can't help it.'

Jonathan talked for a long time and I listened. Then there was silence, even though the music was still frolicking and the crowds chattering. Jonathan's phrasing may have been eccentric but if you spent time with him, and felt your way into what he was saying, it was almost always possible to understand him. On this afternoon in the park, he was particularly lucid.

I looked up. Jonathan was grinning, with his head on one side. He looked quite old and wise. 'It was a good try wasn't it? Thank you for listening. That was very brave of you. The point is why do you want to be brave? It's just silly, you know. People have to learn that underlying business, the message of everything is love. Which is why society sticks together. You and I have love.'

Somewhere in the middle of this long hot summer I was approached to apply for the position of director of the Australian Film, Television and Radio School, a national tertiary institution which also ran a broad program of industry training. I had been on the council of the school, I believed in what it was doing, and I knew I would find the work stimulating. It would mean returning to Sydney to live, but that wasn't a bad idea, as it was time I put down roots again, and I had become tired of scrabbling for a living as a freelance. It wasn't good timing for Josh, as he still had his final year at school, so I compromised and said I couldn't start the new job in Sydney till the second half of the year.

Betty, who was still coping with her family saga of schizophrenia, thought it was a good idea. She had written to me from Adelaide. *You've got Neptune in your house, Saturn says get yourself organised, Neptune says let me float, Uranus says there's a big production coming up – so get off your arse and get going.*

Just before the interview I went to have my hair cut. The hairdresser told me his name was Bruce and that he had heard me on the radio talking about schizophrenia. He launched into promises of God's holy redemption. He said he could cure Jonathan by the laying-on of hands.

A girl wandered in wearing green satin pants and a leopard chiffon top. Her hair was teased out into a white peroxide fizz with roots a startling black. Bruce said to her, 'What do you want, all-white or all-black?'

Then he turned to me and said, 'What do you want, God or the Devil? God sent you, that's how you knew about us. I think your son is possessed by the Devil. I was. I was that violent, people would shake. I was gay, a drug addict and a prostitute. I used to frequent public toilets. Now I am married. I have a lovely wife, two cars, three hairdressing salons, and I have received the Word of the Lord. Such peace and beauty, Anne, I cannot say.'

He teased a piece of hair, cut a bit more. 'My parents are called Mervyn and Ruby, and they live in Cabramatta. They have beer-swilling, suburban lives. Ruby says, "Give over talking. I've that much of a migraine. Give over," she says. 'Just bring your son in here. Any time – he doesn't have to have his hair cut. After 5.30 or at home, I'll talk to him and see if he wants to be saved. I've saved that many people.'

I told Jonathan but he was not impressed. He said he could shave his own head and that he was already friends with God.

When the summer holidays were over, I returned to Adelaide with Georgia and Josh. I opened the front door, switched on the answering machine, and heard the voice of an unknown doctor telling me that, between my leaving Sydney and arriving in Adelaide, Jonathan had been committed.

I read my diary for that period: *You think you have put it behind you. You think you have stopped feeling. But here it is again, the panic and the fear.*

The hospital put me straight through to the ward sister. The ward sister put me straight through to Jonathan. That wouldn't have happened a few years back: then, they would have said, 'We can't disturb the patient.'

Jonathan said in his slow, medicated voice, 'How are you, Anne? I am all right except I had these bumps on my arms and they were eating me up. They have stopped.'

I said I was glad the bumps had stopped eating him up. A doctor came on the phone and said the police had brought Jonathan to the hospital because he was sitting down in the middle of Kings Cross in front of oncoming traffic. He had been given medication and was no longer psychotic, so the hospital could not keep him much longer on an involuntary basis. What was his history?

I said he had first been diagnosed as having schizophrenia when he was seventeen. I listened to myself emphasising that Jonathan had a home and a family who loved him and then felt ashamed that I still felt the need to justify myself.

The doctor said that as Jonathan had a history of being in and out of hospital, it looked as if it might stay that way. 'All you can do is ride with the present,' he said.

'What about half-way houses, for rehabilitation?' I asked.

'There's not much going,' said the doctor. 'He's probably as well at Matthew Talbot as anywhere: they can keep an eye on him.'

Later that night I went for a walk round the block, glad that the sky was without stars. I needed the darkness. I thought of the darkness of Jonathan's eyes when he was a baby, of feeding him and staring down at him, of wanting to shake him, to find out who and what was there. Had he been brain-damaged? Apparently not: he had recovered. So what about now? Is the intact person still there or has he gone forever? On those rare occasions when Jonathan seems to pull himself together, how is it that he can find that person and then lose him again?

I went to Canberra for a few weeks to take up a fellowship with the Australian National University. I used much of the time to put together a series of radio documentaries on schizophrenia. My room was festooned with tapes about schizophrenia: about the nature of the illness; about research; about having the illness, and about living with it. The edited offcuts wrapped themselves around me and hobbled my ankles. The university put a notice in the paper – without warning me – saying that I was in residence and would like to talk with people. I had no protection from callers and I was deluged. I lectured at the university, and I also talked to schools and community groups on everything from mental illness to the media.

Returning to Adelaide to prepare for our move, I drove via Sydney, and stopped at a roadside café for a cup of coffee. I also bought a newspaper. There, on the front page, was a large picture of Jonathan. I remember the gasp that I gave, the lurch in my stomach, my haste to read, the way the lines of print were jumping because of my fear. The photograph of Jonathan was underneath banner headlines which read *NOTHING'S CHANGED IN HOPE LANE*. The story was about the public face of heroin, of street-corner drug deals and drug overdoses, and of hopeless addicts injecting themselves in sordid back lanes.

I have the picture in front of me, this evening in Sydney, four years later. Jonathan is sitting on a step, side view, his face hidden by his straggle of hair. His feet are bare. He leans against a wall on which is a piece of graffiti: *MEN AND WOMEN UNITE TO CREATE A WORLD OF PEACE, LOVE, WISDOM.*

There is no mention of Jonathan's name, so how do I know it is him? Heroin was never his addiction. I knew it was Jonathan then just as I know it is Jonathan now. I know the hang of his head, his nose, the way he is wearing his raggy clothes, his jumper which has shrunk so that his back is exposed, and his feet – oh those long, thin, vulnerable feet. The photo makes me feel as sad and as tender now as it did then, and so close that I feel I could reach out and touch him. But I cannot, because Jonathan is dead, and I am looking at a piece of newsprint, yellow round the edges.

Back in Adelaide I had to get ready to move to Sydney. We had decided that Georgia and Joshua would stay on in the Adelaide house, and that I would go home for weekends every two or three weeks. Josh was then seventeen and had almost finished school. Georgia was twenty and was in her third year at university.

Some time in the preceding months I had managed to buy us a house in Sydney. It was a ramshackle Federation house on the water, with magnificent views right up the harbour so that dawn came up in rosy splendour, and evenings brought mysterious bird-calls from the water's edge and flying foxes swooping through the trees.

The house had been owned by a melancholic artist who had painted the front silver and had festooned the inside with neon lights. His melancholia seemed to have been passed on to the house, and I never really settled there. My pictures remained un-hung, my boxes unpacked. I used to wonder at the chill and depression I felt whenever I went into the downstairs part of the building. Later I found that someone had committed suicide there not long before I moved in.

In order to achieve this magnificent waterfront house, I had taken on a magnificent mortgage, so much so that I never had any spare cash to do any repairs, even though my job as director of the Film School paid well. I arrived in Sydney on Friday, I went to work on Monday, and fell sick on Tuesday. On Wednesday I struggled to work, and came back to the house to find the ceiling had fallen in.

I found the job difficult. My management experience was patchy and the School was full of intrigue. I went to a wise and experienced friend for counsel and, instead of giving me management lectures, he cooked me dinner and told me to begin looking after myself. Lesson number one, he said.

I saw an advertisement in a shop window for a kitten: *to be destroyed if no home available*. I took the kitten because I was missing the children and was needy, but so was the kitten. It scratched and bit me and I wanted to hit it.

On the day I arrived in Sydney, while I was unpacking, Jonathan arrived and flung his arms around me and we sat on the verandah in two rickety chairs. Jonathan was now suffering from chronic ill health. He coughed constantly. He smelt dank and depressed. His arms and his feet were covered in sores. I longed to say, Come back and live at home, but I dared not because of all the disasters of the past. I spoke with Andy who said Do not, and the Matthew Talbot psychiatrist who said Do not, and with Frank in Adelaide who said Do not. I asked Georgia, who said 'Over my dead body', and Josh, who said, 'Don't be silly, Anne, he wouldn't stay.'

I was worried about Jonathan's teeth again. They were becoming black and decayed. Every time I tried to persuade him to go to a dentist he would say, 'Thank you, thank you, but I don't want anything like that, thank you.' Once or twice I had made appointments but he had never turned up. Jonathan said that in jail he was subjected to capital punishment: 'They took out a tooth,' he said.

So now, one Sunday afternoon when I had been in Sydney about a month I asked, 'How about going to the dentist again?'

'Yes, I do want to go to the dentist,' he said. When the time came for his appointment he was nowhere to be found. I remembered that some weeks previously I had received a call from Bill Windspear at the Sydney Dental Hospital offering to help people with schizophrenia. Windspear had left a prosperous private practice to give some time to upgrading the service at the Dental Hospital. He said he was concerned that people with mental illness were not being assisted; the hospital had to accept that many of them would not be able to keep to appointments, and the system had to be flexible enough to cope with this.

The theorists say you must make people behave normally, otherwise you are reinforcing their aberrant behaviour. This means that mentally ill people are often locked out of programs after the first misdemeanour, in the expectation that this will teach them conformity. It won't, especially if we are trying to make them conform to something that seems neither essential nor pleasant. In Jonathan's case, I remember being reprimanded by a doctor because he felt that yet again I had become over-involved in Jonathan's concerns. I said, 'If I were ill and you allowed my teeth to rot in my head, I wouldn't thank you.'

Even with the blandishments of the social worker at the Talbot, and a young dentist at the Dental Hospital, Jonathan refused to let anyone treat his teeth. He allowed them to be looked at, but when he was told that they would need filling and that two might have to be removed, he said firmly but politely, 'With respect, sir, thank you, sir, but I have a magic eye and I can heal my own teeth. Thank you, sir. And madam.'

I had gone back to Adelaide for the weekend and was digging in the garden on a Sunday afternoon when Ray Bourke phoned from the Talbot in Sydney. Jonathan was in hospital. He had taken an overdose.

'He's all right, dear,' said Ray. 'We've seen him and he's recovering.'

I returned to Sydney on Monday and went straight to the hospital. Jonathan had already been released, twelve hours after being admitted. I was angry about this and so was Ray. Jonathan was sitting on the footpath outside the Talbot, head in hands. He wouldn't say much except, 'Yeah, it was silly.'

He had overdosed with a mixture of Serepax and alcohol, and

had taken himself off to the hospital to have his stomach pumped out. 'I have a death-defying wish,' he mumbled, his head drooped so low it looked as if it might tumble off.

Since he had been ill Jonathan had played Russian roulette with his life on many occasions, but this was the first time he had overdosed to the point of danger. I guess it was remarkable that he had then sought help, but at the time my head was full of the import of what had just happened. Up until then Jonathan had always appeared as a survivor. He had grown into his cloak of madness and wore it with a certain style. He had not shown any inclination to suicide. Whenever I had been in a panic and lamented about how he might end up, Georgia or Joshua or friends would say, 'He'll turn up: he always does.'

This time had been different. I lay awake for several nights, and during the day I embarked on another round of seeking alternatives. Jonathan still refused to go into hospital. Hospitals said they would not keep him. There was little in the way of hostel accommodation or rehabilitation programs. Anyway, he wouldn't have gone. He came home that weekend and slept most of the time, curled up on the couch in my front room. He looked ill and exhausted.

Three weeks later I had another phone-call from Ray, and this time I was in Sydney. Jonathan had taken a second overdose. This one wasn't as bad, but he had been found unconscious at Matthew Talbot and had been taken to the hospital. I rang the psychiatrist in charge who said, 'We know your son. He's sleeping it off. He'll be able to leave in the morning.'

My anger burned like a blowtorch. 'That's absurd,' I shouted.

'He'll be quite all right by then.'

'This is the second time he has overdosed. Keep him in.'

'What would be the point?'

'But you know he has schizophrenia. His general health is lousy. Surely it's a chance to work with him to get him back onto medication.' My voice was rising. I was both angry and tearful. I was sitting at the same desk I am sitting at now: I remember the dark polished wood, the coffee-cup stains, the paper clips I was twisting and throwing on the floor, the hard knot in my stomach, the sense of rage.

'Being delusional isn't grounds for scheduling him under the Act.'

'He can be scheduled because he is a danger to himself.'

'But your son is not a danger to himself.'

'He's nearly died. Twice in one month. What else does he have to do? Does he have to die?'

'He'd have to be suicidal, and when he goes before the magistrate he'll simply say that it was an accident. That's not being suicidal.'

'It's a form of suicide if you are not taking care of yourself to the extent that you overdose and nearly die.'

'Your son has trouble with his drug habit.'

'He also has trouble with his schizophrenia, remember?'

'I have to act in the spirit of the Mental Health Act.'

'The spirit of the Act is to safeguard people's rights. Jonathan has a right to life.'

'My hands are tied.'

I was shouting by now. I was not going to give in. 'You have a young man who has been schizophrenic now for seven years, who has nearly died twice in the last month, who was in here on commital two weeks earlier, and you say you can do nothing. That he's not a danger to himself. Am I crazy, or is he, or are you?'

'I can't send him to Rozelle Hospital, there's a strike there, and I have only one bed, and six to nine people sleeping on the floor.'

'So what do I do? Tell me that, what do I do?'

There was a long pause. 'We could try talking to him, together perhaps.'

I arrived at the hospital the following morning. Jonathan was having a shower. I met the doctor, who was courteous and measured.

He said that perhaps I did not realise what my son had been doing. That my son was a heroin addict. That he prostituted himself at the Cross. That he sold drugs. I said that every time Jonathan had been tested he had not been found to be a heroin addict. That even if he were a heroin addict, that was no reason for letting him die. That he was unlikely to be a prostitute because no one would have him in his present condition. That even if he were, again that was no reason for letting him die. And did he not know that half of Jonathan's talk was delusional?

The doctor wiped his glasses. 'He says he knows Jane Fonda.'

'Doubtless.'

At this point Jonathan had joined us. He wore a white gown and his hair was still wet.

'Jonathan, your mother thinks you should stay in hospital to get better,' said the doctor.

I thought, *Stuff it, Dr L, what about your views? Why don't you take some responsibility in all this?* Jonathan gave me a sharp look. 'I'm not going into hospital because I'm a normal-fearing citizen and I know my rights.'

'What good are your rights if you are dead?' My voice was beginning to sound tired.

'It was an accident.'

'Second time round, and I am frightened, Jonathan. I don't want you to die.'

'I am addicted. I am an addicted human rights leader and I have a black belt for valour.'

The doctor turned to me and said, 'If you want to get him into hospital the only way would be to charge him under the Inebriates Act. It will mean taking him to court.'

Jonathan said, 'Fuck off, if you do that I'll kill you, I'll ...'

'Stick a gorilla knife up your arse,' I said wearily. Dr L looked startled.

'I would charge you if I thought it would keep you from dying.'

'Fuck off!' he shouted, standing over me and waving his arms.

'Okay, so I won't. Because I feel defeated.'

'Fuck off.'

I went. I went to Ray and wept, and he put his arms around me and said, 'We'll keep an eye out for him, dear.' Ray was angry. 'Where is he getting it from, Anne? There's some damned pharmacists dishing out sedatives like hundreds and thousands. They're killing our people.'

Schizophrenia Fellowships receive hundreds of phone-calls from parents who tell of sons or daughters who are able to get seemingly limitless quantities of drugs like Valium, Serepax, Mogadon, Tegritol, Dilantin, Largactil, just by going from doctor to doctor and demanding them. These tablets are obtained on Pharmaceutical Benefits or Health Care Entitlements. A prescription for 200 tablets is not unknown. Ray said that when he or any of the Matthew Talbot staff tackled these doctors, their response was usually, 'If I don't prescribe them, someone else will.' Is this a responsible answer, or do they just want to get rid of difficult people from their surgeries, especially if they are unkempt and perhaps noisy?

Chemists then dispense these drugs. Do any of them question these quantities? How many cases of overdosing from this cause are handled each week by our hospitals?

Hospitals sometimes discharge mentally ill people by putting them in a taxi with one month's or more supply of sedatives, without asking them whether they have anywhere to go, and without telling their families they have been discharged. The family is told this is not a hospital responsibility because the patient is a legal adult. Yet imagine the outcry if people still suffering from a serious physical illness were discharged without ensuring they have a roof overhead and follow-up care.

People with schizophrenia are far more impaired in functioning than mental health professionals often accept or understand. Many are dependent to some extent, and they need lots of supportive counselling. It does not help confused people to load them up with sedatives on top of their already strong medication, and then to give no follow-up care. Many discard their proper medication and become dependent on illicit drugs, alcohol, concoctions of all kinds, whatever they can get their hands on, all of which exacerbate their illness, perhaps irrevocably. For one period, while he was in Sydney, Jonathan was shooting up vitamin syrup, using rusty syringes he had found in the streets.

Ten to fifteen per cent of people with schizophrenia kill themselves within the first five years of diagnosis. They do so because the struggle to survive becomes too great. The majority are young people, still in their teens or twenties. I knew the statistics full well: I had often quoted them.

One month later I had to give a paper about schizophrenia and stigma at the ANZAAS Conference in Melbourne. It was the first time I had spoken publicly about Jonathan's illness and I was nervous. I said that he had twice overdosed, that on each occasion he had been kept in hospital less than twenty-four hours and that there had been no follow-up. 'What more has to happen? Does he have to die before anyone will listen?' I asked.

At a Human Rights seminar in Brisbane, I heard this statement, which had been made by a Canadian mother at a similar conference in Toronto only a few months previously:

*We are the parents of the throwaway schizophrenics, the disposables, the ones who are the most difficult to treat; who are often, as a result of their disability, unable to ask for or accept help. They refuse it.*

*Left without treatment they continue to suffer. Relatives must stand by and watch, unable to alleviate the suffering which in the main is ignored by the mental health care system until it is sometimes too late. It seems to be the same story the world over. We are the people who are told you can't help those who won't help themselves, and we reply under our breath that it seems to us that you won't help those who can't help themselves.*

*We are the people who mop up the blood of our sons and daughters when they have killed themselves, released from hospital all too soon, or not considered sick enough to be hospitalised ... When we ask psychiatrists why they do not declare our obviously ill relative incompetent, they reply that the Mental Health Act ties their hands. When we ask the bureaucrats and the politicians how such a law can be passed, they tell us that the psychiatrists are interpreting the law too narrowly. When we turn to the lawyers they tell us that the rights of the individuals are paramount ... We are left helpless and hopeless, alone in our struggle to save the lives of our children.*

# Nine
## *Stuff for My Pain*

*For long you live and high you fly*
*But only if you ride the tide*
*And balanced on the biggest wave*
*You race towards an early grave*
                    PINK FLOYD

***February 1986*** I began this year with a sense of profound
melancholia. I felt hunted by the need to find some way of stopping
Jonathan's deterioration but, because of my heavy work-load, I had
little time to start another round of 'saving Jonathan'. It may sound
foolish to write about 'saving Jonathan' after all those other abortive
attempts but Jonathan needed saving. He was unwell. He had a
constant bad cough. His arms and legs were covered with abscesses.
He wasn't eating properly and was painfully thin. He often had
injuries because people would set upon him and he would never
defend himself.

He would come to see me two or three times each week.
Occasionally he turned up at the Film School; mostly he came home.
If I wasn't there, sometimes he would break in but mostly he would
curl up on the front doormat and sleep there until I arrived. He was
often quiet and sad. All his anger and all his energy seemed to have
burned away.

Early in the term, I was at the Film School when he rang me reverse
charges and said in a thin tired voice, 'Excuse me, excuse me, but
I'm in trouble with the police.'

I sighed. 'What's up?'

'I suppose you could say that, mildly speaking, I was picked up
because my pants were falling down. I told them that to a mild extent
I have schizophrenia but they didn't believe me. I was held all night.'

Ian Webster, the Professor of Community Medicine who ran a
weekly medical clinic at Matthew Talbot, was so concerned about

245

Jonathan's condition and the fact that he was always being picked up by the police, that he wrote a letter for Jonathan to carry on him, should he be arrested. The letter said:

*Jonathan has attended the clinic at the Matthew Talbot Hostel intermittently over the years. He is a very disturbed young man, and has permitted only limited contact by our nursing staff for incidental problems related to his use of drugs, intravenous administration of vitamins, and neglect.*

*He has many delusions and these incorporate the use of drugs. He has irrational thoughts, abnormal behaviour, and is often withdrawn.*

*He becomes very disorganised in appearance and needs treatment for skin infections, injuries, sub-cutaneous abscesses, and poor nutrition.*

*On many occasions, the staff here have felt that he is a danger to himself and we have been most disappointed that the formal psychiatric services have either been unable or unwilling to take a stronger line in confining him to a treatment centre for sufficient time to improve his mental state and physical condition. In my opinion, he suffers from schizophrenia complicated by drug dependence.*

As the mental health services had proved to be so ineffectual, I went to Odyssey House, an organisation for drug addiction, which works particularly well with young people. The Director, Milton Luger, was sympathetic. He said that by all means Jonathan could come and talk with him. The program did sometimes have young people who also had a serious mental illness, but Jonathan would have to be self-motivated. I had known that was what Milton would say, and, in the light of Odyssey's philosophy, it was quite appropriate. So I went through the routine of telling Jonathan about Odyssey House, and he said, 'Yeah, yeah, I'll go along, but I'm giving up heroin for Lent.' Needless to say, he never went.

Milton rang me a little later to find out how Jonathan had reacted. When I told him, he said sadly that was what he had expected, and then, said in a kindly voice, 'Hang on in.' Now, so many years later when people say, 'But I don't know how you stood it', the answer is that you stand it because you have no option. You do hang on, precariously, to any small ledges of hope. You cling with your fingernails, with your breath tightly held, and you cling, you bloody well cling.

I remember a BBC documentary on schizophrenia, made by Marjorie Wallace, now head of the national British organisation SANE, where an elderly man spoke of his son in such a sad, resigned voice: 'You start off with hope. He goes in for treatment. He comes out. And you hope that eventually it's all going to be fine. But after a little while, you find it isn't. He has to go in for more treatments. He comes out. And again you hope. You sink back into apathy. And it all starts again and again. And you hope because that's all you have. Hope.'

That year, 1986, we established Schizophrenia Australia, a national foundation for education and social research, based in Melbourne, with Margaret Leggatt as its director, and a Schizophrenia Fellowship in New South Wales. When we held our first public meeting in Sydney, some four or five hundred people came, even though it was a wet cold night. What struck me that evening was the courage of people with schizophrenia who stood up and talked about their illness for the first time in public, and who said it felt as if they were 'coming out of the closet'. Relatives spoke who had been silent for years.

I had begun to get phone-calls and letters from all over Australia, mostly seeking help. One night at home, when Jonathan was lying on the floor fast asleep, a man rang and said in a taut voice that his only son, aged twenty-two, was in jail.

'Do they ever get into trouble with the police?' he asked.

*Do they ever,* I thought.

'I've taken him to England, America, everywhere. He dived in his wet suit through a plate-glass window. He said he was going to surf round the world, and the policeman tried to stop him. Now he says he has the key to the sun, but he is in jail and he doesn't see much sun.'

In February, or it might have been March, a well-known Aboriginal storyteller and painter called Nosepeg came to the Film School to be filmed for a television documentary.

Nosepeg set up two canvases on the floor and showed students and staff how to follow a method of painting that had been derived from sand paintings but which now involved making dots on the canvas with acrylic paint. We all made dots, while Nosepeg sang the paintings into life. Making the dots was soothing. One of the students said, 'I can't tell you how good dot paintings are for your head.' I found myself fantasising that perhaps if I took Jonathan into central Australia to live with an Aboriginal community, he might get better. Alas, the reality of schizophrenia amongst Aboriginal communities is that it is just as much of a problem to deal with as in white communities, and that ignorance of the illness is perhaps even more profound.

Perhaps by now you are thinking, *What has happened to this woman if by now she is even considering that making dot paintings is going to fix up her son?* But there are few parents who would not go to the utmost limits to try to save the life of their child. And was Jonathan still a child now that he was twenty-four? To me he was both child and adult, for as Toni Morrison writes in her splendid book, *Beloved*: *Grown don't mean nothing to a mother. A child is a child. They get bigger, older, but grown? What's that supposed to mean? In my heart it doesn't mean a thing.*

On Tuesday, April Fool's Day, I came home late from work and found a jagged star-shaped hole in one of the etched glass panels of my front door. I opened the door. A trail of blood led along the hallway, down the side passage, and into the living-room. My eyes followed the trail and stopped at the sight of Jonathan, sitting cross-legged and holding up his right hand in the air. He was watching as blood dripped into a gathering pool on the floor.

He looked up and said, 'Hello Anne.'

I shouted, 'Why did you have to break the glass?' And then I thought, *God, how awful, what the hell does it matter about breaking the glass.* I took his hand which was deeply cut and lacerated. 'Does it hurt?'

Tears fell down his face. 'No,' he said. 'But I'm sorry about the door.'

'It doesn't matter.' I kissed his hand. 'Let's go to the hospital.'

He jerked his hand away and his eyes darted around the room. 'No,' he said.

'Your hand needs looking at.'

'I'm looking at it.'

'But they're deep cuts.'

'I can heal them. I'm magic.'

By now I had found bandages and plaster and I was trying to stem the flow of blood. I said that I promised the hospital wouldn't lock him up. All they would do was fix up his hand. He wobbled to his feet and began shuffling out of the room, blood still dripping. 'See ya, Anne,' he called over his shoulder. I remembered the psychiatrist at Yale when he had talked about terror. I came up and put my arms around him.

'How about coming to Andy then?' I was referring to Andy, our community psychiatrist friend who had first persuaded Jonathan to go into hospital seven years ago.

Jonathan stopped. He thought for a moment. Then he said, 'No.'

'He likes you. He won't hurt you.'

'No.' He kicked the door, and some more glass cascaded on to the wooden floor.

'Oh, okay,' he said.

Andy and his wife Chris were still up, even though it was nearly midnight. Chris made tea and Andy looked at Jonathan's hand.

'It'll need a few stitches,' he said. 'Hospital job.'

'No, no,' said Jonathan, eyes on the ground. And then he repeated, 'I'm magic.'

'Okay, you're magic, but how about a few magic stitches as well?'

Jonathan laughed. He liked the idea of magic stitches. 'Yair?' he said.

'Won't hurt,' said Andy. 'They'll give you an injection.'

'No.'

'So what are you going to do? Risk it not healing?'

Jonathan's eyes filled with tears again. And then I became alarmed. As I watched him, his neck seemed to be going into spasm and he was having trouble breathing.

'Need some Cogentin?' said Andy quietly.

Jonathan was twitching all over, the muscles in his neck were in severe spasm and his head was jerking round to the back of his body, much as it had those several years ago in Adelaide when I had first seen the side-effects of anti-psychotics, and learned that Cogentin was one of the drugs used as an antidote. Clearly Jonathan had taken some medication recently and had either not been given any Cogentin tablets or, more likely, had lost them.

'Best get to hospital, eh?' said Andy gently. Jonathan nodded. His face was contorting and he looked grotesque.

Andy and I managed to spoon him into my car, which wasn't easy because he was so tall, and because of his muscle spasms. At the small local hospital, near where I lived, a nurse appeared in Casualty, looked at Jonathan's twitching frame and bloodied hand, and said, 'Goodness!' The young woman doctor who attended to Jonathan and the two nurses were gentle, kind and patient. They first gave him a Cogentin injection, which quickly eased his spasms , and then a second injection so that they could stitch his hand. Jonathan's feet stuck out over the end of the bed, and there were large holes in his mismatched socks. His ankles were stick-like and so were his wrists. He held tightly to my hand. The doctor wanted him to stay the night, but after about two hours, he suddenly jerked himself off the bed and said, 'Excuse me, excuse me, I have to go. Thank you for being kind.' He strode off down the street and into the night.

I managed to catch up with him in my car, and persuaded him to come home at least until morning. He ended up staying for a further two nights and Joshua spent quite a bit of time with him. On the third morning, as I was leaving the house for work, I noticed that the back door to the downstairs part of the house was wide open. This had once been a separate flat, and Jonathan occasionally stayed there. I looked inside. Jonathan had gone.

'Anne, he doesn't stay anywhere for very long. You know that,' said Joshua gently. By now Joshua was the same age that Jonathan had been when he first became ill. With Joshua, I was finding it hard not to be over-protective, and to realise that I was dealing with someone whose reactions were gloriously normal. If I asked Josh not to do something, it still amazed me when he complied. I found it both distressing and reassuring to mark the difference in these two young men. The only good analogy I could come up with was to liken them to two model aircraft. One had been put together the right way and consistently flew on track and flew well. The other had some in-built vulnerability, so whether it was the engine that wasn't properly working, or whether the wings were a little awry, it always ended up crashing.

Two weeks later, Jonathan overdosed again. It was not as serious as earlier times, and he had taken himself to the hospital to have his stomach pumped out. Ray Bourke, from the Talbot, tried to sound reassuring when he told me, but then admitted that he was increasingly worried about Jonathan. 'He's going downhill, dear.'

'Ray, what can we do?' I wailed the question. Ray said he didn't know. Jonathan was still getting hold of vast quantities of Serepax or Valium, and mixing these with cheap cask wine. Ray said that a few months previously, Jonathan had been to Alcoholics Anonymous and made an immense effort to stay clear of drugs and alcohol, but one day he turned up at an AA meeting stoned, and he was asked to leave. He never went back.

When I spoke with Jonathan at the Talbot about what he was doing to himself he turned away, and then shouted at me, 'People get me in the head and tell me I'm crazy, and it sends me crazy. How could I smell of death if people weren't trying to kill me?'

In May I went to a Conflict Resolution workshop and met a woman who had taught Jonathan at primary school. She asked after him with affection and was distressed to hear he was ill. Zoe had become a psychotherapist and was running a therapeutic community at Oberon, in the high country beyond the Blue Mountains. She suggested seeing if Jonathan would go and stay there. I said I would try.

Jonathan said, 'Yes, I'd like to stay in the country. Can I ride horses?' So I took time off from work and arranged to take him to Oberon, but when I went to call for him at Matthew Talbot he had disappeared. He turned up one week later, and when I reminded him of our arrangement, said irritably that he was too busy to go. On this particular evening, I was trying to get my things together for the Duke of Edinburgh's Study Conference the following morning where I was a keynote speaker. I had just realised that I had miscalculated the importance of the conference which was being opened by the prime minister. I had nothing prepared. I tried to write my speech while Jonathan lay on the floor in my study, sometimes talking to himself, sometimes laughing. He said no, he didn't want to go into the other room. No, he wouldn't stay the night. No, he didn't want to listen to music. No, he wouldn't be quiet. In the end I drove him back to Matthew Talbot. The speech was never written. I was sick on the drive from Melbourne airport to the Conference building, and my address was high on faked animation and low on content.

At the Film School, two staff and I had introduced lunch-time meditation. It was guided meditation, but I was in such a state of distress that every time we were taken through fields of flowers, I never got beyond the first meadow without wanting to burst into tears. I used to cheer myself up afterwards by reading the student graffiti: *Do not frolic. Please do not put butter down the lavatories. It is impossible to retrieve.*

One Sunday afternoon when the winter sun had a fragile brightness, Jonathan came knocking on the door. His visits had acquired a certain ritual. He would roam around the house for the first ten minutes or so, usually talking quite incoherently, and then head for the couch in the living room where he would cover himself with a rug and fall asleep, curled up in a foetal position. He seemed too exhausted even to listen to music. Nor would he eat. Very occasionally he would come for a walk in the park. He would put his arm round my shoulders or sometimes take my hand. On this particular afternoon we had been for a walk and Jonathan was back on the couch when my Irish friend Clare unexpectedly arrived. Clare always looked like an elegant Edwardian, with her red hair piled on top of her head, her long skirts, and her fine white skin. She went and sat beside Jonathan and began massaging his poor sore feet. He looked up at her. 'Would you like me to go on?' she asked.

Jonathan smiled, and wrapped his arms tighly around himself. He had stuck a feather in his hair and wore pieces of dirty white rag around his wrists. There were sores on his face. Clare massaged first his feet, and then his back, his shoulders and his head. The memory still shines, for not many people would touch Jonathan by now. He smelled. He was dirty. He looked strange. After she had gone I looked down at him as he lay, sleeping peacefully. *Dear God, don't let him die.*

Four days later, I was at work when I had a phone-call from someone I did not know. Her name was Kay and she was a social worker at Kings Cross Community Health Centre which Jonathan sometimes attended. She said that Jonathan had overdosed once more. This was the fourth time. She said she and her colleagues were desperate, and I said so was I. I went round the following day and we met at the Centre, which was once an old house, in a side street at the top of a hill. We sat in a small, sparsely furnished room, with its wilted pot-plants, black-stained ashtrays, and a gas fire but no coins for the gas. Why is it that these places are always starved of funds, and have to beg year after year in order to keep going?

Kay was dark and small, wore glasses and was heavily pregnant. Jonathan was supposed to be present, but had gone. 'He always does,' said Kay sadly. She clearly had a good relationship with Jonathan and kept repeating, 'We have to get Jonathan away from the Cross or he will die.' We decided that we would have another attempt at getting him out of the city.

We looked up a tattered directory of hostels and half-way houses and refuges, city and country, and found they all made demands about self-motivation. Kay pulled a wry face. There were very few places prepared to have people who had a mental illness as well as drug addiction. You could have one problem or another, but never both, and more than two put you beyond the pale. We found four places that were a possibility, and the Oberon community made five. We agreed that I would try Oberon again, and if that failed Kay would try the next place.

I said, 'Well, I give it a seven per cent chance.'

Kay said, 'At least you're realistic.'

On my way out of the Centre, we passed two old men who were sitting in wicker chairs by the unlit gas fire, rocking backwards and forwards. I do not remember much about them except that they looked like characters out of some Shakespearean tragedy. Perhaps I am being melodramatic but it was no longer the time for comedy.

Kay said, 'Have you seen Jonathan?'

'Jonathan? Didn't you hear, he died in the night,' said one old man, with stubble on his chin and a battered hat over his eyes.

'Jonathan, Jonathan, died in the night,' said the other.

'Died in the night.'

'Died, died.'

I turned to Kay with horror. 'Don't be absurd,' she said to the old men. 'He's not dead. He was here earlier.'

The old men cackled again. 'Died at the Edward Eger,' said one.

'The Edward Eger,' echoed the other. And they rocked with laughter. The Edward Eger was a night refuge similar to the Talbot, and another of Jonathan's haunts.

I stood outside in the street. I was shuddering with cold, a cold so appalling that I wondered if I would ever get warm. I started walking; I walked for over two hours, with no recollection of where I went nor even how I managed to cross the roads. The intensity of my foreboding was surprising, for I had lived through so many alarms with Jonathan that I usually brushed them to one side. This one was too heavy to brush aside; this one was stone.

At the weekend I had to visit Adelaide for some screenings of student films, and saw Georgia, who was disturbed when I told her about Jonathan. She said there was little we could do except hope.

On Monday 9 June, I had come home from the School at about six o'clock, together with Pablo Albers, the head of training. We went in to my study to work on the new curriculum. Joshua was in the front room, watching television. When the front door-bell rang, and I saw that it was Jonathan, I momentarily cursed because I did not have time for him, and I was already tired. But because I had been trying to find him since his overdose a few days earlier, I had a strong sense that it was important to give him all my concentration. I apologised to Pablo and asked if he minded leaving.

Jonathan went into the kitchen to get a glass of water. It was a small badly lit room that barely had room for both of us, and I remember looking up at him as I said that I felt desperately upset about his overdosing.

'Listen,' he said, 'Listen, I don't want to kill myself because I've got a drug tolerance, see, I can handle more pills and take in more fear than anyone else can.'

'Then how come you had to go into hospital?' I was crying.

'Because it was a mistake, see. I know what I'm doing. I say, Joe, you've had enough. And I go to hospital.'

'I am afraid. I am afraid that one day you will not get to hospital. One day you will die.'

Jonathan doubled up as if in pain, then he shouted at me, 'No, listen – I have a life-affirming desire, and that's why I go to hospital. You'd have to have a life-affirming desire to want to have fucking tubes put up your nose. Have you ever had fucking tubes put up your nose? I don't want to die, see.'

He had a large bundle of white pills, wrapped in polythene, and he went to take two of them.

'Please Jonathan,' I begged, 'put them away.'

'Listen,' he said, 'they gave my father morphine for the pain in his cancer, and it helped him, right, and no one's going to tell me not to take stuff for my pain, right?'

I said, 'How about going to hospital and see if they can help with pain? Or Andy?' I had this desperate sense that I must try everything, even if they were such well-known routines.

To my surprise Jonathan hesitated, his head with that familiar tilt to one side. Then he said, 'Nuh.' He put his arms around me and cradled me as if I were the child, and he the parent. 'Don't cry, Anne.'

'Well, what about the country?'

'Nah, 'cos I've got my friends, forty prostitutes and they're depending on me. I stop people from beating them up, and I'm a gentleman, see, and it's God's honour not to let them down.'

'They won't mind if you go somewhere for a break.'

'Nuh.'

'Then bring them too.'

He laughed at that, 'Well, maybe I do need a break away, maybe I do. But I can't leave my friends.'

I thought, *But Jonathan does not have any friends.*

Josh had earlier asked if he could go up to the shops and get some pizza for himself and for Jonathan, and he had just returned. I presumed that Jonathan was in the front room and that they were eating together. They were. But then Joshua burst into the kitchen, calling out, 'Come quickly. Jonathan's collapsed.'

I rushed into the front room to find Jonathan sitting at the end of the table with saliva and pizza falling from his mouth and tears running down his face, rocking back and forth, banging his head on the table and against the wall.

I took him to the couch and held him in my arms and stroked his head and kissed his head, and all the while his body was heaving with sobs, while he shuddered out disconnected statements like, 'I can't go on . . . the pain in my head . . . terrible, terrible . . . look at me . . . look at what I've fucking become . . . oh God!' He was choking on his tears, choking in a river of despair.

I cradled him close and rocked him, singing to him as if he were a small child, singing inside my fear as well as his, singing sweetness to the sour of his breath, singing softness to the sores on his body, singing love and life into his whole being, and willing, with all my heart, with all my mind and with all my strength that I would keep him safe from harm. But deep inside I already knew that I had failed.

After a long time during which he lay peacefully in my arms, Jonathan stirred and said that he needed to sleep. I made him some hot milk and he went to the downstairs part of the house. We had no internal stairway, so he had to leave by the front door. After he had gone, it began raining heavily.

About fifteen minutes later, I heard a knock on the door. Jonathan stood there, the rain pouring down his face. He was naked, and wrapped in a blanket. He asked for a clean T-shirt to wear to bed and insisted that was all he wanted. Five minutes later he returned. I asked, 'Do you need something warmer?'

'No,' he said. 'I came to say another goodnight.' He hugged me close to him, and I felt the wet from his body, and reached up and touched the wet of his hair.

I left for work very early next morning, at about 6.30 am. I had peered in through one of the windows of the downstairs flat, but it was dark and hard to see. As Jonathan always slept at least until midday if he were allowed, I did not worry, but rang Joshua at a reasonable hour and asked him to hang onto Jonathan. I think I still had faint hopes of getting him to the country. But Joshua said, 'Jonathan has already gone.'

On Tuesday 10 June, I rang a doctor and said, 'I know that Jonathan is going to die soon. Get him into hospital.'

He said, 'I can't. He won't stay and we can't force him.'

On Wednesday 11 June, I had dinner with a radio colleague and friend whose daughter had schizophrenia. She was about the same age as Jonathan. We said with forced humour that perhaps we had better send them away together.

On Thursday 12 June, at about ten o'clock in the morning, I was at the Film School when the nice woman operating our switchboard rang through and said tentatively, 'The police have just rung. They are coming to see you.' I heard myself calling out in a strange harsh voice, 'It's Jonathan, isn't it? He's dead.'

My hands shook as I rang the Kings Cross Health Centre and asked to speak to Kay. She was crying. 'Oh Anne, he was alive until about eleven, but he didn't want to go to sleep. He was woozy. So they left him downstairs, and found him in the morning, by the lift.'

'Where?' I said.
'At the Edward Eger.'

> *Jonathan Jonathan, died in the night,*
> *Died in the night,*
> *Died, died,*
> *Died at the Edward Eger.*

I put down the phone, and heard from within me a primitive cry, a cry of astounding energy, over which I had no control.

The police came and were young and awkward and extraordinarily kind. They drove with me to the mortuary to identify Jonathan's body. I went and was frightened until I saw Jonathan, and then I was frightened no longer. They told me at the mortuary that I could 'view the deceased on a video monitor,' that I did not have to go inside the morgue.

I said, 'But he is my son.'

They said, 'His face is covered in blood, from where he fell.'

I said, 'He is my son.'

He lay on a raised platform, like a votive offering, covered in a white sheet. His feet protruded. His long, slender, poor scarred feet. He was in one room, and I was in another. We were separated by a wall of glass. I said, 'I want to touch him.'

They said, 'You might get upset.'

I said, 'I will be more upset if I do not touch him.'

His face was streaked with dark blood like a birthmark. His mouth was calm. His eyes were closed. He no longer looked like a child. He was a young man. I touched his cheek, and his matted fair hair. I kissed his forehead, and I said, 'Goodbye, you silly old thing.' I don't know why I called him a silly old thing, but it came from a well-spring of deep love and tenderness. Then I left.

What can I say about the next few days, except that friends gave us their love and their strength. And that when I told Georgia, she said, 'You must never blame yourself. You were the most marvellous mother to him and to us. You did everything you could.' And when I sobbed to Joshua, 'But he never had a home,' Joshua replied, 'True, he never had a home but, Anne, he had so much love.'

We held the funeral service by the side of his grave, in a new part of the cemetery, where the wind was tossing the leaves of a grove of eucalypt trees. It was raining slightly, and the rain stung our faces as we walked, Georgia and Joshua on either side of me, our arms linked, up a small hill to the graveside.

Through the rain I saw the faces of loving friends and people who had tried to help Jonathan. Neil and Icia had come, and Neil brought his guitar. I had asked him to play 'The Lord Is My Shepherd,' but he could not remember it, so instead he played 'Swing Low Sweet Chariot.' This was somewhat unexpected, but appropriate to Jonathan's delight in the unpredictable. Neil and Icia's baby threw her bottle almost into the open grave. The minister likened Jonathan to an instrument, too finely tuned to bear the vicissitudes of life. I thanked everyone for their love and support over so many turbulent years. And then it was over. Or I thought it was over, until I looked up and saw through the rain, standing on the other side of the grave, Ray Bourke and a collection of people whose faces I did not know. I saw the people who were homeless, who were crazy, who were sick. They had come from the Talbot, from the other shelters, from the Cross, and they had come to say goodbye. They were Jonathan's friends. With their coming they brought me peace, for they brought the knowing that within the tortuous journey of Jonathan's short life there had been meaning. The meaning was life itself, with all its paradoxes, its joy and its pain, its weakness and its strength, its anger and its love.

# EPILOGUE
## *Into the Light*

*We shall not cease from exploration*
*At the end of all our exploring*
*Will be to arrive where we started*
*And to know the place for the first time.*

T. S. ELIOT

I needed to write this book: to lay before myself the richness of the experience and the bleakness. I needed not to deny the bad aspects because these were a part of the whole and, for me, serenity rests in the whole. I still feel distress when I think of the terrors that Jonathan endured. I miss him. But I no longer feel despair. People are talking more openly about their experiences with schizophrenia, and seem to have better insight into it than they had in the past. The stigma of mental illness, like a dark shadow, is beginning to move away.

When I made a television documentary on schizophrenia, in 1991, the experience affected me profoundly. As I worked closely with people who had the illness, I became aware of their courage, of their struggle to hold on to the fragility of themselves. I also became aware that their responses when psychotic were quite understandable within the context of the way their minds processed information. Different yes; mad, no – not within their scheme of things. It was the first time I had fully integrated my intellectual and emotional acceptance of the illness. When Jonathan was alive, there were too many anxieties in the way. The extent and nature of past and present discriminations suddenly became outrageously clear.

As long as schizophrenia is treated like some evil and frightening nemesis, not as just an illness, we shall continue to spurn those who are afflicted, and to abandon their families.

Young people with schizophrenia are still dying. I wrote this book to try to understand why.

I wrote it because I believe that most people have little idea of what happens when someone you love goes mad, of the maelstroms that can engulf you. I believe there is still a distressing gap between the professional perception of living with schizophrenia and the actual experience of what occurs.

I wrote it because, whenever I speak about the illness, I am overwhelmed by letters of distress, both from people with schizophrenia and from their families. For each one that I receive, the number could be multiplied a thousandfold, again and again, around the world.

Yet we know enough about schizophrenia now to understand that it is a physical malfunctioning of the brain, in which genetics, chemistry and environment interact in fathomless permutations. We know that schizophrenia is an illness; it is nobody's fault; it could happen to any one of us, or to those we love.

It is morally indefensible to treat people with serious illness as outcasts of society; to treat them with any less sympathy and care than we treat those with a physical illness.

It is indefensible that people should be in jail or living on the street because there is nowhere else for them to go.

It is indefensible that they have less protection in human rights legislation than any other group in society.

It is indefensible that their families are still left to flounder in isolation and despair.

It is indefensible that there is so little research into schizophrenia, when one person in a hundred suffers from it, and when it takes up more hospital beds than any other single illness. Ten times more per patient is spent on research for heart disease and over fifty times more for cancer.

Yet schizophrenia is a treatable illness. We may not know how to prevent it, nor how to cure it, but in the last few years we have made remarkable progress in helping people learn to manage their differences in brain functioning, just as we can help people manage differences in physical functioning. There are many ways to walk gently in the world.

If we accept the obvious—that people with schizophrenia do not present themselves as a homogeneous kind, and that the illness has chronic and acute phases, it should be easy to accept that we need a range of services, as flexible as possible. It is not simply a question of hospital versus community; we need both. We may also need a new positive concept of asylum, for those not coping with independent living. Perhaps the most important factor affecting the success of people living within the community is whether they have a place to live—literally a place they can call home. We need to bridge the gap between the bureaucratic perception of how services are working and the day-to-day traumas of supporters, who often struggle alone.

The fact that distress continues is partly because help is patchy, or inappropriate, or not enough, but it is also because we are still fearful of mental illness. We continue to separate mind from body, and to see in part, not as a whole. It is surely time that we let go of such limiting concepts of ourselves. We are both mind and body, and we live within an environment which is also part of ourselves. Only now, as I approach this whole picture, can I begin to understand Jonathan's illness.

For too long, mental illness has been kept in the shadows. Instead of rejection, we need acceptance. Instead of shame, we need love. Instead of despair, we need solid and unwavering support. It is time to come out of the shadows and into the light.

# Further Information

If you need help or further information on schizophrenia, or wish to help or to make a donation, please contact the National Alliance for the Mentally Ill. NAMI is a grass-roots, self-help support and advocacy organization of families and friends of people with serious mental illness. NAMI's mission is to eradicate mental illness and to improve the quality of life for those who suffer from these no-fault brain diseases.

To learn more about NAMI, contact the National Alliance for the Mentally Ill, 2101 Wilson Blvd., Suite 302, Arlington, VA 22201, 1-703-524-7600.

NAMI Helpline 1-800-950-NAMI

ADDRESSES OF STATE AFFILIATE GROUPS

**Alabama** AMI
3322 Memorial Parkway S.
Huntsville, AL 35801
(800) 626-4199
(205) 880-3918

**Alaska** AMI
4050 Lake Otis Pkwy., #103
Anchorage, AK 99508
(907) 561-3127

**Arizona** AMI (AAMI)
2441 E. Fillmore Street
Phoenix, AZ 85008
(602) 244-8166

**Arkansas** AMI-Help and
Hope, Inc.
4313 W. Markham
Little Rock, AR 72205
(501) 661-1548

**California** AMI
1111 Howe Ave., Suite 475
Sacramento, CA 95825
(916) 567-0163

**Colorado** AMI
1100 Fillmore St.
Denver, CO 80206
(303) 321-3104

**Connecticut** AMI
62 Alexander St.
Manchester, CT 06040
(203) 643-6697

AMID
2500 West 4th St.
Wilmington, DE 19805
(302) 427-0787

AMI DC Threshold
422 8th St., SE
Washington, DC 20003
(202) 546-0646

**Florida** AMI
308 Tequesta Dr. #21
Jupiter, FL 33469
(407) 575-3054

**Georgia** AMI
1256 Briarcliff Rd., NE
Atlanta, GA 30306
(404) 894-8860

**Hawaii** AMI
1109 12th Ave., Suite 5
Honolulu, HI 96816
(808) 737-9069

**Idaho** AMI
313 N. Allumbaugh
Boise, ID 83702
(208) 376-4304

AMI **Illinois** State Coalition
110 W. Lawrence, Suite B
Springfield, IL 62704
(800) 346-4572
(217) 522-1403

**Indiana** AMI
7768 Eagle Valley Pass
Indianapolis, IN 46214
(317) 298-9291

AMI of **Iowa**
Box 495
Johnston, IA 50131
(515) 254-0417

**Kansas** AMI
PO Box 675
Topeka, KS 66601
(913) 233-0755

**Kentucky** AMI
The Speed Building
333 Guthrie Green, Suite 310
Louisville, KY 40202
(502) 584-2009

**Louisiana** AMI
2431 S. Acadian Thruway, Suite 28
Baton Rouge, LA 70808
(504) 928-6928

AMI of **Maine**
PO Box 222
Augusta, ME 04332
(800) 464-5767
(207) 622-5767

AMI of **Maryland,** Inc.
2114 N. Charles St.
Baltimore, MD 21218
(410) 837-0880

AMI of **Massachusetts,** Inc.
27–43 Wormwood Street
Boston, MA 02210
(617) 439-3933

AMI of **Michigan**
592 Foxboro
Saginaw, MI 48603
(517) 799-1467

AMI of **Minnesota,** Inc.
1595 Selby Avenue, #103
Saint Paul, MN 55104
(612) 645-2948

**Mississippi** AMI
215 Edinburgh Ct.
Brandon, MS 39042
(601) 992-1227

**Missouri** Coalition of AMI
204 E. High Street
Jefferson City, MO 65101
(314) 634-7727

MONAMI
103 S Strevell
Niles City, MT 59301
(406) 232-1553

AMI of **Nebraska**
PO Box 371
Red Cloud, NE 68970
(402) 746-2746

**Nevada** AMI
PO Box 85373
Las Vegas, NV 89185
(702) 457-7238

AMI of **New Hampshire**
10 Ferry St. Unit 314
Concord, NH 03301
(603) 225-5359

**New Jersey** AMI
114 West State Street
Trenton, NJ 08608-1102
(201) 329-2888

AMI—**New Mexico**
PO Box 9049
Santa Fe, NM 87504
(505) 983-6745

AMI—NYS
260 Washington Ave.
Albany, NY 12210
(800) 950-3228
(518) 462-2000

**North Carolina** AMI
3716 National Drive, #213
Raleigh, NC 27612-4863
(919) 783-1807

**North Dakota** AMI
Box 637 1st Avenue NE
Kenmare, ND 58746
(701) 385-4355

AMI of **Ohio**
979 S. High Street
Columbus, OH 432066
(614) 444-2646

**Oklahoma** AMI
1140 N. Hudson
Oklahoma City, OK 73103
(405) 239-6264

**Oregon** Alliance for the
   Mental
161 High St., SE, Suite 212
Salem OR 97301-3610
(503) 370-7774

AMI of **Pennsylvania**
2149 N. 2nd St.
Harrisburg, PA 17110-1005
(717) 238-1514

AMI of **Rhode Island**
PO Box 28411
Providence, RI 02908
(401) 464-3060

**South Carolina** AMI
PO Box 2538
Columbia, SC 29202
(803) 736-1542

**South Dakota** AMI
Box 221
Brookings, SD 57006
(605) 692-5673

**Tennessee** AMI
1900 N. Winston Rd., #511
Knoxville, TN 37919
(615) 877-4109

**Texas** AMI (TEXAMI)
1000 E. 7th Street
Austin, TX 78702
(512) 474-2225

**Utah** AMI
PO Box 58047
Salt Lake City, UT 84158

AMI of **Vermont**
67 Main Street
Poultney, VT 05764
(802) 287-5566

**Virginia** AMI
PO Box 1903
Richmond, VA 23215
(804) 225-8264

AMI of **Washington** State
4503 Lacey Blvd., Suite 11
Olympia, WA 98503
(206) 438-0211

**West Virginia** AMI
1418 MacCorkle Ave.
Charleston, WV 25303
(304) 744-5562

AMI of **Wisconsin**, Inc.
1245 E. Washington Ave.,
  Suite 290
Madison, WI 53703
(608) 257-5888

**Wyoming** AMI (WYAMI)
1949 E. A Street
Casper, WY 82601
(307) 234-0440

# Notes and References

This book is not the appropriate place for a comprehensive bibliography on schizophrenia. The publications listed below are some of those that I found useful. The other references relate to specific information which is in the text.

## BOOKS

ALEXANDER, K. *Understanding and Coping with Schizophrenia.* Schwartz & Wilkinson, Melbourne, 1991.

CARR, V. *Understanding Schizophrenia.* Schizophrenia Fellowship of South Australia, Adelaide, 1986.

HATFIELD, AGNES B. *Coping with Mental Illness in the Family: A Family Guide.* NAMI Book No. 6, Arlington, VA, 1991.

LAMB, RICHARD H. *The Homeless Mentally Ill.* American Psychiatric Press, Washington, D.C., 1984.

LINTNER, B. *Living with Schizophrenia.* Macdonald & Co., London, 1989.

MENDEL, WERNER M. *Treating Schizophrenia.* Jossey-Bass, San Francisco, CA, 1989.

NAMI. *Experiences of Patients and Families: First Person Accounts.* NAMI Publication No. 2 (second series), Arlington, VA, 1989.

PRIDMORE, S. *The Case of Joshua Kirk.* Schizophrenia Fellowship of Australia, Melbourne, 1984.

SEEMAN, M. V., LITTMAN, S. K., PLUMMER, E., THORNTON, J. F., & JEFFRIES, J. J. *Living and Working with Schizophrenia.* New American Library, New York, 1984.

STYRON, WILLIAM. *Darkness Visible: A Memoir of Madness.* Random House, New York, NY, 1990.

TORREY, E. FULLER, M.D. *Nowhere to Go: The Tragic Odyssey of the Homeless Mentally Ill.* Harper & Row, New York, NY, 1988.
———. *Surviving Schizophrenia: A Family Manual.* Harper & Row, New York, rev. edn, 1988.
WALSH, MARYELLEN. *Schizophrenia: Straight Talk for Families and Friends.* Morrow Press, New York, 1985.
WASOW, M. *Coping with Schizophrenia.* Science and Behavior Books, Palo Alto, CA, 1982.

TEXT REFERENCES
**Chapter 3**   Torrey, E. Fuller. *Surviving Schizophrenia: A Family Manual.* Harper & Row, New York, rev. edn, 1988.

**Chapter 4**   Brodoff, Ami S. *Schizophrenia Bulletin,* 1988, vol. 14, no. 1, pp. 113–16, a publication of the US Department of Health and Human Services, Public Health Service, Alcohol, Drug Abuse and Mental Health Administration, Washington, DC.
For information about Athma Shahkti Vidalaya, write to Cathexis India Society, No. 445/A, 3rd Block, Koramangala Layout, Bangalore 560–034, India.
Carey, E., & Leggatt, M. *Coping with Schizophrenia: The Relatives' Perspective.* Schizophrenia Fellowship of Victoria, Melbourne, 1987.

**Chapter 6**   Herrman, H., McGorry, P., Mills, J., & Singh, B. *Severe Mental Disorders and Psychiatric Service Use in Sentenced Prisoners in Melbourne.* Department of Psychological Medicine, Monash University, and the National Health and Medical Research Council Schizophrenia Research Unit, Royal Park Hospital, Melbourne.
Teplin, L. A. 'The prevalence of severe mental disorders among urban male jail detainees: comparison with the epidemiologic catchment area program'. *American Journal of Public Health,* 1990, vol. 80, pp. 663–9.
Whitmer, G. 'From hospitals to jails: the fate of California's deinstitutionalized mentally ill'. *American Journal of Orthopsychiatry,* January 1980, vol. 50, no. 1, pp. 65–75.
McFarland, B., Faulkner, L., Bloom, J., Hallaux, R., Bray, J., Donald,—'Chronic mental illness and the criminal justice system.' *Hospital and Community Psychiatry,* July 1989, vol. 40, no. 7, pp. 718–23.

**Chapter 7**   *Homeless People with Severe Mental Disorders in Inner Melbourne.* Council to Homeless Persons, Victoria, 1988.

Torrey, E. Fuller. *Nowhere to Go.* Harper & Row, New York, 1988. (For a detailed and scathing indictment of the issue of homelessness and the mentally ill).

National Alliance for the Mentally Ill (NAMI), 2101 Wilson Blvd., Suite 302, Arlington, VA 22201.

Harding, C. M., Brooks, G. W., Ashikaha, T., Strauss, J. S., & Breier, A. A. 'The Vermont longitudinal study of persons with severe mental illness—1: methodology, study sample, and overall status 32 years later'. *American Journal of Psychiatry,* 1986, vol. 144, pp. 718–26.

Wasow, M. *Coping with Schizophrenia.* Science and Behavior Books, Palo Alto, CA, 1982.

Wasow, M. 'The need for asylum for the chronically mentally ill'. *Schizophrenia Bulletin,* 1986, vol. 12, pp. 152–7.

American Mental Health Fund. *Quarterly Report,* Spring 1989, vol. 6, no. 1, Washington, DC.

*Schizophrenia Survey,* conducted by ICM Research for Guardian Newspaper, National Schizophrenia Fellowship and SANE, London, 1990.

(SANE: 5th floor, 120 Regent St, London W1R 5FE).

*Schizophrenia Study,* conducted by Dr. Rob Hall of Environmetrics and Newspoll market research for Schizophrenia Australia, 1991 (first national survey of community attitudes in Australia).

'Public attitudes toward people with chronic mental illness', prepared for the Robert Wood Johnson Foundation program on Chronic Mental Illness, Boston, 1990.

Laing, R. D. & Esterson, A. *Sanity, Madness and the Family.* Pelican, London, 1960.


**Chapter 9**   Morrison, T. *Beloved.* Chatto & Windus, London, 1987.

# *Spinning Out*

A 55-minute documentary film, produced and directed by Anne Deveson.

One in a hundred people will develop schizophrenia at some time in their lives, forty million worldwide. Schizophrenia fills more hospital beds than any other illness. *Spinning Out* is unlike any other film on the subject: it speaks directly to the experts – people with schizophrenia. *Spinning Out* goes inside the locked wards, joins the crisis teams, the self-help groups, and the families, to see how they deal with the knife-edge existence of their lives.

*Spinning Out,* an Anne Deveson Production, 1991, made with the assistance of the Australian Broadcasting Corporation, is distributed by The Cinema Guild, 1697 Broadway, Suite 802, New York, NY 10019, tel: (212) 246-5522, fax: (212) 246-5525.